FUNDING WHITE SUPREMACY

In *Funding White Supremacy*, Robert B. Williams shows how current federal policies have perpetuated and expanded the racial wealth gap in the United States. Through the lens of stratification economics, Williams explores how twelve tax expenditures buried in the federal tax code shower over $1 trillion annually to mostly wealthy, White households, while federal estate and gift taxes have been systematically dismantled. The book reveals how these policies originated in a period of overt racial oppression and have evolved in the modern, post-Civil Rights era, not only contributing to the expanding racial wealth gaps over the last fifty years but also fostering the growth of White wealth at the expense of Black wealth. This book is a must-read for anyone seeking to understand how federal policies contribute to the vast and expanding racial wealth gap at the core of the American system of White supremacy.

Robert B. Williams is the Stedman Professor of Economics at Guilford College, North Carolina. He is the author of *The Privileges of Wealth: Rising Inequality and the Growing Racial Divide* (2016) and *Greening the Economy: Integrating Economics and Ecology to Make Effective Change* (2010).

CAMBRIDGE STUDIES IN STRATIFICATION ECONOMICS: ECONOMICS AND SOCIAL IDENTITY

SERIES EDITOR: William A. Darity Jr., *Duke University*

The *Cambridge Studies in Stratification Economics: Economics and Social Identity* series encourages book proposals that emphasize structural sources of group-based inequality, rather than cultural or genetic factors. Studies in this series will utilize the underlying economic principles of self-interested behavior and substantive rationality in conjunction with sociology's emphasis on group behavior and identity formation. The series is interdisciplinary, drawing authors from various fields including economics, sociology, social psychology, history, and anthropology, with all projects focused on topics dealing with group-based inequality, identity, and economic well-being.

Funding White Supremacy

Federal Wealth Policies and the Modern Racial Wealth Gap

ROBERT B. WILLIAMS
Guilford College

Shaftesbury Road, Cambridge CB2 8EA, United Kingdom

One Liberty Plaza, 20th Floor, New York, NY 10006, USA

477 Williamstown Road, Port Melbourne, VIC 3207, Australia

314–321, 3rd Floor, Plot 3, Splendor Forum, Jasola District Centre, New Delhi – 110025, India

103 Penang Road, #05–06/07, Visioncrest Commercial, Singapore 238467

Cambridge University Press is part of Cambridge University Press & Assessment, a department of the University of Cambridge.

We share the University's mission to contribute to society through the pursuit of education, learning and research at the highest international levels of excellence.

www.cambridge.org
Information on this title: www.cambridge.org/9781009367844

DOI: 10.1017/9781009367851

When citing this work, please include a reference to the DOI 10.1017/9781009367851

First published 2025

A catalogue record for this publication is available from the British Library

A Cataloging-in-Publication data record for this book is available from the Library of Congress

ISBN 978-1-009-36784-4 Hardback
ISBN 978-1-009-36786-8 Paperback

There isn't a Negro problem; there is only a white problem.

Attributed to Richard Wright

Your ancestors dragged these black people from their homes by force; and in the white man's quest for wealth and an easy life they have been ruthlessly suppressed and exploited, degraded into slavery. The modern prejudice against Negroes is the result of the desire to maintain this unworthy condition.

Einstein, *The Negro Question*

For more than a decade through books, magazines, newspapers, TV and radio, the white man has been trying to solve the race problem through studying the Negro. We feel that the answer lies in a more thorough study of the man who created the problem. In this issue we, as Negroes, look at the white man today with the hope that our effort will tempt him to look at himself more thoroughly. With a better understanding of himself, we trust that he may then understand us better – and this nation's most vital problem can then be solved.

John H. Johnson, *Ebony Publisher's Statement*

Contents

Figures

Tables

Abbreviations

AGI	adjusted gross income
BEOG	Basic Educational Opportunity Grants
CEEB	College Entrance Examination Board
FHA	Federal Housing Agency
GRA	guaranteed retirement accounts
GRAT	grantor retained annuity trust
GST	generation-skipping transfer
HOA	homeowners' association
HOLC	Home Owners Loan Corporation
IPS	Institute of Policy Studies
IRA	Individual Retirement Account
JCT	Joint Committee on Taxation
KKK	Ku Klux Klan
LCH	Life Cycle Hypothesis
NAACP	National Association for the Advancement of Colored People
NCES	National Center for Education Statistics
SALT	state and local tax
SCF	Survey of Consumer Finances
TCJA	Tax Cuts and Jobs Act
TRB	tuition, room, and board
VA	Veterans Administration
WP	Wealth Privilege

Acknowledgments

As I finish this book project, I can see the contributions of so many colleagues and friends.

One of my earliest mentors, Bob Hall, long-time publisher of *Southern Exposure*, continually encouraged me to "follow the money." Those words reverberate throughout this book. Bob, that you continue to do so even to this day is inspiring.

Two colleagues in particular, Drs. Adrienne Israel and Carolyn Beard Whitlow, encouraged me to explore my White privilege. Many others – including Jada Drew, Sekinah Hamlin, Deena Hayes-Greene, James Shields, Monica Walker, Jorge Zeballos, and Drs. Naadiya Hasan and Barbara Lawrence – continued to challenge me to go deeper even as I resisted. Other colleagues – including Drs. Tom Guthrie, Mark Justad, Lisa McLeod, and Barton Parks, as well as Judy Harvey – offered important support and mentoring through this journey. To all of you, your insights are woven throughout the pages of this book.

Among the many National Education Association colleagues who have welcomed and supported my work, I want to give special acknowledgment to Drs. William Spriggs, Samuel Myers Jr., and Nina Banks. Bill, your untimely death leaves a vast hole in many of our lives. Sam, your timely advice that I stop neglecting the insights of past Black economists has paid obvious dividends. And Nina, your tireless and important work in organizing the annual Freedom and Justice conferences along with your own research on Sadie Alexander have leavened this work.

I want to thank my Wednesday afternoon group. Your honest criticisms and continual support have helped me find my voice and express it more directly and forcefully.

Thank you, Sandy, for your encouragement to tackle this project. That it took me two-plus years to conceive what you saw from the beginning is probably about par.

In the peer review process, we have all experienced the "anonymous reviewers from hell." In this instance, I benefited from the "dream" reviewer. Thank you for your insightful feedback as well as your generous offer of suggestions and source citations. I would welcome your help anytime.

Thank you to my editors, Rachel Blaifeder and Jadyn Fauconier-Herry, for your assistance in navigating the publication process. Thanks also to my copy editor, Robert Holden, who cleaned up many of my mistakes.

Many thanks to my students over the years. You have been willing participants as I have revealed to you the "first drafts" of my thinking. Your insightful feedback has helped me hone my ideas.

Over several years, this project has received the generous support of Guilford College's Kenan Faculty Development Fund. Colleagues and administrators alike across our community have offered me nothing but vocal support for this project.

Lastly, I want to thank my creative and supportive wife, Mary Beth Boone. Throughout, you have been encouraging and patient during the many hours I've spent working to complete this book. Thank you.

1

Recognizing the Wealth–Race Nexus

PRODIGIOUS BUT STINGY

Sometime during 2021, the US economy passed a momentous milestone virtually unnoticed. Buried in a government report, in this case the Federal Reserve's *Financial Accounts of the United States – Z.1,* is the revelation that US household wealth had reached $142 trillion by year's end.[1] This is one of those mind-numbing statistics that defies any real understanding. Yet, when paired with another statistic, that the current number of US households is 131 million, its significance takes shape. Combining the two figures demonstrates the prodigious bounty of the US economy as they reveal average household wealth now exceeds $1 million. So much for the 1920s slogan that aspires for "a chicken in every pot." A century later, the US economy is capable of making every American household a millionaire! Consider for a moment the possibilities.

In an ancillary appendix, opaquely named the *Distributional Financial Accounts,* the Federal Reserve offers insights into the distribution of this wealth; not evenly, I can assure you. According to the publication, the richest 1 percent of households garners nearly one-third while the bottom half of households claims less than 3 percent of that wealth. These lopsided shares demonstrate the acute stinginess, even cruelty, of the American economy. Although capable of generating vast amounts of wealth, its parsimony is striking. When we consider the wealth shares by race, we find a similar imbalance. White households account for just under two-thirds of American households, yet they hold 86 percent of household wealth. In contrast, Black households comprise almost 12 percent of the total

[1] See the Federal Reserve Board of Governors, 2022. Table B.101.h Balance Sheet of Households, Line 27.

population while their share is a paltry 2 percent.[2] These lopsided distributions should raise alarm.

LINKING RACE AND WEALTH

That there exists a strong link between race and wealth shares should come as no surprise; they have been inextricably linked from the very beginning. No doubt when the English colonists first landed on the shores of Virginia, they viewed the land and its bounty as a source of great wealth. Of course, the land was already occupied. Possession of this valuable source of wealth could only be obtained by the removal of the Indigenous peoples, whether through negotiation, intimidation, or violence. The settlers quickly learned that simple possession was insufficient to unlock the land's great rewards. Rising demand back home for tobacco, indigo, and other crops meant hard labor in a hot climate, generating the need for cheap labor. Enslaving local Indians initially and later captured Africans offered a means to expanded harvests, large landholdings, and great wealth. The rising trade between local plantations and European markets enabled colonial merchants, insurers, and financiers to grow rich as well. On the backs of the enslaved, a colonial elite emerged to challenge the English king on any taxation without representation. Clearly, they were unwilling to see the irony in their position. By 1774, the enslaved Africans themselves represented the most important source of wealth in the Southern colonies and the second most important, after land, across all thirteen colonies.[3]

That revered document the US Constitution codified this tight link between race and wealth. Although always in coded language that surely reflected ambivalence among the founders, the Constitution made numerous concessions to slavery. It prohibited federal interference in the international slave trade for at least twenty years.[4] By stipulating that slave revolts would be deemed as domestic insurrection, it bound the federal government to help in their suppression.[5] Further, the Constitution required every state – even those that might abolish slavery – to return any enslaved persons who may have fled for their freedom, thereby placing the property rights of enslavers above any civil rights.[6] Worried that

[2] All of these figures are based on the 2022 Survey of Consumer Finances (SCF).

[3] See US Census Bureau (1975) Chapter Z 169–191 Components of Private Wealth Per Free Capital for the Thirteen Colonies, by region, 1774.

[4] See US Constitution, Article I, Section 9, Clause 1.

[5] See US Constitution, Article I, Section 8, Clause 15.

[6] See US Constitution, Article IV, Section 2, Clause 3.

abolitionists might try to tax slavery to extinction, supporters of slavery inserted a prohibition against direct taxes, or those on property, whether chattel or land,[7] as well as against taxes on state exports.[8] Lastly, the Constitution imposed the infamous three-fifths clause that gave the slaveholding states added representation in both Congress and the Electoral College. This provision further protected the slaveholding South against a majority of free states abolishing slavery throughout the country. All of these provisions lead some to consider it an enslavers' Constitution. Further, they demonstrate the government's intention to protect and expand the personal wealth of (some) Americans.

Even the celebrated Bill of Rights functioned to tighten this link further. While these early amendments enshrined various rights broadly applied to any "person," it is clear the founders had in mind White, male persons only. The Fifth Amendment's prohibition against any deprivation "of life, liberty, or property, without due process of law" clearly established the enslaved as chattel property. In the notorious Dred Scott case, Judge Taney argued that Congress could not abolish slavery anywhere since it would represent an undue taking of property. Not until passage of the Reconstruction Amendments, particularly the Thirteenth and Fourteenth Amendments, would this legal bond between race and wealth be severed, even if the actual link would continue unabated in practice.

Federal policies continued to widen the racial wealth gap. The often-praised Homestead Act of 1862 offered up to 160 acres of free land – land taken from Indigenous tribes – to those who could work the land for five years and make improvements. As initially written, only Whites could apply. Although this restriction was modified in 1870, few Black freedmen could take advantage of this opportunity given their destitute status and physical distance from the available land on the Great Plains (Deverell, 1988). In force until 1976, the Homestead Act offered 270 million acres of land to 1.6 million homesteaders (National Archives, 2021). In contrast, General Sherman's Field Order 15 offered the freedmen a more accessible opportunity. Using land that had been confiscated from openly rebellious White planters along coastal Georgia, it offered the freedmen a less generous "forty acres and a mule." Nearly 40,000 freedmen accepted the offer and settled these lands, only to learn nine months later that President Johnson would vacate the order and return the land to its antebellum owners. There is no better proof of the continuing link between race and wealth than the

7 See US Constitution, Article I, Section 9, Clause 4.

8 See US Constitution, Article I, Section 9, Clause 5.

design and legacy of these two land grant programs. Such disparate treatment by the federal government continued throughout the twentieth and even the twenty-first century, but their discussion must await subsequent chapters.

TODAY'S LEGACY

The consequences of this early linkage between race and wealth remain with us today in so many forms. White Americans enjoy substantial advantages in almost every measure of physical, social, or economic well-being. Focusing on just four metrics, Figure 1.1 illustrates the current gaps in college attainment, professional employment, median income, and homeownership rates.[9] In each case, White households achieve levels that are between 30 and 70 percent higher than Black households. Arguably, these four metrics represent the most important ladder for upward mobility currently available. As the thinking goes, earning a college degree will increase one's chances of landing a professional job that pays well and offers generous benefits. Such gainful employment should generate stable and ample income, enough to provide access to homeownership. Collectively, these achievements should lead to greater wealth accumulation and subsequently financial security.

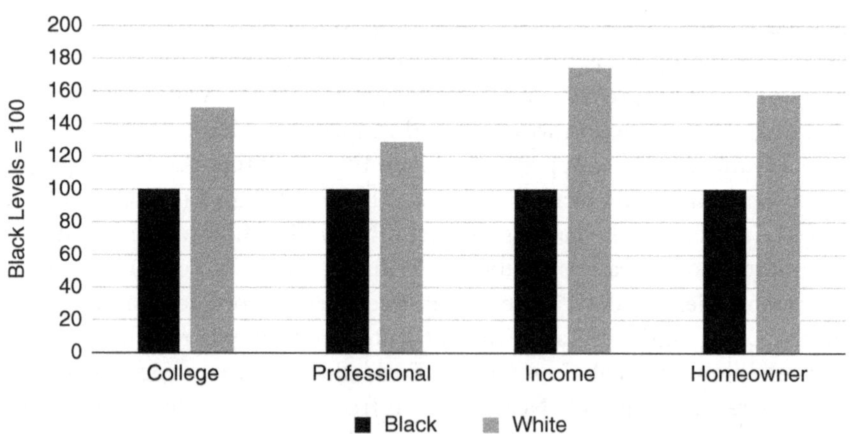

Figure 1.1 Racial disparities, Take I
Source: Author's calculations; Federal Reserve Board, 2022 Survey of Consumer Finances

[9] Each of the gaps is estimated by comparing the White to Black levels, with the latter indexed at 100.

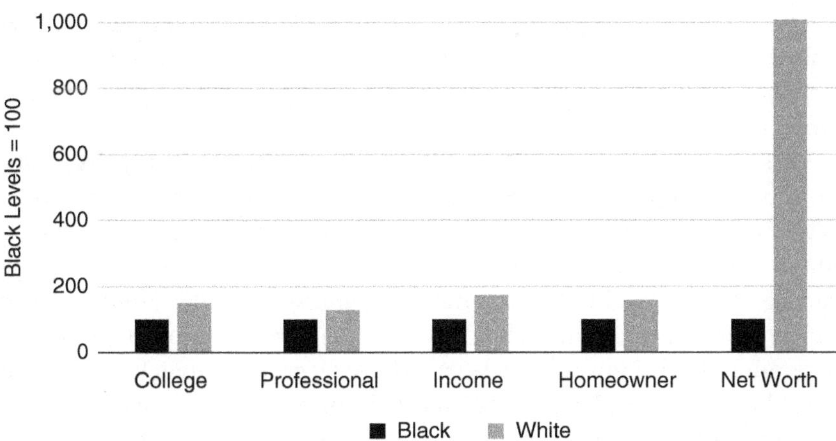

Figure 1.2 Racial disparities, Take II
Source: Author's calculations; Federal Reserve Board, 2022 Survey of Consumer Finances

However, adding one further metric reveals a flaw in this thinking. Including the racial wealth gap transforms the perspective, as illustrated by Figure 1.2. Whereas the previous figure suggested that Black households may still be in "catch-up mode," this one illustrates an imposing obstacle. Unlike the earlier gaps, the ratio in net worth is closer to 10:1. The bond between race and wealth persists today and casts a large shadow.

No doubt, some readers will find Figure 1.2 surprising and confusing. The prevailing narrative is that despite the disturbing racism that prevailed deep in our nation's past, the Civil Rights laws of the 1960s ended legal segregation and opened new doors to Black Americans. Have not circumstances for Black Americans changed for the better over the past two generations? Has not the removal of past legal obstacles to Black opportunity led to a reduction of economic disparities experienced in the past? Simply put, yes and no.

To be sure, Black Americans have experienced substantial improvements in many areas. Since 1950, Black adults have seen their college graduate ranks swell from 2 percent to 25 percent and their professional ranks increase from 4 percent to 18 percent today; both represent notable improvements. Despite these remarkable gains, Black adults currently find themselves further *behind* their White peers. Among White adults, college graduates now number 41 percent, and professionals 33 percent. Similarly, median Black household incomes more than doubled from over $20,077 to $45,870 in real terms since 1950, while the Black homeownership rate rose from 34 percent to 44 percent. Once again, the luster of these gains is tarnished as we recognize the absolute racial gaps have widened. Currently, median household income among Whites is nearly $75,000, and the homeownership rate has stabilized at over 72 percent.

These statistics reveal important insights about our economy. Its prodigious bounty has raised the material circumstances of most Americans by a substantial margin. Compared to the mid-twentieth century, more young adults matriculate and graduate from college. Many more find employment in professional or managerial occupations that offer ample salaries and benefits. Far more households today own their own home than several generations back. However, these gains have disproportionately redounded to White Americans. Despite the expected consequences of the Civil Rights legislation of the 1960s, the elimination of Jim Crow segregation, and a token application of affirmative action policies, Whites have maintained or expanded their absolute advantage in each of these areas. Yes, the rising tide of the American economy has lifted many boats, but it has elevated White yachts more fully. This disparate treatment is most apparent when we consider its impact on household net worth.

TRACKING THE RACIAL WEALTH GAP

Sixty years ago, the Federal Reserve pierced the veil that shrouded how the nation's wealth was distributed across American households. Prior to this moment, national surveys had gathered minimal information on household wealth. In the spring of 1963, trained interviewers surveyed 2,600 targeted households after years of discussion, planning, and pilot studies. They asked detailed questions on household assets, debt, income sources, and related circumstances. This effort, known as the 1962 Survey of Financial Characteristics of Consumers, represented a notable achievement. Even then, much of the nation's wealth was held by a small number of households, who were reluctant to reveal the extent of their good fortune. To capture this group, the survey administrators combined an oversample of wealthy households with an improved questionnaire design and field procedures to obtain a more accurate snapshot (Projector, 1968). It offered our first peek into how wealth was spread across American households, as well as how asset ownership and debt were distributed.

Remarkable in many ways, the survey reflected its era on one notable issue. The years of planning were conducted while Jim Crow remained ascendant. The published reports examine the distribution of wealth by householder age, employment, and poverty status, but no mention was made of race or ethnicity. Survey respondents were designated as "White," "Non-White," or "Not Ascertained."[10] The surveys were conducted a full year before the 1964 Civil Rights Act would outlaw de jure racial discrimination, thereby providing us with a snapshot of Jim Crow America. From that picture, we learn the median White household possessed a net worth of $7,620 ($73,701 in 2022 dollars), while the typical Black household held only $295 ($2,853 in 2022 dollars).[11] Fully 78 percent of White households had more wealth than the typical Black household. Almost one-third of Black households held zero wealth or worse, while less than one-fifth of White households suffered the same. One striking result of the survey is that White households – on average – were expecting an inheritance currently held in probate of $208 ($2,012 in 2022 dollars), while the figure for Black households was $1 ($10 in 2022 dollars). White Americans were preparing to inherit almost the same amount of wealth held in toto by Black Americans. Given the time in our nation's history, these results generate little surprise.

What many may find more astonishing is how the racial wealth gap has evolved over the past two generations. The usual narrative is that our nation's racial history – at one time sordid and worthy of condemnation – has been transformed in the modern era by laws outlawing discrimination and market forces encouraging meritocratic outcomes. This chronicle argues how the 1960s Civil Rights legislation outlawed Jim Crow racial exclusion and forced segregation. Dismantling the barriers to Black opportunity and progress opened the doors to higher education and professional occupations. Affirmative action policies were enacted to redress past abuses by ensuring colleges and businesses took active roles in augmenting their numbers of Black students and professionals. Economists insisted that competitive markets surely would eliminate any persistent vestiges of racial discrimination. Many hailed President Obama's election in 2008 as a harbinger of a "post-racial" society.

The evidence tells a different story. After waiting twenty-one years before implementing a second survey, the Federal Reserve quickly

[10] Like Aliprantis et al. (2019), I assume that "Non-White" is similar to more recent survey definitions of Black or African American.

[11] I use the terms net worth and wealth interchangeably despite their differences. In this case, my definition of net worth includes real and financial assets minus debt. I follow the conventions of the SCF by excluding any defined benefit retirement funds and any claims to future Social Security benefits. I also exclude any vehicle assets as they, like household furniture and appliances, are both depreciating and less fungible assets.

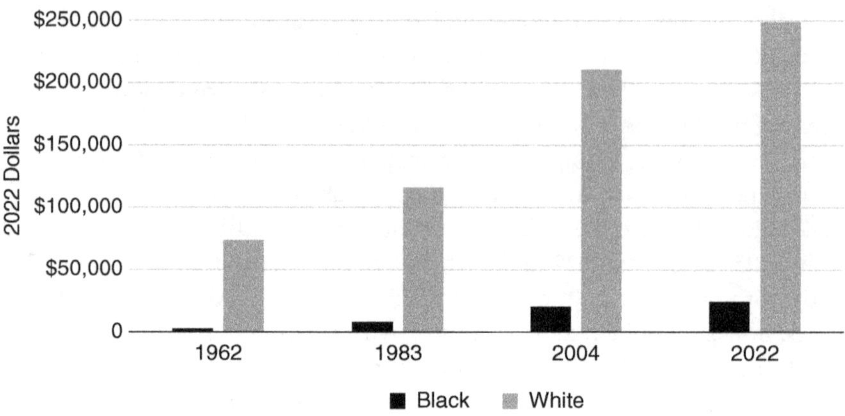

Figure 1.3 Tracking median household net worth
Source: Author's calculations; Federal Reserve Board, 1962 Survey of Financial Characteristics of Consumers; Survey of Consumer Finances

developed a regular, triennial wealth survey, starting in 1989. Using the available sources, one can track the Black–White racial wealth gap over the period. Figure 1.3 illustrates the changes in median Black and White household wealth after making adjustments to control for inflation. Using 2022 constant dollars, typical Black household wealth rose from $2,853 in 1962 to $24,698 in 2022, an overall increase of nearly $22,000. Over the same period, typical White household net worth increased from $73,701 to $248,880, a net gain of over $175,000. Despite the image suggested by the figure, the gains in household wealth were not always steady nor positive. Both groups were clearly harmed by the Great Recession of 2008–2009, although there is significant evidence that Black households were hammered harder (Williams, 2016). Most important is what has happened to the racial wealth gap. During this period of supposed movement toward racial equality, the absolute difference between typical Black and White household wealth has more than *tripled*, from around $71,000 to over $220,000 *in real terms*.

This expansion in the racial wealth gap has the ability to upend the upward mobility ladder discussed earlier. Family wealth determines which opportunities are truly available. Without ample savings, households must forgo additional education and training that can open occupational doors to higher-paying careers. Unable to access family help, their children face the stark choice of graduating with substantial student loan debt or forgoing college altogether. Without a diploma in hand, they find most doors to well-paying jobs closed. Instead, they are relegated to jobs that offer uncertain tenure, modest pay, and limited benefits. Each of these limits their ability to develop retirement savings or to attain homeownership, key steps in building wealth and achieving financial security. Indeed, the swelling wealth gap threatens to stall and undo much of the material progress made to date by Black households. And it threatens such progress over multiple generations.

CONTRASTING PERCEPTIONS WITH REALITY

Most Americans believe our country has witnessed steady and significant progress toward racial equality over the past sixty years. In a recent poll, half of White Americans said that Black Americans experience equal treatment in gaining access to good jobs.[12] A similar percentage feel there has been substantial progress made in equalizing access to education and health care. In another poll, only a minority of White respondents believe they have benefited as much or more than Blacks over the years.[13] Whites who report they have gained little help outnumber those who think they have benefited a great deal. In both surveys, Black respondents offer very different answers.

To gauge public perception of the racial wealth gap, a recent study queried individuals about their views. Respondents were asked to estimate the net worth of a typical Black household assuming White households held \$100 (Kraus et al., 2019). They could select among answers that ranged from \$10 to \$200 and were invited to make comparisons both in the past – as far back as 1963 – as well as currently. The typical answer among the more than 1,000 study participants was that Black households have \$90 for every \$100 held by Whites. Looking back to 1963, they believed that Black households held just under half (\$50) for every \$100 held by Whites. While closer to the reality, even these estimates substantially underestimate the extent of the racial wealth gap. Nonetheless, these figures confirm belief in the dominant narrative that progress over the years has largely eliminated any racial disparities in wealth.

In a follow-up survey, the researchers provided half of the White respondents with materials that explain how both explicit and implicit racial bias would deter racial progress (Onyeador et al., 2021). Once again, most believed that the country had experienced substantial progress in eliminating the wealth gap. Among those who read the materials on racism,

12 See AP-NORC Center for Public Affairs Research (2022).

13 See Pew Research Center (2021).

they offered a curious response. Relative to the control group, they tempered their optimism on how much progress had actually been achieved. However, they did so by reducing the extent of the wealth gap in the past rather than revising their perceptions of the current gap. These results suggest that Whites are resistant to changing their perceptions on the size of the current racial wealth gap.

What explains why White Americans are so clueless regarding the extent of the nation's racial wealth gap? Various arguments have been advanced. Wealth, even more than one's salary or income, remains shrouded from view. We rarely speak openly about such matters in public. Among our colleagues at work, we can make informed guesses on their salaries, but their wealth remains far more elusive. One obvious marker of people's wealth is their home, yet most White Americans live in neighborhoods that are predominantly White (Massey & Denton, 1993; Hadden Loh et al., 2020). Two-thirds of White Americans report having no friends of color, thereby indicating even greater racial isolation (Brumley, 2022). Very few Whites interact with Blacks on a regular basis and therefore they have little experience in assessing any wealth gap. Some contend this racial isolation among Whites is so severe and influential, they label it as "White habitus" (Bonilla-Silva et al., 2006). Absent meaningful cross-racial relationships, White Americans have little knowledge from which to accurately assess the extent of the racial wealth gap.

There is a motivational cause for White myopia on this issue. An essential feature of our national narrative is that we are a just, egalitarian, and meritocratic society. Holding these beliefs not only supports our country's sense of exceptionalism, but also offers individuals strong incentives and a dose of self-protection (Kraus & Tan, 2015; Kraus et al., 2017). The lure of expected economic advancement offers encouragement to work hard even when the material consequences are not immediately clear. Viewing our economic system as fair and meritocratic offers those who achieve material success a defensible rationale for their good fortune. It provides a bulwark against the argument that their success is simply the result of privilege and favoritism. For this reason, White Americans have a pressing need to view racial exploitation as relegated solely to our sordid past while our contemporary society moves quickly toward racial equity. Doing so protects White, particularly affluent Americans, from the psychological threat that their material success is largely the result of White privilege (Kraus et al., 2019). Thus, White Americans have a strong incentive to minimize the racial wealth gap even when confronted with persuasive counterevidence.

FOCUS OF THIS BOOK

The purpose of this book is to document and explain why the racial wealth gap is widening during a half century that many view as a period of racial progress and reconciliation. To do this, one must view the growing racial wealth gap not as an unfortunate consequence of our prodigious economy, but as an intentional objective of our current system. This requires delving into this system, which I label as White supremacy in the book title.

Many may find my using the term White supremacy to describe our contemporary society as provocative and even alarming. In recent decades, the term has been used to describe the goals and methods of the Klan and other White nationalist/terrorist groups that, until recently, were somewhat marginalized. Yet, a century ago, White politicians spoke freely using the term. Speaking to a crowd just days before the infamous 1898 election, Furnifold Simmons, chairman of the North Carolina Democratic Party, described the stakes of the impending vote: "The battle has been fought, the victory is within our reach. North Carolina is a WHITE MAN'S State and WHITE MEN will rule it, and they will crush the party of negro domination beneath a majority so overwhelming that no other party will ever again dare to attempt to establish negro rule here" (Rippy, 1936, p. 86)[14]

Two years later, Simmons spoke to a crowd to raise support for a North Carolina state amendment – one that was popularly referred to as "the Simmon's Election Law" (Watson, 1989, p. 144) – that would effectively end Black voting rights for sixty years. He explained:

> There is no use mincing matters. This amendment discriminates against the Negro in favor of the white man. We intended that it should so discriminate and I am here today to defend that discrimination. This is a white man's state. We have raised the white flag here. Who will haul it down? The Negro can't do it and the white man that does, spot him. Write on his brow traitor – traitor to country and race; to wife and child, aye to the father and mother. Let him be an outcast on the face of the earth. (Christensen, 2010, p. 29)

Simmons went on to serve in the US Senate for thirty years, rising to chair the powerful Senate Finance Committee. In that role, he will return in later chapters. Even thirty years later, in a radio address that billed him as "our Old Chieftain of White Supremacy" (Watson, 1960), he referred to the election of 1898 in the following way:

[14] Capitalization is the author's.

> Instantly, upon surveying the situation, I raised the question – it was not raised in the Democratic platform – of black or white supremacy in North Carolina. (Great applause). I set about to effect a union of all white people of every occupation, of every class and every condition, in the Democratic fold for the purpose of redeeming the State from disgrace which had been cast upon it. (Simmons, 1936, p. 179)

As these quotes demonstrate, mainstream politicians like Simmons, himself a credible presidential candidate in the 1920 election, spoke forthrightly about the importance of maintaining White supremacy.

At its core, White supremacy embodies a social system that produces and reproduces racial hierarchy and domination. This dominance operates within political, cultural, social, and economic spheres. In her book *Caste: The origins of our discontents*, Isabel Wilkerson (2020) offers a useful framework to examine how this system functions. From her research, she argues that caste hierarchies rely upon eight pillars for their support and persistence.[15] Two pillars, the inherent superiority of certain castes that result from the natural order, are clearly manifest in our culture wars. There is no need for a White History month since what has always been packaged as American history is a focus on White accomplishments from a White perspective. Modest challenges to this dominant narrative, like the 1619 Project, Critical Race Theory, and the Advance Placement (AP) class in African American History, have triggered bellicose responses revealing the importance of maintaining cultural domination. Two more pillars, status heritability and occupational hierarchy, are clearly revealed as one considers the power corridors of Washington or corporate board rooms. Intergenerational wealth functions to ensure that those born into privilege have the means to exert that privilege throughout their lives. More to come on this issue. Two other pillars, endogamy and maintaining caste purity, function less importantly today, although wealth disparities do encourage economic homogamy and cement residential and educational segregation. The last two pillars, stigmatizing and imposing cruel conditions on subordinated castes, are evident throughout the media as well as by the breadth and depth of financial hardship amidst such a bountiful economy. Each of these pillars can be applied to the racial divide that currently exists. We will return to these issues.

Additionally, this analysis uses the lens of stratification economics to examine the issues. Racial stratification requires some mechanism by

[15] They are divine will and the laws of nature; heritability; endogamy and the control of marriage and mating; purity versus pollution; occupational hierarchy; dehumanization and stigma; terror and cruelty; and the inherent superiority versus inferiority of castes.

which resources and opportunities are disparately distributed. Household wealth provides a suitable means. Even more than income, household wealth offers its holder an expansion of opportunities, agency, and power. Ample wealth provides households the means to respond to educational or entrepreneurial opportunities that may increase future income. Parents can access the best local schools for their children as they are able to purchase a home in select neighborhoods. Moreover, household wealth is easily transmitted across generations, ensuring its power will extend into the future. In this way, the system is capable of reproducing the disparities generation after generation. Acknowledging this important transmission, recent policy changes have worked to make this transfer easier and less subject to any tax bite.

Equally important to this system of unequal treatment is the perception that these disparities are themselves "earned" and not the result of favoritism. As suggested by the polling data, any structural advantages that redound to Whites must be viewed as the result of a meritocratic system. Once again, household wealth meets this need effectively. According to conventional wisdom, households accumulate wealth by saving prudently for the future, investing those funds wisely, or gaining some modest help from their families. Few of us receive large inheritances from our forebears, but many of us gain some help. The potential to save and invest funds is nominally open and accessible to all households. Consequently, if we conveniently ignore those structural advantages that redound to the wealthy, one can attribute the unequal wealth shares as the result of laudable self-discipline and astute financial literacy. More on this to come.

An additional element of the stratification framework is the recognition that status and well-being is assessed both relatively and absolutely and that it reflects both our intragroup position as well as our between-group comparison. According to one explanation, "in the context of the Black–White dichotomy, each Black American will be concerned simultaneously with how Blacks as a collective are doing relative to Whites and how they are personally doing relative to other Black Americans. Similarly, Whites will have a parallel set of concerns" (Darity, 2022, p. 4). This means that Whites will view any perceptible reduction in racial disparities with suspicion and even a sense of threat. To the extent that any improvements gained by Blacks are attributable to specific policies, Whites will argue that they represent "unearned" improvements. White reaction to modest affirmative action policies offers a compelling example of this. Similarly, any revision of the structural advantages currently favoring Whites will generate comparable responses.

This particular component of stratification economics offers some instructive predictions. During periods where the intergroup disparities between White and Black Americans are vast, the framework predicts that Whites will focus more on their relative position among other Whites (Darity, 2022). This prediction takes on particular interest as one considers the early twentieth century. At this time, White supremacists across the South and beyond had eliminated Black political participation using legal barriers backed by local terrorism. One wonders whether the enactment of the federal income and estate taxes – two topics of consideration in later chapters – owe their birth to these White supremacist achievements. Additionally, stratification economics predicts that as the intergroup disparities narrow, Whites will respond to this perceived threat to their status by rallying to White tribalism. Of course, one response will be to attack the sources of Black group improvement as unearned and unmerited.

Lastly, stratification economics views race prejudice and discrimination as critical elements to maintaining the White supremacy system. Racial discrimination – whether in educational systems, labor markets, credit markets, or wherever – functions to maintain and expand those intergroup disparities that support the status of Whites. Racial prejudice is necessary to offer an explanation for why these disparities exist and persist. Both elements focus more on maintaining intergroup disparities than on limiting individual access. This view of racial animus explains the behavior of many Whites who might welcome specific Black colleagues and acquaintances while holding deeply biased views about Blacks in general.

THE REMAINDER OF THIS BOOK

Although income and wealth are frequently confused as identical twins, the singular qualities of wealth cannot be overstated. Wealth offers its holder, at minimum, reduced vulnerability to the threats that emerge from an uncertain world and, at maximum, a source of power that can be wielded across and over lifetimes. In Chapter 2, I explain how households accumulate wealth. At one level, this explanation is both simple and intuitive. Households may receive wealth in various forms from their families; they may save some of their current income; and they may invest those savings into assets that appreciate over time. This is not rocket science. Under this simple view, these opportunities are largely accessible and subject to individual discretion, discipline, and determination. Bluntly put, this view contends that wealth is earned.

Yet, households experience each of these avenues toward wealth accumulation in very different ways. Some households find themselves sharing their wealth *back to their parents and grandparents* who find themselves in economic distress. Other households earn incomes that are either too irregular or inadequate to support regular savings. Many households invest their limited resources in essential assets that do not appreciate over time, like furniture, appliances, and cars. In these cases, something other than individual discretion, discipline, and determination is driving wealth outcomes. In large measure, household wealth itself drives these outcomes. Put simply, wealth begets wealth.

In Chapter 2, I introduce the Wealth Privilege (WP) model to provide a more nuanced explanation on the role that wealth status plays in the wealth accumulation process. After attaining a modest wealth threshold, households find it increasingly easier to save and invest in assets that appreciate more rapidly. Numerous institutional and systemic factors favor the affluent, making their efforts all the more fruitful. Across generations, families take whatever gifts they have received from prior generations, build wealth upon this base, and offer their children even larger gifts of support. All of this functions as a virtuous cycle as more wealth enables greater wealth accumulation. As our prevailing cultural beliefs argue the wealthy have earned their good fortune, the system's beneficiaries can indeed feel virtuous. At the same time, households with little or no wealth find these avenues threatening and unrelentingly stingy, offering only discouragement to their efforts to get ahead. These contrasting circumstances illuminate why even modest family gifts can have such powerful consequences on life outcomes. Sixty years ago, the typical White household had the means to buy a modest home, while the typical Black family had enough to buy a used car. This significant head start has allowed White households to benefit more fully from the privileges of wealth, thereby widening the racial wealth gap.

A key omission of the WP model is the role that federal policies have played throughout our nation's history in supporting the wealth-building efforts of American households. In Chapter 3, I redress this omission as I describe landmark policies that helped families build wealth. Almost without exception, these policies intentionally targeted White families. These include the already mentioned constitutional protections to enslavers as well as the differential treatment given to White homesteaders and Black freedmen. During the twentieth century, the GI Bill and federal housing policies funneled vast sums to help millions of White households earn a college degree, start a business, or become homeowners, all while ignoring and even harming Black households. Moreover, federal acquiescence and participation in legalized segregation further helped White households as these policies limited the educational, occupational, business, and residential opportunities afforded to Black households. Given this lopsided assistance provided to White households and their descendants, it comes as little surprise that the racial wealth gap in 1962 was as large as it was. Indeed, the real surprise is that it was not even larger.

In the post-Civil Rights era, federal wealth policy took a new turn, one that has remained largely unnoticed. Over the vehement disapproval of then Treasury Undersecretary Surrey, lawmakers increasingly relied on federal tax expenditures as the way to help households build wealth. According to Surrey, such tax expenditures lack either transparency or accountability, causing him to view them as the hidden back door to the US Treasury. Their relative obscurity makes them the perfect vehicle to dispense favoritism without attracting notice. In Chapter 4, I examine twelve tax deductions and explain how their design targets the needs of the wealthy. Initially modest in scale, these tax expenditures now cost the US Treasury more than $1 trillion annually, with the bulk of this aid assisting the wealthy. Given the tight link between wealth and race, targeting assistance to the wealthy is simply another way to funnel funds to White households. As I document, these twelve tax deductions provide the largest contribution to the growth of White wealth over the past generation.

The growing generosity of these tax expenditures experienced increasing resistance from another tax obstacle. While these tax deductions fueled the accumulation of vast sums of wealth, existing federal estate and gift taxes limited their transfer across generations. Chapter 5 examines this issue as it describes the trinity of federal wealth taxes: estate, gift, and generation-skipping transfer (GST) taxes. Given the growth and concentration of wealth, these taxes were poised to take larger roles as federal tax sources. However, several bouts of *tax reform* over the past fifty years have undermined their effectiveness. These taxes have been pierced by so many loopholes that some see them as "voluntary taxes." Any who want to avoid paying them generally can do so. Moreover, changes in state tax laws are allowing the very rich to create "dynasty trusts" that will assure future descendants financial security fully guaranteed from birth.

The next two chapters examine the origins of both sides of the federal wealth policy: tax expenditures and wealth taxes. Chapter 6 traces the source of many of the contemporary tax deductions back to the creation of the federal income tax enacted over a century ago. Without exception, these tax deductions were created largely as afterthoughts and often as pragmatic solutions to thorny tax accounting problems. In most cases, these decisions raised little controversy and their future consequences went unrecognized. Only after the federal income tax's transition from a "class tax" to a "mass tax" did they assume any real importance. Throughout the bulk of this period, state and federal laws ensured that Black political participation was either nonexistent or severely marginalized.

Chapter 7 replicates this historical examination as it sketches the birth and evolution of the federal wealth taxes. It discusses the circumstances that gave rise to the federal estate tax (1917), the gift tax (1924), and the GST tax (1934). It is no coincidence that their implementation occurred during a period of overwhelming suppression of Black political participation. This vacuum permitted the emergence of class divisions among Whites over the appropriate role of wealth in society. During this early period, shifting political winds favored one side and then the other in this debate, thereby causing substantial revisions to these taxes. After the Great Depression, these taxes remained relatively untouched and reasonably effective in both limiting the intergenerational transfer of wealth and filling the US Treasury. It is not until the 1970s with the threat of Black resurgence that the attacks on their effectiveness manifest in tax policy changes.

Chapter 8 returns to the modern era as it examines federal policies attempting to remedy the rising cost of higher education and its impact on accessibility. Our nation's experience with the GI Bill demonstrated how opening college to eligible matriculants broadens the middle class, expands access to financial security, and boosts economic growth. Even by the 1970s, the cost of attending college was beyond the means of many college-ready students and their families. When first introduced, the Pell Grant program was heralded as opening the doors of higher education to all who were ready. Yet, its actual history and diminished accomplishments offer us a cautionary tale. Early reforms that extended its aid to recipients from middle-class households diluted its assistance to those recipients with the greatest need. Rather than build broader political support for the program, these changes inaugurated an era of increased underfunding. Today, the financial obstacles to obtaining a college diploma are far greater as the cost of college attendance has far exceeded the Pell Grant aid and family resources. Many graduates leave with student debt loads they cannot possibly repay, creating a new source of economic stratification.

Chapter 9 examines a range of potential solutions that might help close the racial wealth gap. Of course, any substantial effort to close the gap requires that an increasing number of White Americans become aware of the gap as well as how it both benefits them as it harms Black Americans. Without such an understanding, it is difficult to see how any truly effective solution to the problem will become enacted. To be sure, there are a number of nonracial policies that have been advanced that could reduce the gap, at least modestly. These include revamping the current tax deductions to retarget their assistance to households seeking financial security rather than to already affluent households. It also includes a doubling of the largest Pell grants as well as a proposal for funding Baby Bonds. However, it is unlikely that any of these policies, even working together, will dramatically reduce the wealth gap. Thus, the chapter recommends the enactment of reparations as the only way to make amends for our nation's past and bridge our racial divide.

CONCLUSION

Throughout our nation's history, wealth and race have experienced multifaceted, complex, and important links. Racial classifications emerged largely to justify the forced removal of one people and the enslavement of another, all in the pursuit of profit. Concerned about the stability of this link, Southern delegates demanded provisions to the Constitution that would protect slaveholding. A half century later, the federal government was offering 160 acres to Whites while rescinding its offer of only forty acres to the freed people. Other federal policies, including support for Jim Crow segregation, targeted aid to White households to the detriment of others. By 1962, a carefully conducted household survey revealed the extent of the resultant racial wealth gap. Given the survey's careful preparation, its offhand attention to race reveals much about the link between wealth and race. Despite the "conventional wisdom" and certainly public perceptions among Whites, the racial wealth gap has only widened over the past sixty years. White ignorance of this reality is in part caused by the federal policies that led to racial residential segregation and kept White and Black households separated and isolated. Perhaps equally important is the willful ignorance among Whites who likely acknowledge unconsciously how the racial wealth gap both supports their group status and threatens their meritocratic narrative. Yes, this link between wealth and race is very complicated.

Given all of this, it makes sense to move next to understanding the unique benefits that wealth brings its holder. While the ways that households can accumulate wealth on their path to financial security are well understood, the particular circumstances that different households face depend on their position and resources. All of this is the focus of Chapter 2.

2

Understanding How Households Get Ahead

LIVING PAYCHECK TO PAYCHECK

On September 23, 2016, the US Treasury Department convened the Freedmen's Bank Forum to commemorate the opening of the National Museum of African American History and Culture. Named for the bank created after the Civil War to provide Black Union soldiers a safe haven for their accumulated pay, this day-long event attracted experts and luminaries from inside and outside of government. Hosted by Treasury Secretary Jack Lew, the discussions targeted various strategies needed to bring greater opportunities and increased financial inclusion to Black and other marginalized communities. When asked by Derek Dingle, editor-in-chief of Black Enterprise magazine, about the racial wealth gap, Secretary Lew acknowledged its importance in the issues highlighted by the forum. Yet, at that point he explained how households could accumulate wealth:

> A lot of people say they can't afford to save. I understand. Living on a paycheck-to-paycheck income is really challenging. I experienced it at the beginning of my career and I know how hard it is. By the same token, most people buy a cup of coffee without thinking about it. Most people buy an extra magazine or video without thinking about it ...If you take the accumulated decisions people make lightly and in one of those occasions say, I am going to put money away for retirement, you'd see more people start out with more. ... I think financial education, financial literacy, is about understanding that some people buying a home may not be a good idea. (US Department of Treasury, 2016, as cited in Baradaran, 2017, p. 253)

Secretary Lew's explanation of how households get ahead raises several interesting issues. First, his emphasis on disciplined, individual saving and financial literacy as the solution to the racial wealth gap mirrors much of what passes for conventional wisdom. Yet, the evidence offers little support for this view (Darity et al., 2018). Neither financial discipline nor astute decision making, *by themselves*, can offer much help to households earning low incomes and holding no wealth. In addition, Secretary Lew's understanding of living paycheck to paycheck suggests a confusion regarding the differences between income and wealth. After starting at Carleton College and eventually graduating from Harvard University and Georgetown Law School, Secretary Lew likely lived from one pay period to the next. However, he is ignoring his sources of wealth. Both his educational pedigree and law degree would open doors unavailable to most Americans. Further, his parents, Irving and Ruth Lew, worked as legal professionals and owned not only a home in tony Forest Hills, but also a rare book business. They could easily offer Jack a secure safety net if he found those occupational doors challenging to open. Either source of wealth insulated him from the worst stresses that accompany living truly paycheck to paycheck.

What makes Secretary Lew's comments even more striking is that he is someone that mostly understands the economic realities facing households. As host of the Forum, he undoubtedly was aware of the panel discussions highlighting racial and economic disparities. Just nine months earlier, he opened the new Treasury Annex building as the Freedmen's Bank building.

Likely he heard the history of the federal government's disengagement with the Freedmen's Bank as well as the freed people themselves. The former contributed to the bank's eventual demise while the latter left the freed people with nothing to start their new lives. As Treasury Secretary he certainly knew of the discriminatory practices that Black creditors face when seeking car, home, and business loans. Despite his understanding of these and other systemic disparities, his answer that day reflected a very individualistic focus. Undoubtedly, our day-to-day decisions do impact our capacity to get ahead; however, they play a minor role as compared to the systemic forces that either support or hinder household efforts to gain financial security.

DIFFERENTIATING WEALTH AND INCOME

Getting ahead in this country has long been associated with achieving the American Dream. While this evocative concept eludes any singular definition, it usually includes owning one's home, gaining middle-class status, helping one's children get through college, and contemplating a comfortable retirement. Many focus on earning an ample income to achieve these aspirations, yet attaining these goals is really about accumulating wealth. As income and wealth represent two parts of an intricate relationship, many blur their important differences, including Secretary Lew. Nonetheless, their distinctions are substantial and worth noting.

Among the media and policymakers, the focus on household income has long overshadowed any attention given to wealth. Recent acknowledgments of the growing patterns of economic inequality in American society generally focus on income disparities and differences in earnings. While these gaps are substantial, they pale in comparison to the widening gulf in household wealth. As of 2022, the top 10 percent of income earners captured nearly half of all earned income while the wealthiest 10 percent held almost three-quarters of the nation's wealth. Clearly, different forces are influencing our nation's wealth distribution from income shares. Recall from Chapter 1 that these disparities are even more alarming when one considers them across the racial divide. As a reminder, the typical Black household earns about 57 percent of the typical White household while holding less than 10 percent of the wealth. As large and daunting as the racial income gap is, the racial wealth gap is five times larger. Given this contrast, it makes sense to investigate it further.

One reason that so many blur the distinctions between income and wealth is because they are so tightly interrelated. Indeed, the link between income and wealth resembles the iconic chicken-and-egg relationship. Many forms of wealth, whether savings accounts, stock portfolios, or commercial real estate, generate regular sources of income. Bank deposits yield interest, stocks generate dividends, and commercial buildings produce rental income. Other forms of wealth, like gold, generate income as they gain value. Assets like rental property and stock portfolios can generate income in both ways. Any income that goes unspent becomes the source of new wealth, whether deposited in one's bank or retirement accounts or used to purchase new assets. Income and wealth relate in an intricate dance in which each is capable of reinforcing the other in an iterative fashion. More wealth begets more income, which if unspent can generate even more wealth and more income. For those fortunate enough, this relationship is experienced as a virtuous cycle in which both facets of this relationship continue to support each other. Of course, this cycle can be experienced in reverse. Reductions in wealth generally result in less income generated. If this income is insufficient, households might consume more of their wealth with the concomitant reduction in future income.

Although income and wealth are inextricably linked, wealth offers households far more security than income. For most of us, our wages and salaries provide the largest source of income by a large measure. We depend on the regular replenishments of income that our jobs provide. Yet, as we learned during the COVID-19 spring of 2020, our regular earnings along with our jobs can disappear overnight and without warning. Employment income, the primary source of income for most households, is extremely tenuous. Wealth, on the other hand, is prized due to its durability and reliability, particularly in times of crisis. While some forms of wealth are vulnerable to theft or unexpected destruction, various protections limit our exposure. Federal insurance safeguards bank deposits while various forms of private insurance protect real property from specific threats. Indeed, humans have long cherished wealth for its protections during periods of crisis and disruption. Its durability and capacity to retain value positions wealth as the true source of financial security.

In addition to serving as a financial safety net, wealth also serves its holder as a source of power (Browne, 1972). Owning a dependable car expands one's search area for potential employment and generates income directly as a Lyft driver. Not only can savings cushion the trauma of unanticipated expenses or income loss, but they can also be deployed to exploit potential opportunities. Household savings can finance new training or educational opportunities that may open doors to more lucrative careers. Or households can use these funds to finance new business ventures that are too small, novel, or risky to attract outside investors. Wealth serves as collateral that can access credit much more easily and at lower cost; with such credit in hand, households can leverage investments, whether in their own home or commercial ventures. Those with more wealth to dispense can impact their community visibly as they decide which charitable organizations to support or influence public policy through their political contributions (Hall, 2024). In these and other ways, wealth serves as a source of power as it expands opportunities and agency. Raymond Franklin made the point bluntly when he wrote, "Ownership carries with it domination; its absence leads to subordination" (Franklin, 1991, p. xviii).

The reach of wealth's power and influence extends far beyond one's lifetime. Even during volatile periods, modest savings can help parents provide their young children necessary nutrition as their bodies and brains undergo rapid development. Family wealth can assure safe and stable housing and thereby avoid the disruptions caused by housing insecurity, household moves, and school changes. Wealth offers parents the choice to reside in communities known for their strong and well-funded public schools. As many of these communities use restrictive zoning to limit rental properties, they will likely need the necessary down payment to purchase a home. Or they can use their wealth to pay tuition at elite, private schools. Additionally, they can afford needed educational resources or special programs that might nurture their child's interests or talents. In these and countless other decisions, parents can use their wealth to prepare their children for college. Once accepted, their wealth can pay the tuition even at the elite colleges with their daunting price tags. None of this provides any guarantees, but it does increase the likelihood their children will reap job offers that provide professional status, ample salary, and attractive benefits. In some instances, parents can make this happen directly by offering employment in the family-owned business. Each of these examples illustrates how current family wealth can affect future opportunities quite dramatically. Interestingly, none of this help would be viewed as an intergenerational gift or inheritance, strictly speaking.

Family wealth brings other advantages as well. Wealth often brings an associated network of influential friends and colleagues. With this network, parents can use it to assist their children in getting into select schools, elite colleges, coveted training programs, and desired jobs, all instances where personal references can make a difference. This same network also yields a number of associations and social events that introduce their children into a world of status and power. Exposure to exclusive country clubs and elite summer camps prepare their children to become comfortable in rooms with powerful people. Wealthy parents have greater opportunities to share their financial wisdom and experiences, whether the intricacies of corporate finance or the complexities of running a business. Each of these influences can be instrumental in their impact on the career trajectories of their children. Again, none of these sources of help are considered forms of taxable inheritance. Yet, each of these enable parents to transfer their status and privilege to their children consistent with one of the key pillars of Wilkerson's caste requirements (Wilkerson, 2020).

Parents can deploy their accumulated wealth to help their children even after they have started their own careers. During times of economic distress, parents can offer their adult children free room and board or simply provide financial assistance. This safety net limits the financial bottoms that job loss or business failure can generate, thereby offering their children greater resiliency. By co-signing the mortgage or providing the down payment – often conveyed in the form of loan that may never be repaid – affluent parents can jump-start their children's financial journey as they provide early access into the financial world of appreciating assets. Such timely gifts can help their children buy homes in exclusive communities with coveted public schools. Labeled "transformative assets," these gifts can increase dramatically the wealth trajectory of subsequent generations (Shapiro, 2004, p. 2). Most of this help can be provided outside the normal channels of in vivo gifts and inheritances. When these transfers are forthcoming, they simply add to the help already received.

UNDERSTANDING HOW WEALTH IS ACCUMULATED

Secretary Lew's emphasis on the importance of household saving as a remedy for the racial wealth gap is unsurprising. Most economists would respond similarly given the broad acceptance of the Life Cycle Hypothesis (LCH) as a model of wealth accumulation. Introduced in the 1950s, the LCH offers a rather simple and intuitive understanding of how households build net worth (Modigliani & Brumberg, 1954). It acknowledges that some household wealth stems from family gifts and inheritances while far more results from the rising value of assets. Yet, at its core the LCH is primarily a savings model and therefore emphasizes saving as the key to wealth status. Although households may face incomes that are uncertain and erratic, they prefer consumption that is steady and, of course, high. Taking this cue, the model contends that households seek to smooth out their consumption at the maximum amount that circumstances permit. As such, the model views wealth merely as a store of value that one consumes during lean times.

The LCH model argues that household wealth follows a predictable pattern over the life cycle of households. It predicts that very young householders will actually dissave as they acquire debt to invest in their education and training to increase their human capital. As they approach middle age, they save an increasing share of their current income, first to pay down their debt and then to expand their financial portfolio. Now in their highest income-earning years, they continue to augment their wealth as they anticipate retirement. At retirement, households supplement their lost employment income by drawing down on their accumulated savings. Under the model, they ideally exhaust their wealth just as death approaches. In this way, they have utilized their wealth to the fullest by consuming it completely. Figure 2.1 offers evidence of this life-cycle pattern to household wealth as it illustrates the asset value and net worth of the median household for each age cohort. It clearly shows households accumulating assets and net worth until retirement and then experiencing some decline in both.[1] In this case, the evidence appears to support the LCH model, although it does suggest that aging households liquidate their wealth more slowly than the model predicts.

[1] The difference between the two figures is household debt. After rising through middle age as households purchase homes (and mortgages), it declines as householders continue to age.

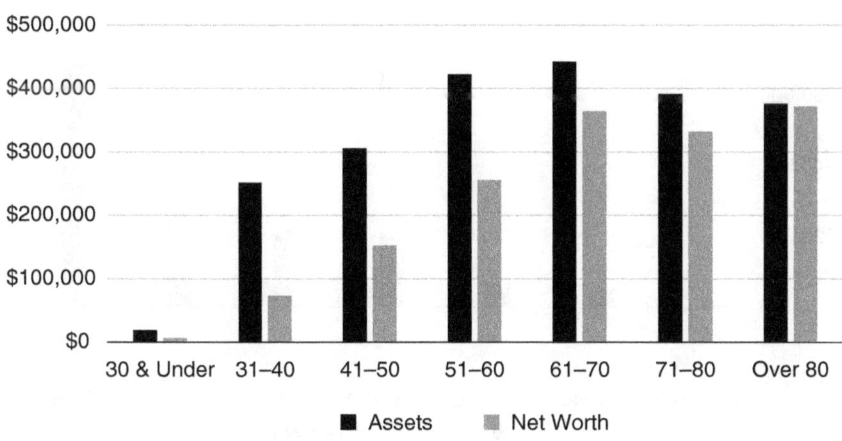

Figure 2.1 Household wealth over the life cycle
Source: Author's calculations; Federal Reserve Board, 2022 Survey of Consumer Finances

Other evidence raises doubts regarding the LCH model's predictive powers. Many years ago, one study found the model was applicable to professional, White households but did not apply to marginalized groups including Black and wealth-poor households (Wolff, 1981). In neither case did these households experience the arc of wealth accumulation illustrated in Figure 2.1. We can find contemporary corroboration of this result by examining the wealth of households that reside toward the bottom of the wealth continuum. Figure 2.2 depicts the asset values and net worth of households residing at the seventeenth percentile, about the middle of the bottom third of wealth holders. As you can see, there's little evidence that age alone enables many households to accumulate much wealth. Indeed, this figure depicts a disturbing, if unsurprising, consequence of household wealth – that it promotes longer life expectancy (Demakakos et al., 2016). Clearly, this group does not experience the life-cycle pattern of wealth accumulation as predicted by the LCH.

Other evidence poses further challenges to the LCH model. The model predicts that the distribution of wealth across households should reflect differences in household income, holding for age. Higher-income households will use their good fortune to increase their levelized consumption above those households earning less. Even as they experience an unanticipated increase in their income, particularly if they view the increase as permanent, they will raise their consumption spending accordingly. Similarly, households who expect or have received family wealth will increase their consumption relative to their less fortunate peers. The model argues that

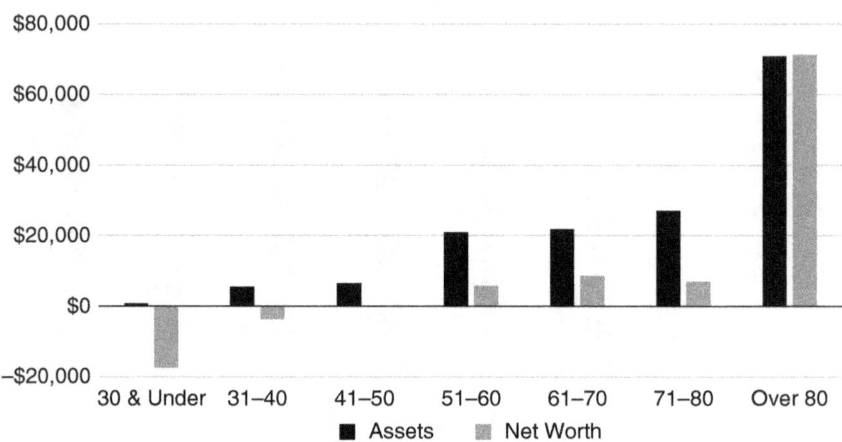

Figure 2.2 Life-cycle household wealth among the wealth-poor
Source: Author's calculations; Federal Reserve Board, 2022 Survey of Consumer Finances

higher-income households will differentiate themselves from their lower-income neighbors more by their consumption levels than by their accumulated wealth. Yet, in defiance of the model's predictions, wealth disparities far exceed income differences whether we consider intraracial or interracial distributions.

The apparent conundrum posed by the large and growing racial wealth gap has attracted many possible explanations. In one extensive study, Scholz and Levine (2004) investigated a number of reasons that might explain the growing gap. After rejecting the offered suggestions, they wondered whether *cultural differences* like reduced patience or risk tolerance among Black households might explain the vast discrepancy between the racial income and wealth gaps. According to another view, Black households place greater value on attaining a standard of living similar to their peers.[2] This emphasis on maintaining current consumption levels might explain lower household saving, limited financial discipline, or reduced risk tolerance, any of which could explain a larger wealth gap (Yao et al., 2005). While cultural differences might account for the unexpectedly wide wealth gap, so might differences in economic circumstances. As such, those trying to make the cultural differences argument face a difficult challenge as culture itself defies easy measurement. Unable to measure it directly, scholars aim to capture all of the noncultural arguments with the assumption that

2 The interested reader may want to look at Burlew et al. (1992); Yao et al. (2005); Gutter and Fontes (2006).

any unexplained remainder can be attributed to cultural differences. More troubling, these perceptions that Black households engage in conspicuous consumption as well as lack both fiscal discipline and financial acumen align well with broadly held racial stereotypes.

Nonetheless, let us examine these arguments. The contention that Black households save less than their White peers remains unsupported by the evidence once key controls like household income are considered (Hamilton & Chiteji, 2013). Various studies, conducted by economists who represent the full spectrum of economic thinking, ranging from Milton Friedman to Marcus Alexis, have found that Black households save slightly more than their White counterparts.[3] More recently, researchers wondered whether reduced access to credit, retail desertification in Black neighborhoods, and customer discrimination might all depress Black household consumption significantly. The authors concluded that White households outspent their Black peers by 30 percent when controlling for similar incomes (Charron-Chénier et al., 2017). Yet, the canard that Black households simply do not save enough to close the wealth gap persists.

Many researchers have shown that Black households typically hold a less diversified financial portfolio, with more of their wealth held in their home and less in higher-return assets like stocks and business equity. There is broad agreement that these differences in asset portfolios can explain some portion of the wealth gap (Boshara et al., 2015; Williams, 2016). There is disagreement on whether these choices result from poor or uninformed financial decisions, greater risk avoidance, or simply – again – the reality of modest resources limiting household options. A recent Federal Reserve study investigates these issues by evaluating the routine, day-to-day decisions that every household makes (Boshara et al., 2015). The authors find substantial differences between how Black and White households report whether they save, miss paying bills, carry credit card balances, hold adequate savings and limit their overall debt. They conclude that these differences in household behavior can explain portions of the racial wealth gap. Curiously, while the authors control for household age and education levels, they neglect to consider either household income or family wealth. One would expect either would influence saving behaviors, debt loads, and credit histories. Indeed, one can argue that their financial metric is more reflective of household distress than a determinant of wealth accumulation (Hamilton & Darity, 2017).

[3] See Darity et al. (2018) for a review. Among some of the studies are Friedman (1957); Alexis (1962); Galenson (1972); Gittleman and Wolff (2004); Hamilton and Chiteji (2013).

Still remaining is the argument that differences in racial attitudes toward risk might contribute to the wealth gap. One study finds interesting results after the researchers controlled for a long list of economic and demographic factors. They conclude that Black households were less inclined to take moderate risks as compared to White households, but a larger minority of Black households expressed a willingness to take *substantial* risks (Yao et al., 2005). One wonders whether this mixed result reflects fairly nuanced differences in risk tolerance or simply the result of imprecise metrics. Nonetheless, the authors call for increased financial literacy to prevent the fleecing of these risk-taking households since they "might be susceptible to financial scams" (Yao et al., 2005, p. 59) as they are unsophisticated investors who have little to lose. Just as we saw with Secretary Lew, there is the assumption that poor financial literacy *must* be at play. This natural tendency toward stigmatizing Black households reflects another of Wilkerson's caste pillars.

THE WEALTH PRIVILEGE MODEL

What is missing from this discussion is the possibility that systemic differences – whether social, racial, economic, or otherwise – may impact opportunities for accumulating wealth and getting ahead. The Wealth Privilege (WP) model aims to redress this void as it seeks to understand and explain the realities of wealth accumulation across the wealth spectrum (Williams, 2016, 2017). In its simplest form, the model can explain the persistently expanding racial wealth gap across generations without reference to overt racial discrimination. At the same time, it can include and accommodate the robust literature documenting the evidence of persistent racial bias in education as well as labor, credit, and housing markets. Further, it offers a persuasive explanation of how wealth functions as a form of economic stratification within and across generations (Darity, 2022).

Similar to the LCH, the WP model suggests that households accumulate wealth in three ways: household saving out of current income, the appreciation of assets held by the household, and any intergenerational transfers of family wealth. Unlike the LCH, this model argues that households accumulate wealth not simply as a store of future consumption, but also a source of power that can reach across generations. As such, the WP model does not emphasize Household Saving over the other two wealth pathways. Indeed, the evidence suggests that Household Saving may be the least important source of wealth accumulation. In further contrast from the LCH, the WP model argues that each avenue of wealth accumulation is influenced by a household's wealth status. While affluent households experience each of the three pathways as virtuous cycles, wealth-poor households find them forbidding and unforgiving. Thresholds exist to delineate the two experiences and thereby create distinctly different outcomes, leading to stratified results. Simply put, households experience each of these pathways in vastly different ways depending on their wealth status.

Let us start with the Household Saving pathway as it is the one pathway of which likely all households have some experience. When we consider this pathway, most of us consider what economists call *active saving*. This means that we divert some portion of our current income from buying groceries, paying the light bill, or taking in a movie. Or as Secretary Lew suggested, the coffee, movie, or video that is purchased without thought. Of course, this type of saving requires substantial discipline and self-control, which we exhibit in varying degrees. Although this form of saving is what most people consider, it is unlikely to be the most significant.

For those of us with ample savings, banks and other financial institutions design their services with our interests in mind (Mullainathan & Shafir, 2009). Bank accounts enable employees to get paid through direct deposit, thereby mitigating the step where their pay burns a hole in their pocket. Even better, bank customers can divert part of their pay directly into a savings account, thereby making the "saving decision" automatic. While one can always countermand this intention by spending the funds later, people are less likely to do so (Thaler, 1999). With online banking, bank customers can set up bill-pay alerts and online bill-pay services, thereby limiting late fees and finance charges. These largely unnoticed services reduce unwanted fees and streamline our savings decisions, all without an explicit cost.

Households with ample and stable earnings can experience the savings pathway as a virtuous cycle in which saving gets easier incrementally. As households deposit funds into bank accounts and other assets, these investments supplement their current income, thereby making future saving easier. Although this cycle works incrementally, it does so relentlessly until there is a change in one's earnings or expenses. The accumulated savings foster future saving in other ways. Not forced to live paycheck to paycheck, households use their savings to meet unexpected major purchases without resorting to borrowed funds and interest charges. When the car breaks down, they can fix it immediately rather than rely on undependable transportation that can lead to job loss. As needed, they can borrow funds at lower interest rates and easier terms than those less well off. They can use their savings to buy items in bulk, particularly when such purchases offer substantial discounts in price. Accumulated savings allow one to afford precautionary medical care which can prevent more expensive health problems down the road. None of these advantages are major sources of wealth accumulation, but they work relentlessly and seamlessly.

More important are employer-sponsored retirement plans. In some cases, these plans simply allow employees to direct a portion of their pay to a dedicated retirement account, while other times the employer will offer matching deposits. In either case, this option offers the employee another automatic savings option that limits the temptation of discretionary spending. Any earnings remain within the fund, while financial penalties discourage early withdrawals. Similarly, homeownership provides another savings option not available to renters. Under conventional amortizing mortgages, the *principal* portion of the monthly mortgage payment pays down the outstanding debt on the property. Over the life of the loan, this portion gets larger as the debt is reduced. Frequently, homeowners make monthly mortgage payments similar to what renters might pay in rent; however, the principal portion of the mortgage payment is really a form of involuntary saving. Similarly, any loans taken out on other commercial properties offer the landlord/borrower the same opportunity to build equity.

Each of these advantages mitigate the temptations of impulsive spending and encourage greater saving of one's current income. These benefits accrue even if one's employment income remains the same. For those households who experience promotions and raises at their job, the additional income adds further opportunities for household saving.

Asset Appreciation provides households with a more substantial source of wealth accumulation. While households invest their savings in durable assets that retain their value to gain financial security, these assets generate income, appreciate in value, or both. Bank savings, money market accounts, and bond funds generate regular interest payments. Real estate can furnish regular rental income and appreciate over time. Stock funds often increase in value more dramatically, but are subject to increased volatility and risk. Business ventures, whether funded by sweat equity or invested funds, may bring riches or fall flat on their face. All of these options enable households to deploy their current wealth to generate additional wealth, sometimes spectacularly.

A key characteristic of the Asset Appreciation pathway is the risk/reward trade-off. Those investments that yield steady returns do so at a lower rate than those whose yields are volatile. For good reason, most wealth-poor households choose to invest their modest wealth in safe but low-yielding assets. These investments allow them to recover their money as the need arises. As households accumulate more wealth, they can safely take more chances. Increased wealth enables households to diversify their assets across a range of investment options, all of which reduces their actual risk. This capability to assume greater risk opens wider opportunities to invest in assets that generate higher yields. Similar to the Household Saving pathway, the Asset Appreciation pathway functions as a virtuous cycle as greater wealth enables increased diversification, which then allows more risk taking and increased returns.

Increased wealth enables households the means to utilize *leverage* in their quest to accumulate wealth. *Leverage* is simply *the ability to use other's people wealth to increase your wealth.* To demonstrate its importance, I offer a simple example. An investor buys a $100,000 condominium to use as a rental property. Normally, they put 20 percent down, or $20,000, and borrow the rest from the bank. For simplicity's sake, let us suppose they get an interest-only mortgage. Further, their monthly rental exactly covers their mortgage payment as well as any fees and taxes. Thus, they are simply breaking even on the deal. Over the next five years, the condo appreciates 20 percent, or $20,000. If our investor decides to sell the condo at that price, they will double their investment, since their only investment is the original $20,000. Although the bank technically owns 80 percent of the condo, the investor gets to claim all of the increased value. By using leverage, investors can deploy their wealth far more productively than simply depositing funds into a bank. Yet, one must have access to credit to take advantage of leverage. Wealth clearly helps here. Viewed as better credit risks, wealthier households can borrow at lower rates and easier terms as well as in larger amounts. Access to credit along with the capacity to take risks provides affluent households with the means and motive to augment their wealth in spectacular fashion.

The third avenue for wealth accumulation – the Family Support pathway – functions like the other two, although it does so over longer periods. Many of us can look back into our family history and observe a progression over the generations. While it is unlikely we know the details of family wealth with each generation, we can view proxies like property ownership and college attainment. At least until recently, most families have experienced absolute mobility across the generations as children attained more than their parents. Although there are exceptions, this general pattern can be easily explained by understanding how the Family Support pathway functions.

It is true that every parent can bequeath their children character and moral development while sharing those life lessons that guide them throughout their lives. Yet, wealthy parents have many other ways of promoting their kids. Affluent parents can provide their children with the necessary education and upbringing to secure well-paying employment as an adult. They can supply the necessary funds to finance a first home or business start-up. They can make regular gifts or leave an inheritance upon their death. Simply their presence as a safety net allows their kids to take greater risks in their own lives. All of this help enables their children to take greater advantage of the privileges available in both the Household Saving and Asset Appreciation pathways. Parental help that is offered early or in substantial amounts magnifies these opportunities. In most cases, parents expect little in return. Instead, they wish their kids will pay it forward to their own children. As each generation leverages this help, they have more to offer the subsequent generation. In this way, intergenerational wealth can support one of Wilkerson's eight pillars of caste as it ensures an immutable birthright from parent to child. As parents have fewer kids, this expansion of intergenerational wealth merely increases. Across generations, family wealth can grow in the same iterative fashion we have observed several times already.

At least to this point, the WP model's primary conclusion is that we should all get richer together. It does not explain, like the LCH model, why so many wealth-poor households are unable to accumulate wealth over time. Yet, the WP model includes another key narrative. The experiences discussed above occur only as households attain some measure of wealth. For wealth-poor households, their experiences of the three wealth pathways are considerably different. Households who experience income that is inadequate, irregular, or uncertain find the Household Saving pathway relentlessly unforgiving. Without sufficient income to meet their household expenses, they are forced to liquidate past savings or suffer mounting debt, either of which contribute to future peril. Liquidated assets no longer generate income, while increased debt spawns larger debt payments. Until their circumstances improve, they have little recourse but to pursue these "remedies." Unlike the virtuous cycle discussed previously, these households find the Household Saving pathway as an unrelenting vicious cycle.

Wealth-poor households face other obstacles as they strive to save some portion of their income. Their modest savings along with their need use these funds frequently make them unwelcomed by banks (Mullainathan & Shafir, 2009). High minimum balances, regular account fees, and substantial overdraft charges serve to discourage wealth-poor customers, causing 20 percent of households to remain unbanked. These households not only forfeit the banking services discussed previously but also must rely upon alternative financial institutions like check-cashing services or payday lenders. These businesses charge hefty fees that deplete whatever limited resources their customers might have to save.

Wealth-poor households face other demands on their limited funds due to their financial vulnerability. Often, they must pay deposits to gain electric and gas service, making these funds unavailable. When borrowing, they face higher interest rates as their low credit scores alert lenders of their increased risk. Just as often, their credit requests are denied, forcing them to make other arrangements. Without access to credit, they are forced to defer major purchases until they have saved the needed funds. They are required to use local services like the laundromat, causing them to spend money that could be used to repay the loan on a new washer and dryer. For unbanked households, accumulating cash savings may be thwarted by impulse purchases or pilfering by a household member. Many households view the lottery as a more reliable vehicle to gain needed funds to purchase an appliance than this traditional method.

These challenges that siphon their limited income means they are unlikely to have any financial cushion. All of us face income and expenses that rarely match over time. Lacking any savings cushion, wealth-poor households must rely on other remedies when their expenses exceed their income. Sometimes households will delay payments, often with a clear strategy (Desmond, 2016). Inevitably, they suffer disconnect fees and then subsequent reconnect charges. While these behaviors meet their short-run imperatives, they create longer-run problems as their credit scores plummet.

Wealth-poor households experience the Asset Appreciation pathway quite differently than their more affluent neighbors, although the treatment is less draconian. Instead, they are treated indifferently. The assets that most households initially purchase are furniture, appliances, and motor vehicles. While these meet basic household needs, each decline in value over their operating life. No doubt these assets offer comfort, lower expenses, or even employment opportunities. Yet, none of them offer what many assets provide: a direct source of increased wealth. Wealth-poor households get little assistance from the Asset Appreciation pathway until they gain the means to invest in those assets that do appreciate. Some may benefit from more welcoming credit unions or banks as they deposit their savings, although the returns are modest.

More rewarding investments like homeownership entail substantial capital requirements, such as a down payment. With their shaky financial circumstances and modest credit scores, wealth-poor households are unlikely to find much help in overcoming this obstacle. To these households, access to credit and the rewards of debt leveraging may appear as a distant mirage.

Households that come from wealth-poor families can experience the Family Support pathway as equally treacherous as the Household Saving avenue. Only one-third of households report receiving or expecting a family inheritance.[4] Many more households do benefit as parents help with college expenses, slip a cash gift on special occasions, or gift them the family car – transfers rarely viewed as inheritances. Those who come from wealth-poor families do not simply miss the possibility of receiving these gifts; in many cases, they find themselves the target of family requests. Their parents may need help as they drain their meager savings. Siblings may experience challenging illnesses that generate unpayable medical bills. Their relative success can make them the family safety net. As they loyally respond to these requests for help, they limit their own efforts to get ahead. Just as the legacy of family wealth can propel their descendants, so can the legacy of wealth poverty limit their children's prospects.

Even those fortunate to receive an inheritance may find a bequest gift of real estate fraught with challenges. Low-income and non-White households are more likely to die intestate with no will guiding how their estate should be distributed (DiRusso, 2009). Many find the cost of paying an attorney to draw up a valid will beyond their means, while those from marginalized communities have experienced an unwelcoming and even rapacious financial sector (Henderson, 2020). Absent a valid will, any real property is divided in common among any heirs recognized by the controlling state law. Under this legal arrangement of tenancy in common, each heir has the right to use the whole property, none can be excluded from its use, and all must agree to any important decision. Any heir that dies intestate transfers their in-common tenancy to their successors, further fragmenting property ownership. This clouded title to the property lowers its market value to creditors, lessees, or buyers. Often unable to use the property as collateral, owners find it challenging to raise cash to make needed improvements to prevent property decline (Henderson, 2020). Rather than serve as a catalyst for further wealth, these inherited properties can function as emotional and financial deadweight (Dobbs & Gaither, 2023).

The narrative predicted by the WP model is that households experience very different circumstances as they strive to get ahead and find some measure of financial security. Those starting out with means – and without substantial student loan debt – may find the path initially challenging, much like Secretary Lew. Securing employment that brings ample income

[4] According to the 2022 SCF, 23 percent of households report receiving past transfers, while 14 percent expect one in the future. Some households are included in both groups.

will enable young householders the means to invest their savings into productive assets that yield income. Family help can hasten the move to homeownership, business ventures, or retirement savings. Earlier attainment of these milestones offers greater opportunities for households to reap their long-term rewards. With increased wealth, households experience greater privileges that make their efforts less exerting and more fruitful. Each of the wealth accumulation pathways functions in synergistic ways as they complement household efforts to get ahead.

Rather than gaining helpful tailwinds, wealth-poor households find the three wealth pathways resisting their efforts to get ahead. At best, they experience brief periods where their uncertain incomes enable them to bank modest savings only to suffer some disruption that undermines their progress. They find themselves largely treading water hoping to avoid the hidden currents that might pull them under. The modest and irregular income along with limited savings marks them as a poor credit risk. Denied access to credit, they are unable to leverage asset purchases like homeownership that might provide financial security. Instead, their most important household assets depreciate over time. Without savings or family resources to draw upon, financial setbacks caused by illness or unemployment may require desperate responses like selling their home, raiding their retirement account, or closing their dream business. Each of these actions means they will be less able to access the privileges of wealth when they overcome the immediate crises. Lastly, those who do experience financial success attract requests for help from less fortunate family members. In each of these ways, the three wealth pathways function as headwinds on their efforts to achieve financial security.

THE WEALTH PRIVILEGE MODEL AND RACE

Although the WP model makes no overt recognition of race, it offers profound insights into the racial wealth gap. Figure 2.3 illustrates this connection. It depicts the percentage of Black and White households that reside in each of the three wealth terciles. Households in the Bottom Tercile have a net worth that is below $47,000. Most households in this group can expect little help from the privileges of wealth. In contrast, households in the Middle Tercile have wealth that ranges from $47,000 up to $395,000. These households generally earn ample incomes, possess varied appreciating assets, and may have family capable of offering financial help. Those in the Top Wealth Tercile can expect the most generous help. Most earn high incomes that enable further saving, own varied investment portfolios,

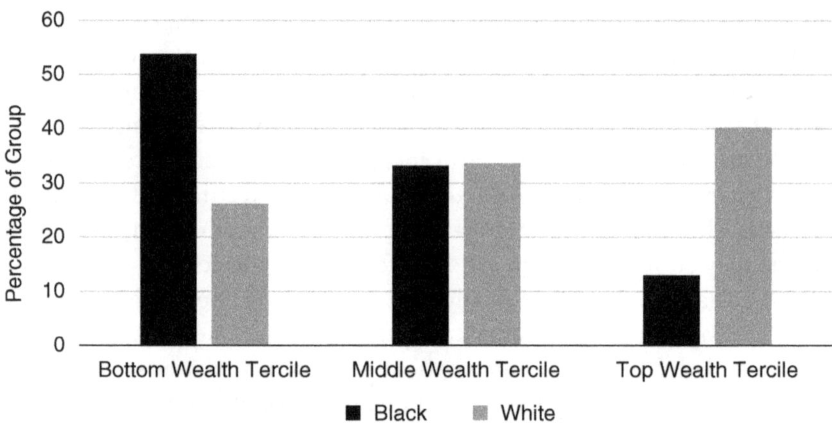

Figure 2.3 Distribution of households by wealth status and race
Source: Author's calculations; Federal Reserve Board, 2022 Survey of Consumer Finances

and have easy access to credit and debt leveraging. As the figure illustrates, a majority of Black households reside in the Bottom Tercile as compared to a quarter of White households. In contrast, most White households have enough wealth to access some or all of the privileges of wealth just explained. Given this juxtaposition, the WP model predicts that the racial wealth gap will only grow over time, *even in a post-racial world.*

Of course, we do not yet live in a post-racial world; there is a robust literature that documents the persistence of racial discrimination, particularly in labor, credit, and housing markets, areas that are critical to getting ahead financially. Black job applicants face greater obstacles in securing employment, as field studies have shown they receive fewer callbacks from prospective employers (Darity & Mason, 1998; Bertrand & Mullainathan, 2004). Often the first laid off, Black workers experience more frequent and longer unemployment spells.[5] They are funneled into lower-paying occupations that offer fewer benefits, including employer-sponsored retirement plans.[6] Even when educational attainment and other factors are considered, Black workers continue to earn wages and salaries that lag behind those of White workers.[7] Indeed, the pay gap widens even further for those who are both Black and female (Darity et al., 1996;

[5] The interested reader should look at Weller (2019); Ajilore (2020); Mason (2023).

[6] The interested reader should look at Copeland (2014); Borowczyk-Martins et al. (2017); Solomon et al. (2019).

[7] See Darity et al. (1996); Paul et al. (2022); Mason (2023).

Paul et al., 2022). We all can understand how much easier active saving is with a higher level of earnings.

Earning less income and holding less wealth already places Black households at a distinct disadvantage when they apply for loans to finance their education, purchase a home, or start a business. Persistent racial bias places further obstacles when applying for credit. Studies show that Black applicants are rejected at higher rates than White applicants even when comparable financial circumstances are considered.[8] Those who gain loan approval pay higher interest rates on car loans, student loan debt, and mortgages than similarly situated White borrowers (Chiteji, 2010). When making the most important investment that most households make, prospective Black homebuyers receive less information and fewer opportunities to view advertised homes (Turner, 2002). As such, Black homebuyers pay around 2 percent more than White buyers even after controlling for income and access to credit (Bayer et al., 2017). After overcoming all of these obstacles, Black homeowners experience less appreciation on their homes due to enduring residential segregation, further limiting their aspirations of financial security.[9]

Black business ownership has long lagged far behind that of Whites. Historically, vibrant Black businesses have suffered destruction at the hands of White mobs, highway construction and "urban renewal" projects, and state-sanctioned seizures (Levin, 2021). More recently, Black business development is hampered by the lack of family wealth to provide adequate start-up funds, causing these enterprises to remain small and financially vulnerable (Fairlie & Robb, 2010; Austin, 2016). Restricted access to credit imperils their survival rates (Bates, 1997; Blanchflower et al., 2003). So does the biased preferences of White customers (Borjas & Bronars, 1989; Myers & Chan, 1996). It seems the disparities in business ownership between Whites and Blacks is less about nerve and risk taking and more about access to capital and receptive customers.

CONCLUSION

Treasury Secretary Lew mirrors the views of many Americans when he offers increased self-discipline and financial literacy as the keys to financial

[8] There is a significant literature on this. See Munnell et al. (1996); Myers Jr. and Chung (1996); Ladd (1998); Charles and Hurst (2002); Chiteji (2010).

[9] Refer to the following: Flippen (2004); Oliver & Shapiro (2006); Williams (2016); Mason (2023).

security. Their actual contribution appears much more modest. To be sure, active saving by households whereby they save some portion of their current income represents one of the three pathways to wealth accumulation. It is the most accessible of the three pathways. However, it is highly unlikely that avoiding the temptation of the $5 coffee realistically leads to financial security. It is more likely that households fortunate enough to have access to an employer-sponsored retirement plan, particularly one with an employer match, will experience greater savings growth. Similarly, gaining access to the full range of banking services will insulate households from the bevy of check-cashing fees, late-payment fees, and overdraft charges that undermine the intention to save. These banking services safeguard us from our impulsiveness and disorganization.

Undoubtedly, most Americans could benefit from a dose of financial education. Yet, there's scant evidence that financial literacy determines whether households become wealthy or remain poor. When initially forming, all households must acquire needed assets like furniture, home appliances, and a car. While none of these assets will lead to financial security, their acquisition should not be viewed as a sign of poor decision making. Until households can amass adequate wealth, they have few options to garner a balanced and diversified portfolio. Until they reach this point, it makes sense for them to invest in safe but low-yielding investments. Doing so, of course, limits their ability to accumulate additional wealth. Only as households are able to accumulate significant wealth should they invest in high-yielding assets. Holding a diversified yet aggressive portfolio is less about financial smarts and more about the capacity to gather adequate wealth. Thus, truly accessing the Asset Appreciation pathway as a source of financial security requires the ability to accumulate a modest nest egg, whether through regular saving or through the Family Support pathway.

Given wealth's durability as well as its easy transfer of opportunity and power across generations, we must consider the contribution of the Family Support pathway, one ignored by Secretary Lew. In 2022, nearly 30 percent of White households reported receiving a family gift or inheritance as compared to only 10 percent of Black households. Among the recipients, White households typically received $110,000 while Black recipients typically got about half that. This help alone can explain why more White households reside in the upper two wealth terciles and thereby garner the advantages of the Asset Appreciation pathway. Even more telling, 13 percent of Black households reported *giving money* to their siblings, parents, and grandparents over the past year, likely to remedy familial distress. This rate exceeded the 6 percent reported among White households. When looking forward, we find a similar pattern. When asked whether they *anticipate* a future family gift, White households respond affirmatively more than double the rate of Black households (17 percent vs. 8 percent). All of these disparities suggest strongly how much influence the past has on current and future opportunities.

Discerning the individual contribution of any of the three wealth pathways is a challenging task given the interlacing ways the three pathways support each other. Nonetheless, a recent study measured how much family gifts and inheritances might contribute to current wealth. Relying on the Survey of Consumer Finance regular household surveys, the authors documented all of the reported gifts and inheritances as well as the year of their receipt (Feiveson & Sabelhaus, 2018). Recognizing that past gifts will appreciate over time, they calculated this growth using a 3 and 5 percent real rate of return. Based on these two estimates, they found that somewhere between 26 and 51 percent of all household wealth in 2016 could be traced back to these gifts.[10] While high, these figures should be viewed as lower-bound estimates. Recall that many intergenerational transfers like parental payment of their children's college tuition are not included in these estimates. Further, one suspects that self-reporting of family gifts and inheritances is subject to substantial recall bias. Whatever the true figure is, the evidence suggests that Family Support through gifts and inheritances represents a substantial contributor to the racial wealth gap. Speaking of financial literacy, one might argue that the most important financial decision any person can make is which parents they select.

With this WP lens in mind, it is evident how effectively our current system meets Wilkerson's eight pillars of a caste hierarchy. Wealth's power, durability, and transferability enables affluent parents and grandparents to bequeath their economic status to their heirs easily and effectively. Investing in their children's educational opportunities will open doors to highly desirable occupations, while family gifts and connections may yield entrepreneurial opportunities that lead to managing and owning businesses. Family wealth will influence where individuals reside, go to school, socialize, and ultimately whom they marry. The dominant narrative that wealth is the outcome of hard work, disciplined thriftiness, financial acumen, and clever risk taking reinforces the social hierarchy. The affluent are to be praised for their inspiring personal character while the wealth-poor should be scolded for their obvious behavioral lapses. This nonrecognition

[10] The vast differences in these two estimates illustrate the dramatic impact of the selected discount rate.

of the privileges of wealth status creates its own form of cruelty, particularly as those without means internalize this dominant narrative. Worse still, much of our current policy is based on the perception that those with wealth are the *deserving recipients* of federal assistance.

The WP model actually acknowledges a fourth source of household accumulation – government support. As discussed in Chapter 1, the federal government, even at its inception, enacted policies to assist households to retain and build wealth. These policies include the infamous fugitive slave laws and Indian Removal Act as well as the heralded homestead laws and GI Bill. In each of these cases, the policy targeted its generosity on the basis of race, usually overtly and sometimes covertly. We often view these policies as part of our nation's distant past; yet, the ease by which wealth can accumulate and later be transferred across generations means that most White households today are the beneficiaries of these policies. Making this argument is the focus of Chapter 3.

While Chapter 3 considers past federal policies designed to help American households build wealth, Chapter 4 examines contemporary wealth-building policies. Today, government support comes in the form of generous tax expenditures that reward households able to accumulate some measure of wealth. All of these tax expenditures are housed within Secretary Lew's Treasury Department. Given their importance, it is surprising and distressing that the Secretary neglected to identify them as important causes of the racial wealth gap. As a previous Treasury Undersecretary noted, these tax expenditures function as a hidden back door to the US Treasury. Perhaps Secretary Lew is simply unaware of their contribution to the racial wealth gap. Making this point clearer is the subject of subsequent chapters in this book.

3

Looking Back

OUTLAWING THE INTERNATIONAL ENSLAVED TRADE

On January 1, 1808, the federal government took a major step against racial oppression and toward justice. Nine months earlier, the Congress enacted legislation quickly signed into law by President Jefferson, himself an extensive enslaver, outlawing the international enslaved trade on this date. The law prohibited the importation of enslaved persons, whether on American or foreign ships, into the newly created United States and imposed heavy penalties on any who engaged in this trade. It permitted the boarding and inspection of ships hovering off the American coastline and authorized the seizure and forfeiture of property if evidence of slaving was found. The law mandated heavy penalties including fines of $20,000 for those outfitting a ship for this purpose, $10,000 for participating in the trade, and $800 per enslaved person. Many of these activities carried prison sentences as well. To encourage enforcement, the law gave informers, privateers, and local port authorities an interest in the seized cargo. A decade later, the federal government raised the stakes even higher by equating the trade to piracy and making participation subject to the death penalty. By these acts, the federal government took substantial steps in limiting the expansion of slavery more widely throughout the United States (Goldfarb, 1994).

Of course, simply making such activities a federal crime did not end their practice. By one estimate, up to 60,000 enslaved Africans were brought to the US after this external trade was outlawed (Goldfarb, 1994). At the time, the United States lacked enough naval ships to patrol its vast coastline. Further hampering enforcement was the continued legality of the *coastwise trade* as slavers transported the enslaved from one state to another.[1]

[1] The law did attempt to regulate, although not discourage, this trade.

As prices for the enslaved rose, the lure of profit encouraged many to ignore the law and its lax enforcement. Many slavers simply brought the enslaved across the border from both Florida and Texas, neither of which were part of the United States at the time of the ban. Those caught were rarely prosecuted since most local authorities supported slavery (Moylan, 2019). On the other hand, local authorities were fully supportive of selling the ship and cargo for money, either to supplement public funds or line their own pockets (Moylan, 2019). The law did little to limit the involvement of American slave traders who were taking the enslaved Africans to Cuba and other parts of the Americas. This substantial trade continued largely unabated.

Two issues undermine the moral stance advanced by the enactment of this importation ban. Few of the enslaved Africans detained illegally on these ships gained any benefit from the law. Certainly, one would expect that the law would recognize their plight and offer them their freedom, either in the US or transported back to Africa. Indeed, one key goal of the law was to limit the flow of enslaved individuals from outside. In most cases, the enslaved were simply viewed as part of the ship's cargo, resold into slavery for money, and therefore a source of profit for others (Finkelman, 2012). Authorities in slaveholding states had little interest in having free Blacks residing within their borders. Even ardent Northern abolitionists had little taste for freeing them. Although deeply offended by the outrage of slavery, most abolitionists feared the freed captives would drain limited public services and threaten White working-class interests (Moylan, 2019). Along with the ship owners who chose to engage in the trade, the enslaved Africans were the primary losers under this law.

Twenty years earlier, the delegates to the Constitutional Convention argued forcefully over the fate of the international slave trade (Finkelman, 2009). Most came to the convention recognizing the federal government would require broad powers over interstate and foreign commerce; the extent and breadth of those powers still needed to be decided. Delegates from slaveholding states were concerned that such powers could be used to restrict the external slave trade and even slavery itself. This conflict gave rise to what has been called the "dirty compromise." At the insistence of South Carolina and Georgia, enough Northern states agreed to limit any federal restriction of the external slave trade for twenty years in order to gain federal regulation of all other commerce by simple majority vote. Given this impassioned debate, it is surprising that Congress voted overwhelmingly to enact the ban before the twenty-year limit had elapsed. With President Jefferson's eager signature, the Act to Prohibit the Importation of

Slaves demonstrated how much Southern resistance had evaporated over the two decades.

Outlawing the external slave trade did not result from any decline in the importance of slavery over the period. Available evidence strongly suggests that a vast number of enslaved Africans were brought to the US during the twenty-year period.[2] One important change was the introduction of the newly invented cotton gin, which made short-staple cotton a more profitable crop than tobacco, rice, indigo, or long-staple cotton. While most Northern states were abolishing slavery by 1808, it was spreading south and west across vast new areas where the short-staple cotton grew best. Still, this does not offer a ready explanation for eliminating a source of cheap labor.

The chattel slavery system that evolved in the United States gave it a unique, and horrific, character that distinguished it from past forms of slavery. Here, enslaved labor was valued not only as a source of inexpensive labor, but as a fountain of wealth. Enslavers used their enslaved wealth as collateral to raise funds to buy more land and more labor. At the time, about one-third of household wealth in the South was based on the value of the enslaved labor.[3] Only the land itself contributed a larger share to household wealth. Unlike the land, enslaved labor was not only productive, but also *reproductive,* thereby generating greater wealth for the enslaver.

Banning the external slave trade produced very different consequences for existing and potential enslavers. The importation ban limited the supply of enslaved persons, thereby raising their price on the still-legal internal market. Those trying to bring more land under cultivation and needing more labor to work that land lobbied against this ban. They would benefit from lower prices for enslaved labor. In contrast, established slaveholders in long-settled lands recognized they would profit from the rising prices. These plantations functioned as "breeder plantations," as the reproduction among their enslaved population exceeded their need for workers. After raising their children, enslaved mothers were forced to see their families sold "down South" so that the enslaver could gain the greatest profit. For example, Thomas Jefferson sold some of his enslaved persons to cover personal debts generated by his lavish lifestyle. The relative ease of outlawing the external trade shows the chattel slavery system was more than a labor system, but one of asset wealth. This perspective suggests the 1807 importation ban was less about moral courage than an early attempt to support

2 As cited in Anstey (1975), Carey (1853) estimates 52,000, while Fogel and Engerman (1974) place the number much higher at almost 250,000.

3 Jones (1980) as cited by Rosenbloom (2018).

wealth-building. In hindsight, it proved an effective policy as over the next half century enslaved prices would triple, with all of the direct gains redounding to White enslavers.[4]

AN ENSLAVERS' CONSTITUTION

The US Constitution is a remarkable document, particularly for its time, in designing a system of governance that protected individual liberties and political rights (for some). The founders were equally concerned with creating a system of governance that promoted prosperity and financial well-being. As stated in the preamble, the Constitution is designed to "secure the blessings of liberty for ourselves and our posterity." At that time, most took an expansive view of liberty that included the rights to acquire, possess, and dispose of property. To ensure these rights, the founders placed limits of whether states could impair "the obligations of Contracts," as well as giving Congress the right to enact patent and copyright laws that would have "limited times." Moreover, they enacted the important Fifth Amendment that outlaws any deprivation of property without due process or taking of property without just compensation. Each of these provisions placed restraints on government's capacity to abridge individual property rights, at least for Whites.

The constitutional limitation on federal regulation of the external slave trade is but one reason that some consider it to be an enslavers' Constitution. Recall from Chapter 1 the other key provisions protecting their interests. Worried that their valuable property in the form of chattel slavery might flee or collectively fight for their freedom, Southern representatives to the Constitutional Convention imposed a fugitive slave clause to ensure federal help in suppressing any enslaved rebellion. Fearful that European migration might produce an abolitionist majority, the Southern delegates garnered prohibitions against direct taxes on property as well as on highly profitable, enslaved-produced crops like rice, tobacco, indigo, and cotton. Each of these provisions made certain that the enslavers' wealth would receive the full support and protection of the federal government. Even this was not enough. To ensure current power and limit future threats, the Southern states brokered the Three Fifths agreement that gave Southern voters disproportionate political power that was wielded on behalf of enslavers. This dominance enabled the Southern states to elect presidents

[4] See US Census Bureau (1975) *Historical Statistics*, Table Bb212 Average Slave Price, as cited in Williamson and Cain (2021).

who were enslavers or sympathizers and control the US Senate until they left the Union in response to the election of President Lincoln.

Some argue that the US Constitution simply reflected the political realities of the times. Northern delegates to the Constitutional Convention worried that any national government would be fatally weakened unless all thirteen states entered the Union. Facing Southern threats to remain separate unless their demands were met, the Northern states had little choice but to compromise on key provisions. This argument concludes that the Constitution took a neutral stance by letting slavery remain only where it was already established. The evidence suggests otherwise.

Almost before the ink was dry, Southern representatives used their considerable political power to enact a fugitive slave law. This law gave enslavers or their agents the right to search and seize any who had fled from their plantations. Further, it imposed substantial fines for any who harbored or concealed the runaways, *even in states where slavery had been abolished.* Over the decades, a growing abolitionist movement in the North encouraged local resistance to this law. Over a half century later in 1850, the slaveholding states still held enough power to pass a more draconian law. This measure reduced the burden of proof on the enslavers' agents while increasing the penalties for any who obstructed the process. Further, it created a federal bureaucracy of judges and commissioners designed to hold status hearings and render decisions that could not be appealed to either state or federal judges (Finkelman, 2012). Free Blacks came under increased threat of being unjustly seized and sent "down South" to slavery. Despite this threat, the law stipulated that free Blacks had no right to testify on their own behalf in any status hearings (Finkelman, 2012).

Both laws certainly reduced the losses experienced by enslavers from those willing to risk the perils of flight and potential recapture. They also held far-reaching consequences. Even states that abolished slavery were bound to help enslavers recapture any persons seeking freedom in contravention of their own state laws. Rather than simply protecting slavery from Northern encroachment, these measures extended its reach throughout the "free" North. In his infamous *Dred Scott v. Sandford* decision, Judge Taney argued the federal government had no power to abolish slavery either in the federal territories or DC itself. This decision overturned a tenuous compromise over an issue that had bedeviled the country for over a half century – the expansion of slavery.

The expansion of slavery to new lands, particularly after the invention of the cotton gin, offered enslavers and the nation at large an even greater source of wealth than the recapture of those fleeing slavery. With their enhanced political representation, the slaveholding states effectively pursued this avenue. Two decisions that predate the Constitution exhibit this new power. Operating under the Articles of Confederation five years earlier, Congress discussed the treatment of lands west of the Appalachian Mountains. As part of the Ordinance of 1784, the representatives developed operating principles that would guide the settlement and eventual inclusion of new states into the Union. One principle discussed was a ban on slavery after 1800 throughout these territories. Unsurprisingly, this proposal drew heated debate. When it came to a vote, all the Northern states voted in approval; three Southern states voted against, while the North Carolina delegation deadlocked and the New Jersey delegation could not vote due to inadequate representation (Berkhofer, 1972). According to the rules, nine states needed to vote affirmatively to adopt a law, causing this provision to fail for lack of one vote (Grubb, 2010). Three years later, the Congress returned to the issue of the western lands. This time they forbade the spread of slavery to lands north of the Ohio River as part of the Northwest Ordinance of 1787. This decision, one that predates the Constitution, represents the apex of those trying to limit the expansion of slavery.

Although no small victory, this restriction on slavery expansion still left vast territories south of the Ohio River ripe for exploitation. New lands resulting from the Louisiana and Florida Purchases, the Treaty of Gudalupe Hildalgo, and the Oregon Treaty created new opportunities to expand slavery. During the antebellum period, both sides on slavery expansion maintained a delicate balance within the Senate by admitting new states under a paired basis, one slaveholding state for one free state. The Missouri Compromise of 1820 maintained this balance but also extended the demarcation line from beyond the Ohio River along the 36° parallel, with an exception given to Missouri. As part of the 1850 Compromise, the South pressed for expansion into the Utah Territory, lands clearly north of the 36° parallel. Four years later, slavery supporters enacted the Kansas-Nebraska Act that repealed past compromises and opened the Upper Plains to slavery based on "popular sovereignty." Only after the Southern states' secession and their subsequent defeat could a constitutional solution to the slavery question be implemented.

The spread of slavery westward across the Deep and Upper South fostered a system that brought great wealth not only to the slaveholders, but to the nation as well. The admission of new slaveholding states more than tripled the land area available for slavery. The new lands provided rich, alluvial soil that could grow the short-staple cotton that was in such demand around the world. High cotton prices encouraged planters to bring as much land under cultivation and to purchase as much enslaved labor as they could afford. This booming demand for labor caused enslaved prices to triple, while high fertility rates caused the enslaved population to grow fivefold over two generations. Both contributed to a massive increase in household wealth throughout the South.

However, the profit of slavery did not stay within the region. Boston merchants got rich transporting the cotton and tobacco to Europe and returning with European luxuries fancied by the plantation elites. Rhode Island cotton mills spun the cotton into Negro cloth that would then clothe the enslaved while Massachusetts shoemakers made their shoes. Slavers would use the ships built in Philadelphia to transport enslaved persons by sea from the Tidewater to the Gulf states. To protect these cargoes, Connecticut insurance companies received lucrative fees as they assumed the risks of shipment. And New York banks provided the credit to finance the purchases of new lands and enslaved workers to keep the system expanding and generating larger profits. The system's profits were so expansive that there was plenty to reap both in the South and North. While Emancipation undermined Southern wealth, all of the wealth generated by slavery in the North remained for future generations.

FEDERAL LAND POLICIES

In the waning months of the Civil War, Secretary of War Edwin Stanton traveled down to Savannah, Georgia to discuss treatment of the freedpeople with General Sherman. At Secretary Stanton's suggestion, Sherman convened a meeting with twenty prominent African Americans from the city (Darity & Mullen, 2022). The group selected the Rev. Garrison Frazier, a Baptist minister who had just eight years earlier bought his own and his wife's freedom from slavery. When asked by General Sherman what the freedpeople needed to best take care of themselves, Rev. Frazier replied:

> The way we can best take care of ourselves is to have land, and turn it and till it by our own labor – that is, by the labor of the women and children and old men; and we can soon maintain ourselves and have something to spare … We want to be placed on land until we are able to buy it and make it our own. ("Newspaper Account of a Meeting," 1865, para. 28)

Four days after the meeting, Sherman issued Field Order no. 15, which identified abandoned land along the Georgia coast to be distributed among the freedpeople "not more than 40 acres of tillable land." Within six months, roughly 40,000 people relocated and began farming the land. Although the order and its transfer of lands was shortly reversed by President Johnson, it has retained its legacy as the source of the iconic promise of "forty acres and a mule."

The Rev. Frazier's answer to General Sherman's question showed his perceptiveness to the realities of nineteenth-century America – the primary way that households might gain the economic security needed to sustain freedom was through access to land. What is equally remarkable about his answer was its modesty. On behalf of his community, he was not requesting the gift of land, but simply access to it. He believed that access alone would enable them to gain "something to spare" and eventually purchase the land outright. Sherman's offer could have been made available throughout the South, thereby giving those newly emancipated some measure of economic independence. Politically, confiscating land from those in open rebellion to the federal government would have been an easy sell. President Johnson's reversal as well as the unwillingness of the federal government to offer any reparations to the freedpeople caused Frederick Douglass to later remind the country:

> When the Russian serfs had their chains broken and were given their liberty, the government of Russia – aye, the despotic government of Russia – gave to those poor emancipated serfs a few acres of land on which they could live and earn their bread. But when you turned us loose, you gave us no acres: you turned us loose to the sky, to the storm, to the whirlwind, and worst of all, you turned us loose to the wrath of our infuriated masters. (Douglass, 1876, para. 3)

Like Rev. Frazier, Frederick Douglass was acutely aware of the importance that land ownership played in securing economic security and individual liberty.

There is an exception where emancipation of the enslaved also brought more than broken chains. Before their forced removal, the Cherokee along with the rest of the Five "Civilized" Tribes adopted customs of the encroaching White society, including slavery. As they brought their enslaved with them west to the Indian Territory, it is estimated there were around 10,000 enslaved persons on the eve of the Civil War (Saunt, 2004). Like the nation that cast them aside, the five tribes splintered over the issue of slavery, with members supporting each side. In the case of the Cherokee Nation, they openly sided with the Confederacy. At the war's end, federal negotiators required the abolition of slavery along with the injunction that the freedpeople be incorporated "into the tribes on equal footing with the original members, or suitably provided for" (Saunt, 2004, p. 72). Under great pressure, the Cherokee leaders reluctantly agreed to extend all tribal rights, which included the right to use and develop any unused land. In this limited case, the newly emancipated gained access to their forty acres, although without a mule (Miller, 2011).

This exceptional case should interest us for two reasons. Federal negotiators, presumably acting on orders from Washington, DC, imposed terms in the Indian Territory similar to those rescinded throughout the South. Of course, explaining this apparent contradiction offers little challenge. Providing land ownership to the four million freedpeople would have offered them economic security while fundamentally upsetting the existing racial hierarchy. Such a change would have threatened White status not only in the South, but in the North as well. Offering a similar opportunity to those in the Indian Territory, land still outside the US, would not produce the same impact. Cherokee reluctance in accepting these conditions was fueled by racial prejudice as well as by the recognition of American duplicity and imperialism that was seen as a threat to tribal sovereignty (Saunt, 2004).

Moreover, this exceptional case offers a rare opportunity to understand how our nation's history might have unfolded differently. Recognizing the potential significance that access to land might provide, Miller (2011) examines how Blacks enslaved by the Cherokee fared in comparison to those in the South that were not given the same access to land. Using various Census sources, the author finds that Cherokee freedpeople typically owned more land in 1880 and had higher homeownership rates in 1900 than those residing in the South. Further, the study finds lower wealth inequality as measured by typical farm size and homeownership rates in the Cherokee areas than in the South at large. None of these results offers much surprise.

Federal land policies influenced the development of our nation's wealth in other important ways as well. Going back to the victory over Great Britain for independence, the Treaty of Paris (1783) ceded over 200 million acres of land between the Appalachian Mountains and the Mississippi River. Title to this land was purely fictional as it was home to various Native American tribes who had lived there for untold generations. Removing the current non-White inhabitants was deemed necessary to make the full wealth of the land available to White settlers flooding in from Europe. Through negotiation, fraud, war, or carried diseases, the Native Americans were killed or relocated through an extensive campaign of "racial cleansing." While it is typically believed that these lands were subsequently made available to masses arriving from Europe, the actual history is more complicated.

At its founding, the federal government was broke, deeply in debt to the tune of $80 million and with few sources of revenue. In one of its first laws, the Funding Act of 1790, Congress pledged this land as security on its debt. All land sales would be used to retire this debt, while federal tax revenues would pay any interest on the remaining debt (Grubb, 2010). Using the land as security enabled the new government to restore its reputation among international creditors, gain new credit on favorable terms, and eventually eliminate the debt by 1834. This financial imperative meant that any land policy was focused more on raising revenue than creating yeoman farmers.

Before the land could be sold, it needed surveying to establish clear and defensible land claims. Rather than use the old metes and boundaries method, in which natural barriers like creeks and ridges were used as barriers, the federal government employed a method of square surveying. Land was sectioned off into squares of six miles by six miles. Each of these was divided into thirty-six plots of a square mile. Each of these plots included 640 acres while half and quarter sections included 320 and 160 acres. This system not only determined the subsequent land policies, including General Sherman's short-lived promise, but remains visible today as one flies over the rigid squares that still mark the landscape.

Initially, the federal government used competitive bidding to auction the newly surveyed land in minimum lot sizes of 640 acres. As most farms at that time averaged one-quarter of that size, the sales were not targeting actual homesteaders. Even more problematic, all sales required cash payment. These barriers limited the sales to the wealthy and land speculators who might resell the land in smaller lots for profit. This system worked well for wealthy buyers and served the specific needs of the federal government. Large minimum lot sizes reduced both the time and expense needed to survey the land. Additionally, some contend that the larger lot sizes enabled the federal government to garner higher prices (Grubb, 2010). Land values depended in large part on the extent and type of nearby development. Larger lots allowed the purchaser to capture more of these external benefits and therefore encourage higher bids. As a consequence, the early land sales benefited the wealthy elite but did little for those with modest means.

Prospective homesteaders who lacked the cash to participate in the auctions simply traveled west beyond the reach of the surveyor and squatted on the land, thereby posing a direct challenge to the federal authorities back east. Their presence complicated federal surveying and threatened needed revenues. Worse, their intrusions generated local conflicts that often spilled into spasms of violence between the White settlers and Native American residents. In response, militias were organized at public expense, further straining the federal treasury. The steady influx of White squatters along with the eroding effects of disease caused any Indian military triumphs to be short-lived and eventually reversed. The remaining Native Americans faced the choice of death or emigration. Either result encouraged more Whites to squat on the "empty land" regardless of whether it had been surveyed or not.

To resolve the challenges posed by squatters, the federal government responded with a stick and carrot. Congress passed the Intrusion Act of 1807, which made squatting a federal crime and subject to fines. The law mandated the local militia to enforce its provisions. Given that many who joined the militias were themselves squatters, enforcement was meager. Using the carrot approach, the federal government lowered the minimum lot sizes in auction to 320 acres in 1800 and then to 160 acres in 1819. The payment was eased to one-quarter payment in thirty days and four years to pay the balance. However enticing, none of these changes could match the lure of squatting for free and hoping for future forbearance.

Forbearance for (White) squatters did come eventually. As early as 1790, Western representatives lobbied Congress to enact preemption rights and even free land policies. Preemption simply means that the squatter has the first right of refusal on paying title to the land. Initially, Congress refused, except in very limited and localized cases, thinking any broad preemption would simply encourage more squatting. As more Western states gained admission to the Union, the calls for preemption rights became more forceful and persuasive. Finally, in 1841 Congress passed the first broad-based Act without a specific sunset clause.[5] Under The Preemption Act of 1841, a squatter could purchase 160 acres at the low price of $1.25 per acre before their land would go to auction. Importantly, this opportunity was available only to "every person being the head of a family, or widow, or single man, over the age of twenty-one years, and being a citizen of the United States, or having filed his declaration of intention of becoming a citizen, as required by the naturalization laws" (The Preemption Act of 1841, Sec. 10). Few states, even including Northern states, granted free Blacks full citizenship rights. In addition, naturalization laws limited this avenue only to "free, white persons." This method of land acquisition was reserved for "Whites Only."[6]

5 Starting in 1830, the federal government passed six Preemption Acts that had one- to two-year time limits.

6 This book narrowly focuses on the divide between Black and White Americans. For a broader analysis, the reader should review Lui et al. (2006) as well as Williams (2016, 2018).

Those advocating for further development of the Western states and territories continued to lobby for free land policies. They got their wish when the federal government enacted the Homestead Act of 1862. The law offered up to 160 acres of unclaimed land to those who would reside for five years and make improvements to the land. The claimant would get a deed to the property after providing evidence and affirming their adherence before two "credible" witnesses to meeting all of the law's requirements (Edwards, 2009). Kept in place until 1976, the law conveyed 270 million acres, almost enough to cover Kansas, Nebraska, both Dakotas, and Montana. As such, it represented a massive transfer of property to private citizens. Today, it is estimated that somewhere between forty-six and ninety-three million Americans today are beneficiaries of this land transfer (Shanks, 2005).

While the Homestead Act is often portrayed as a fable of American egalitarianism, its reality is much less glossy. While the law mandated the land be free, there was no help given to those with modest means. Potential homesteaders needed funds to travel from back east or down south to the local land office. They required funds to buy tools, livestock, and seed as well as supplies to get them through to harvest. Some have estimated that potential homesteaders needed anywhere between $600 and $1,600 to start a western farm (Danhof, 1941; Deverell, 1988). Given an average daily wage of $1.11, this sum would be beyond many who wanted their own farm (Mattheis & Raz, 2019). Like the earlier Preemption Laws, the Homestead Act did not overtly exclude Black homesteaders, but did so covertly. As written, the law stated that only citizens or those eligible for citizenship could apply.[7] This language came on the heels of the infamous *Dred Scott v. Sandford (1857)* decision that ruled Black Americans as ineligible for citizenship. Even as the Fourteenth Amendment gave them citizenship rights, few had the resources or were told of the opportunities for free land in the upper Midwest.[8] Rather than help those with the greatest need for land, whether White or Black, the Homestead Act gave substantial help to those who already had some means.

Scholars have recognized another major problem with the Act. Its implementation and lax enforcement permitted substantial perjury and fraud. Under the law, claimants had the option to purchase the land outright for $1.25 per acre after six months. Called commutation, this allowed the

[7] According to Edwards (2009) women – whether single, widowed, or abandoned by their husbands – could apply.

[8] Painter (1992) recounts the challenges faced by the "exodusters" who did homestead in Kansas.

claimant to resell the land to a land speculator for a profit (Edwards, 2009). Although the law mandated one claim per lifetime, individuals could easily move from one land office to another and submit new claims. Or claimants working cooperatively could relinquish the claim just in time for a speculator to buy the lot in auction. Either of these practices enabled land speculators to elude the 160-acre requirement and acquire much larger parcels. Despite these instances of fraud and abuse, many claimants did exercise their patent rights and work the land. Nearly half of the land in Nebraska was settled by homesteaders, while the figures were 41 percent for both North and South Dakota.

Let us compare for a moment the land policies implemented out west with those used along the Georgia coast. Within months of Sherman's Field Order, 40,000 people took residence on 400,000 acres of rice fields previously abandoned by Confederate loyalists. President Johnson's countermanding meant those who had fought against the Union could regain any confiscated land if they simply obtained a pardon and paid their taxes. This decision produced an irresolvable conflict between themselves and those now residing and working the land. Worried about erupting violence, federal officials suggested the freedpeople work on contract with the antebellum owners. Most refused. When given the choice to work for the White landowners or leave, most left. The very land policies that were recasting the landscape out west were deemed wholly inappropriate on Sherman's land. As this example starkly shows, race trumped either loyalty to the Union or morality itself.

GETTING AHEAD

During the nineteenth century, access and title to land gave households their best chance to attain economic security and material improvement. At minimum, land ownership provided self-sufficiency as households held enough acreage to meet their needs. Children supplied valuable labor while parents imparted key skills and shared local knowledge of soil, climate, and crops. This inherited knowledge enabled the children of farmers to earn a premium over newer arrivals (Laband & Lentz, 1983). Generally, parents kept the farm available for the youngest son to inherit, in part to keep them close during their declining years. They would help the older sons find land nearby or further away as land locally became scarce. The need for farm labor and generally available land meant most of these young men could climb the "agricultural ladder" as they progressed from farm laborer to tenant to landowner (Friedberger, 1983).

While land ownership continued to provide a secure harbor during hard times, it offered new opportunities as the surrounding area experienced development. Nearby markets meant farmers could shift from self-sufficiency to raising commercial crops to generate cash. Expanding commercial opportunities caused local property values to rise. Growing towns and cities brought new educational and occupational opportunities. Rather than work their children year-round on the farm, parents recognized the benefits of allowing them to obtain an education (Ransom & Sutch, 1986). Slowly, parental focus shifted from enabling them to gain their own land to helping them find "a provision in life" (Langbein, 1989, p. 725). With favorable loans or outright gifts, parents steered their children toward professional occupations or business so they might avoid *stoop labor* (Easterlin, 1976). Family inheritances became less about the transfer of property late in life and more about investment in their children's education and commercial ventures. Rising land prices would elevate the value of the family farm, enabling each generation to use it as a springboard to assist the next. At some point, depending on the occupational interests of successive generations, the land might be divided or sold, with the proceeds being distributed among the heirs. For many families, the original homestead served as a safe harbor during difficult times and a catalyst for increasing family wealth over generations.

SEPARATE BUT ABSENT

Over the nineteenth and through the twentieth century, education assumed an ever-increasing role in providing a path toward upward mobility and economic security. Getting a primary school education and learning the three Rs gave hope for a life beyond manual labor. Wages paid to a clerk, machine operator, or craft worker could provide a decent living. Further education could open doors to professional careers as a lawyer, doctor, bank manager, or printer. These professions might pay enough to put savings by in addition to supporting a comfortable lifestyle. Education opened the door to a range of new occupations and opportunities for those who could gain access.

At the time of their emancipation, the overwhelming numbers of freedpeople found themselves liberated but illiterate. Most Southern states had strict laws prohibiting any education for the enslaved. The first true portrait of illiteracy was the 1870 Census, which showed that 81 percent of Blacks ten years or older were illiterate as compared to only 8.5 percent among Whites (Collins & Margo, 2003). With limited access to land, most viewed education as the key to economic and social improvement. Understandably, as the only option available to them, many held "an almost limitless faith in the possibilities of advancement through schooling" (Mathews, 1970, as cited in Kousser, 1980, p. 18).

During Reconstruction, local Black leaders in Augusta, Georgia put their faith into action as they pushed for expansive educational opportunities for their community. Throughout the South, public education was strictly segregated. Even in the North, only a handful of states prohibited segregated education, while some Midwestern states excluded Black students entirely (Klarman, 1998). Given these realities, the local Black leadership in Augusta lobbied effectively at both the state and local levels. At the state level, they pressured the insertion of Section 9 in the 1872 Public Law 346, which specifically directed the Richmond County School Board to "provide the same facilities for both [White and Negro children], both as regards schoolhouses and fixtures, attainments and abilities of teachers, length of term time, and all other matters appertaining to education" (Kousser, 1980, p. 19). Further, in Section 10 they exacted the right to establish high schools and levy a special tax without the need for a referendum. Lastly, they made sure that no general state education law in the future would supersede these provisions (Kousser, 1980). They used this law to organize a number of Black schools in the county and, in 1880, demand the creation of a Black high school to parallel the county's two White schools. In its October board meeting, the all-White school board agreed (Kousser, 1980).

Soon thereafter, Ware High opened its doors to Black students. Offering a classical curriculum similar to White schools, it became a source of civic pride and served as a hub of community activity. As the only high school in the state of Georgia serving Black students, Ware High became an important source of Black educators and professionals (Kousser, 1980). The school achieved a high level of success and notoriety despite contending with higher student–teacher ratios, lower teacher salaries, and poorer school buildings than the county's White schools (Kousser, 1980). Despite its laudable successes amidst great challenges, the school board closed the school after seventeen years, citing a lack of funds.

The local Black leaders responded swiftly and sued the county school board. They cited both the Section 9 provision in the 1872 state law and the equal protection clause of the Fourteenth Amendment as reasons to rescind the closure. Eventually, the case went to the Supreme Court and is known as *Cumming v. Richmond County (1899).* Coming on the heels of the infamous *Plessy v. Ferguson (1896)* that established the constitutionality of "separate, but equal" in public accommodations, the *Cumming* case would determine whether "separate, but absent" would pass constitutional muster. The Court ruled unanimously that the school board's decision was constitutional and did not violate either state or federal statutes. Adding further weight to the decision is the fact that this opinion was written by the sole dissenter to the Plessy decision, Judge John Marshall Harlan. Writing for the Court, Judge Harlan argued that:

> the education of the people in schools maintained by state taxation is a matter belonging to the respective states, and any interference on the part of Federal authority with the management of such schools cannot be justified except in the case of a clear and unmistakable disregard of rights secured by the supreme law of the land. We have no such case to be determined. (*Cumming v. Richmond*, 1899, p. 545)

How the Court could decide that the decision to eliminate high school education is not an "unmistakable disregard of rights" is puzzling. Even worse, the Court argued that:

> We are not permitted by the evidence in the record to regard that decision as having been made with any desire or purpose on the part of the board to discriminate against any of the Colored school children of the county on account of their race ... and if it appeared that the board's refusal to maintain such a school was in fact an abuse of its discretion and in hostility to the Colored population because of their race, different questions might have arisen .... (*Cumming v. Richmond*, 1899, pp. 544–545)

In setting this precedent, the Court shifted any burden of proof regarding equal protection from the school board to the Black community. By striking down the plaintiffs' suit, the Court clearly signaled that it would not countenance any limits to a legalized segregation as initiated by Plessy's "separate, but equal."

The Cumming decision gave school boards around the country the license to limit education to the Black children as much as the dominant White community desired. White employers often supported primary education in order to give their future employees basic skills that would increase their productivity as servants, cooks, and other semiskilled occupations (Collins & Margo, 2003). Others encouraged an "industrial education" for Black children that would benefit them later as they assumed the menial and service occupations of their parents (Klarman, 1998). Of course, this meant school boards could and did limit expenditures on educating the Black children in their communities. They did so by using deficient facilities, paying Black teachers lower salaries, imposing higher class sizes, and shortening the school year. While spending per Black child remained flat during the 1890 to 1910 period, this allowed school boards to increase spending on their White children's education (Collins & Margo, 2003). In the case of Augusta, Richmond County built two new high schools in 1907 and 1908 for White students, while the closure of Ware High left Black students without a public high school until 1937. The refusal to extend high school education to Black children throughout the South had major repercussions given the coming changes. In 1916, at least three Southern states – Mississippi, Louisiana, and South Carolina – had no established public high schools for their Black residents (Klarman, 1998).

At this point, much of the country was embarked on what one scholar has called "the second great transformation of American schooling: the rise of the public high school" (Goldin, 1998, p. 371). Whereas roughly 15 percent of 14–17-year-olds in 1910 were in high school, the comparable figure skyrocketed to 73 percent just three decades later (Snyder, 1993, Table 9). Of course, this educational transformation did not include Black children. Consider the educational attainment of 20–22-year-olds, who are largely expected to be finished with their secondary education. Using the 1940 Census, 73 percent of Whites reported having a ninth grade or higher education as compared to 33 percent of Black young adults. Of these, nearly 14 percent of the Whites reported some level of college education, while only 4 percent of Blacks reported the same. Most disturbing, fully 37 percent of the Black respondents reported a primary education or less (highest grade attended was fifth or below), while only 5 percent of Whites reported the same. This gulf in educational attainment skewed dramatically the opportunities available to each group.

The surge in high school enrollment and graduation rates among Whites offered them unrivaled benefits. Throughout the period there was clear evidence of education wage premiums. Higher-killed jobs that required more education paid more than manual labor and service jobs. The expansion of office work and the demand for clerical workers required individuals who had attained several years of high school education if not a diploma. Even some blue-collar jobs like machine operators needed to know basic math and geometry. The educational and occupational restrictions imposed on Black Americans meant higher wages were necessary to lure those Whites who held the necessary skills. These higher salaries enabled more White households to save for retirement, purchase a home, and fund their own children's education. Earning a high school diploma in the early twentieth century opened doors to better-paying jobs and careers, much like a college diploma does now. Thus, the *Cumming v. Richmond* decision not only limited the prospects of aspiring Black students, it also buoyed the rewards garnered by Whites who faced neither restrictions nor competition.

As Judge Harlan wrote in the *Cumming* decision, education had long been the province of state and local governments, with the federal government having no role. One dramatic exception occurred mid-twentieth century. Just days after the D-Day invasion of Nazi-held Europe, Congress enacted the Servicemen's Readjustment Act as it considered the postwar future. Better known as the celebrated GI Bill, the law offered every returning veteran cash payment for college tuition as well as living expenses while in school. Over the next decade, the Bill enabled 2.2 million veterans to attend college, while another 5.6 million participated in vocational education programs that trained them as carpenters, plumbers, electricians, or auto and aircraft mechanics (Olson, 1973). After completing their education, many veterans took advantage of low-cost loans to start businesses or manage farms. With this help, they commanded higher salaries and built businesses that propelled them into middle-class status and beyond. As President Clinton (1995, para. 13) reflected on its impact, he argued that the "GI Bill helped to unleash a prosperity never before known."

The prosperity unleashed by the GI Bill did not reach all veterans or benefit every community. Despite the Bill's race-neutral provisions, its implementation amidst a racially segregated society curtailed its benefits to Black veterans in particular (Katznelson, 2005). White veterans used their benefits at any university that accepted their application while Black veterans were instructed where they should apply by a Veterans Administration (VA) pamphlet called "Colleges for Negroes" (Turner & Bound, 2003). In the South, Black applicants could only enroll in historically Black colleges and universities (HBCUs). The wave of applications overwhelmed these institutions; they were forced to turn away half of their applicants in 1946 and 1947 even as they doubled their enrollments and pushed their facilities to their limits (Olson, 1973). In the North, some White colleges enrolled Black vets, but always in small numbers. As one example, the University of Pennsylvania enrolled forty-six Blacks among its 9,000 students (Herbold, 1994).

The absence of a secondary education meant that most Black veterans were unprepared for college. They found access to vocational education equally blocked. The GI Bill created a vast network of regional counseling centers ready to assist the returning vets. However, Southern lawmakers required these services be managed by the states in order to comply with local laws and norms. In the South and beyond, state control ensured the delivery of services was strictly segregated. Many counseling centers failed to hire Black counselors to assist the pool of Black vets; in both Georgia and Alabama only a dozen Black counselors were hired to serve the entire state, while Mississippi neglected to hire any (Onkst, 1998). Not only did these barriers limit opportunities for Black veterans, but they also limited any rivals to Whites working in the building trades, creating new businesses, and engaging in the professions. These restrictions on aspiring Black veterans further propelled those White veterans able to access the generosity of the law as they reaped higher incomes and managed successful businesses.

PROMOTING HOMEOWNERSHIP

With the best unclaimed land disappearing and the shift toward towns and cities, homeownership slowly replaced homesteading as a primary path to economic improvement and financial security. The 1890 US Census noted this significance as it introduced specific questions about home tenure (owner-occupancy vs. renting) status. Somewhat remarkably, more than a majority of White households reported being homeowners as part of this Census (Masnick, 2001). In large part this high rate of homeownership resulted from nearly three-quarters of White households living on farms being owners, a clear result of the federal homesteading policies (Collins & Margo, 1999). In contrast, the non-White homeownership rate was below 20 percent.

Off the farm, homeownership looked quite different back then. Higher land prices in towns and cities caused many to purchase properties to meet commercial as well as residential needs. Professionals like doctors and lawyers commonly used part of their home as offices to see their patients and clients. Shop owners frequently lived in quarters above their business. Even employees might rent out rooms to make extra money. Similar to the homesteader on their farm, the home and business were typically molded together. For Black aspiring homeowners, the rise of Jim Crow restrictions on professional occupations and business opportunities would limit this avenue to homeownership.

The Mortgage Credit Market

The home mortgage market – still in its infancy – looked entirely different as well. Many homebuyers avoided a mortgage altogether either with family help, saving enough to pay with cash, or sweat equity. One could get a bank loan, but lenders required down payments of 50 percent or higher. Some might find a secondary lender to bridge the down payment, but they paid a high interest rate. Most relied on family and friends for help with the down payment. This represented an important way that families could pass along their wealth across generations. Absent such help, prospective homebuyers necessarily deferred their purchase until later in life, giving them a shorter window to gain any appreciation (Gordon, 2005). Conventional mortgage loans were short-term, generally 3–5 years; typically, the borrowers made interest-only monthly payments with the outstanding principal due as the loan matured (Fishback et al., 2020). Borrowers were responsible for saving on their own. Many loans carried variable interest rates, creating uncertainty over the size of future payments. As the loan matured, lenders would typically roll it over, although this was never certain. If the borrower could not find a loan elsewhere, they would need to sell their home. Not until householders owned their home outright did homeownership provide much economic security.

Building and loan associations emerged during this period to offer more favorable terms. Small, localized institutions used member savings to make mortgage loans to selected recipients. To qualify for a loan, the borrower would need to be a member with a share deposit. Each month, the borrower would pay both the interest and a deposit to their account. Over time, generally around 11–13 years, the accumulated deposits would equal the loan amount (Snowden, 2013). At this point, the loan was terminated and the borrower now owned their home outright. In this way, homebuyers gained the benefits from loan amortization – a steady and sure payment schedule – although they still typically needed a down payment of 35 percent or higher (Grebler et al., 1956). The presence of family wealth eased the challenge of bridging this gap.

The early twentieth-century home mortgage market did mirror our current circumstances in one important way – the differential treatment given to Black prospective homebuyers. Households with incomes ample enough to consider homeownership still faced the daunting challenge of making a large down payment. Very few had family resources to rely upon, making them even more dependent on gaining access to credit. Many lenders refused to offer loans to Black households looking to purchase in Black neighborhoods, while even fewer made offers to those buying in White neighborhoods (Wiese, 1999). Those fortunate to secure a loan paid higher interest rates and fees. Frequently, they secured a second and even a third mortgage to bridge the gap. With each layer, they were subject to more onerous interest rates and excessive fees (Nier, 2011). Some homebuyers did find better terms from one of the growing numbers of African American–managed building and loan associations that provided mortgages during the period (Mason, 2010). Nonetheless, many Black homebuyers were forced to seek unconventional funding sources, including "pay like rent" schemes. Quite exploitive, these contracts with individual lenders bestowed title to the home only after the last payment was made. Until that moment, the contract offered zero equity to the borrower, and one missed payment jeopardized the whole arrangement. Nonetheless, desperate for some means to homeownership, about one-quarter of Black Philadelphians reported mortgages held by individuals, suggesting this risky and expensive method of financing was widespread (Nier, 2011). In most cases, the recipients of the higher fees and interest rates were White lenders.

Residential Segregation

Prospective Black homebuyers found their choices of where they might reside even more prescribed. In the early decades of the twentieth century, most Northern cities were inundated by new residents, including European immigrants, young Whites from rural areas, and Blacks as part of the Great Migration. Initially, economics and local norms determined the racial residential patterns. Those with little money looked for the cheapest housing, usually adjacent to the city's industrial areas. Existing norms set the boundaries on those enclaves that might welcome the arriving residents based on their race and ethnicity. While prosperous Whites were able to purchase new housing being constructed on the city's expanding perimeter, the growing Black population was restricted to the same neighborhood boundaries. In response, the housing stock in these neighborhoods was subdivided into smaller units, creating increased congestion. Rents skyrocketed, enriching the remaining White landlords. Seeking expanded opportunities, Black professionals relocated beyond the traditional boundaries into historically White neighborhoods, knowing full well they would encounter White threats and acts of violence. White sellers willing to sell to these Black pioneers exacted a premium on their selling price, as much as 28 percent (Akbar et al., 2019). Despite these obstacles, a persistent influx of Black households forced more Black homebuyers to seek homes in previously White neighborhoods. Although these intrepid pioneers continued to pay above-market prices, they stoked fear among the remaining White homeowners – usually with the help of rapacious brokers – that their presence would undermine property values. Again, the financial penalties imposed on Black homebuyers enriched White sellers and brokers.

White fears of shifting racial boundaries encouraged the Baltimore City Council to enact an ordinance restricting residential mobility in 1910. Adhering to strictly race-neutral language, the ordinance prohibited the relocation of Black residents onto White-majority blocks as well as the relocation of White residents onto Black-majority blocks (Power, 1983). Of course, the latter rarely occurred, and when it did it raised little notice. In short order, twenty-seven cities around the country adopted similar ordinances. No doubt more would have followed except for the Supreme Court decision *Buchanan v. Warley (1917)* that struck down such laws as egregious violations of the equal protection clause of the Fourteenth Amendment. The Court's reasoning emphasized the plight of the White homeowner who faced limits to whom (s)he could sell their property. Despite the Court's decision, many of these cities continued to enforce their ordinance (Rothstein, 2017). Other cities, either without their own local ordinance or unwilling to defy the Court, searched for other remedies.

With time, most cities turned to exclusionary zoning laws to limit racial mobility. Zoning ordinances that set minimum lot sizes or prohibited multi-family housing in White areas limited the entry of households needing cheaper housing (Rothstein, 2017). As long as the ordinances were not race specific, they met constitutional muster. While these ordinances were ineffective in restricting prosperous Blacks, they did prop up White property values. When developers proposed multiracial developments adjacent to White areas, some cities responded by condemning the land to develop a public park (Rothstein, 2017). Additionally, local officials located undesirable amenities like landfills and sewage plants near Black neighborhoods while developing reservoirs and parks in the White areas of town (Rothstein, 2017). These decisions would shape further the property values found on either side of town.

To preserve the Whiteness of neighborhoods, particularly in response to prosperous Black homebuyers, neighborhoods and real estate professionals turned to using racially restrictive covenants. Particularly after the Court's *Buchanan* decision, these covenants became the primary tool for limiting who might reside in a neighborhood. Created initially in California to restrict Chinese residents, their popularity spread to the South and eventually to the Midwest and North, particularly after the Supreme Court upheld their constitutionality in *Corrigan v. Buckley (1926)* (Jones-Correa, 2000). Neighborhood associations would sponsor door-to-door campaigns to encourage households to include exclusionary language in their deed. While different regions targeted different groups, most read like this example: "The real property above described, or any portion thereof, shall never be occupied, used, or resided by any person not of the white or Caucasian race, except in the capacity of a servant or domestic employed theron [sic] as such by a white or Caucasian owner, tenant, or occupant" (Rothstein, 2017, p. 78). While widespread throughout the country, these individual covenants required full participation of homeowners to be fully effective. Recognizing their individual gain, some Whites did sell to Black homebuyers willing to pay a hefty premium. In response, local real estate boards encouraged the proliferation of homeowners' associations (HOAs) and enacted "ethical codes" that included protecting the racial purity of neighborhoods (Welsh, 2018). In older areas, neighborhood associations designed ordinances that required membership in the HOA before purchasing a home (Rothstein, 2017). In new areas, developers inserted binding covenants in the deeds to ensure full coverage across the neighborhood. Although the Supreme Court did outlaw them in *Shelley v. Kraemer (1948),* their decision did not end the practice as real estate professionals and home sellers continued to avoid selling homes in White neighborhoods to Black homebuyers.

New Deal Housing Policies

The onset of the Great Depression brought the housing market to its knees, thereby threatening a key component of the American Dream. Housing prices, like everything else, suffered substantial declines. As existing loans came due, lenders chose not to roll them over. Forced to pay the loan balance, homeowners had only one asset valuable enough to sell – their home. Banks were facing their own troubles as well. As their depositors removed their savings to pay essential bills, lenders had less credit to lend. With many sellers and no homebuyers, housing prices plummeted further. Foreclosures spiked to 10 percent of all homes as homeowners could neither sell their home nor find new financing (Rothstein, 2017). To restore financial stability, Congress created the Home Owners Loan Corporation (HOLC) to support current homeowners and later the Federal Housing Agency (FHA) to assist prospective homebuyers.

To stabilize the mortgage market, the HOLC used public funds to purchase existing mortgages from private lenders. It swapped the existing loan agreements for those with a lower down payment, fifteen-year term, fixed interest rate, and fully amortizing payment schedule without any prepayment penalty. These loan terms gave homeowners a certain monthly payment, structured savings plan, and sure path to outright homeownership. Over its brief three-year history, the HOLC reissued over one million existing mortgages, the vast bulk of which were paid back in full

(Rothstein, 2017). This mortgage template not only rescued the private home mortgage market, but it became the model of future mortgages. It brought financial security to the homebuying process as it guaranteed fixed monthly payments and ended balloon payments. Smaller down payments and longer repayments periods meant more households could use bank credit to leverage their home purchase. With no prepayment penalty, borrowers now could refinance with new lenders whenever interest rates fell. These innovations simultaneously lowered the barrier and increased the appeal of homeownership to millions of households.

These features that made the new mortgages more appealing to borrowers were decidedly unattractive to private lenders. Since the federal government had no interest in becoming the nation's lender, it needed to make these new mortgages more appealing to private lenders. With this aim in mind, the FHA guaranteed the loans against default for a modest fee charged to borrowers. Now, private lenders could purchase the existing loans as well as make new loans knowing the federal government would compensate them if the loan went bad. Relieved of any default risk, private lenders could now offer mortgages with lower interest rates. During the postwar period of rising employment and household incomes, these attractive mortgages enabled vast numbers of households to become homeowners and attain an important symbol of middle-class status. While the homeownership rate had wobbled around 45 percent for a half century between 1890 and 1940, it increased over the next two decades to above 60 percent by 1960.

One problem remained. The mortgage guarantee committed the US Treasury and the American taxpayer as guarantor of these loans. To limit their exposure, both the HOLC and FHA established strict appraisal guidelines that required information on the borrower's creditworthiness, the property's condition, and the surrounding neighborhood. This information was deemed necessary to limit the risk of borrower default over the life of the loan. To ascertain local neighborhood characteristics, both the HOLC and the FHA created residential security maps that provided color-coded assessment for each urban neighborhood.[9] By standardizing the financial risk associated with each neighborhood, these maps sped up the approval process as the FHA promised it could make its decision within two weeks (Light, 2011). For those able to qualify, the innovations created by these new FHA loans expanded both access to and the appeal of homeownership. Yet, access to these loans was highly stratified.

[9] See Fishback et al. (2020) for a discussion on whether the two agencies developed these maps in collaboration or separately.

Two FHA officials, Frederick Babcock and economist Homer Hoyt, are credited with developing these residential maps for the FHA. A real estate appraiser, Babcock had championed the idea that appraisers should consider "social influences" as they evaluated the worthiness of a loan. Authoring the FHA's initial *Underwriting Manual,* he instructed local appraisers seeking FHA loan approval to consider the following: "If a neighborhood is to retain stability it is necessary that properties shall continue to be occupied by the same social and racial classes. A change in social or racial occupation generally leads to instability and reductions in values" (Federal Housing Administration, 1936, Pt. 2, Sec. 2, para. 233). He argued that appraisers should make these assessments not simply based on their personal judgments, but rather carry themselves like a "a research investigator occupied solely with the gathering of data and their orderly classification" (Babcock, 1924, p. 77). In contrast, he neglected to offer any facts that might demonstrate the harmful effects of residential integration. Nonetheless, his unstinting advocacy for an "objective" appraisal process gave it the patina of professionalism. His views influenced future editions of the *Underwriting Manual* as he argued that the focus on race was not the result of specific animus, but simply the impact of racial relocation on market values (Brown, 2018).

Homer Hoyt shared Babcock's views on race and property values as well as the need for objective tools to evaluate loan applications. In his book entitled *One Hundred Years of Land Values in Chicago,* Hoyt cites evidence from a West Side real estate broker who ranks sixteen racial and nationality groups based on their impact on property values. Unsurprisingly, the list ranks English, Germans, Scotch, Irish, and Scandinavians at the top with southern Italians, Mexicans, and Negroes landing at the bottom (Brown, 2018). Like Babcock, Hoyt failed to offer any compelling evidence in support of this hierarchy. Instead, he offered an academic argument that urban neighborhoods resembled natural ecosystems as they evolved from high-value White neighborhoods to low-value Black neighborhoods (Gordon, 2005). Similar to Babcock, Hoyt believed that changing demographics represented the greatest threat to local property values. Along with others of his time, he proposed that residential maps could counter this threat as they integrated the key "social facts" from each metro area to reveal underlying "scientific, urban laws." Given the volume of mortgage approvals facing the FHA, he argued that such residential maps would streamline the process and replace the need for site visits for each loan approval. Like Babcock, he aimed to frame the appraisal process as purely scientific.

Given these personal views, it is no surprise that the produced residential maps reflected and hardened the preexisting patterns of racial segregation as they graded and color-coded each neighborhood. Those neighborhoods with a history of stable property values, a homogeneous (White) population, and space for further development obtained the top "A" grade and were colored green. Less desired neighborhoods with less space for expansion were given a "B" grade and colored blue. Neighborhoods graded "C" and colored yellow had an older, deteriorating housing stock and were considered vulnerable to an "infiltration of lower grade population" (Gordon, 2005, p. 17). At the bottom of the appraisal hierarchy were neighborhoods colored red and graded "D." These neighborhoods experienced low homeownership rates, poorly maintained housing stock, and an "undesirable population or any infiltration of it" (Gordon, 2005, p. 17). These grades determined whether one could gain FHA approval of the loan and thereby gain the benefits included in an FHA-approved mortgage. Those buying in desirable neighborhoods faced little difficulty getting approval. However, properties in "C" and especially "D" neighborhoods were judged too risky to gain approval.

The FHA residential security maps took the de facto residential segregation already existing and cemented it with the full weight of the federal government and the mortgage loan industry. Known today as "redlining," these maps ensured a persistent stratification of homeownership among White and Black households as well as functioning to exacerbate the racial wealth gap.

Most new housing developments were being built in the emerging suburbs in areas designated for White buyers only and "earning" an "A" grade. Even if the new development failed to include a racially restrictive covenant, real estate agents, mortgage loan officers, and tax attorneys all worked to steer Black prospective homebuyers away from such areas. All held a vested interest in maintaining the FHA-sponsored norms since any violations could threaten approval of future loans.

This system functioned quite well for White homebuyers. Limiting the pool of prospective buyers caused prices in these new developments to be lower than otherwise. More importantly, gaining an FHA loan meant smaller down payments, lower interest rates, and reduced fees. Those looking to sell their current home in one of the existing White neighborhoods found they attracted multiple buyers, all able to obtain an FHA loan. The appeal and availability of FHA loans in areas graded "A" and "B" caused property values to rise in these neighborhoods. In contrast, neighborhoods graded "C" and "D" experienced languishing values due to the increased challenges that prospective homebuyers faced in obtaining credit. Declining property values in these neighborhoods discouraged real improvements and repairs, causing the housing stock to decline. Homeowners in these neighborhoods experienced little wealth accumulation as compared to the White areas of town.

Fear among Whites that one's property values would collapse as "the Blacks moved in" drove much of this decline. Prominent textbooks on real estate warned their readers about the influx of "undesirable" groups triggering price drops (Jackson, 1987). Indeed, one real estate professional wrote graphically:

> With the increase in colored people coming to many Northern cities they have overrun their old districts and swept into adjoining ones or passed to other sections and formed new ones. This *naturally* has had a decidedly detrimental effect on land values for few white people *however inclined to be sympathetic with the problem of the colored race,* care to live near them. Property values have been sadly depreciated by having a single, colored family settle down on a street occupied exclusively by white residents. (McMichael & Bingham, 1923, p. 181) (italics mine)

While this phenomenon is framed as naturally occurring, there's little evidence of its occurrence. In interviews conducted with real estate agents from that period, there is "the recurring theme that while sellers may not get their price from whites (who are reluctant to consider an area undergoing racial transition), they probably can from nonwhites" (Laurenti, 1960, p. 20). According to a savings and loan office: "Nonwhite entry destroys property values only to whites, not to nonwhites. That is, sellers will lose only if they are determined to sell to whites. They can get their price from colored" (Laurenti, 1960, p. 21). Given that many Black prospective homeowners were willing to pay top dollar to gain greater choice on where to live, the threat of collapsing property values seems unlikely.

Of course, there are examples of rapacious real estate agents stoking White fears and manipulating White racial animus to their advantage. Known as "block busting" agents, they would identify all-White neighborhoods and sell the initial home to a Black household at a premium. They would then solicit door to door making cash offers to those White homeowners willing to move quickly before the "expected" collapse in property values. Assuredly, such mass selling produced the very price decline that was predicted. As encouragement, they hired Black women to push baby carriages and Black men to drive through the neighborhood to make their point (Rothstein, 2017). The ensuing panic enabled the agents to purchase the White properties at a discount and mark them up to the Black buyers. Since FHA guidelines discouraged lending in these transitioning neighborhoods, the blockbusters would transfer the homes using exploitive land installment contracts (Mehlhorn, 1998). One missed monthly payment and the borrower could be evicted and lose any past savings.

The GI Bill Housing Help

In this environment, the generous GI Bill provisions for homeownership widened the disparate opportunities given to White and Black households. Returning veterans had the opportunity to purchase a home with no down payment and favorable rates using a VA-guaranteed loan. By 1956, this program guaranteed loans worth $35.9 billion and helped 4.9 million veterans become homeowners (US Department of Veterans Affairs, 1957, p. 117). For them and their families, this program transformed their prospects as they profited from the postwar housing boom and rising home prices. However, the VA loan program adopted the FHA's appraisal guidelines, thereby skewing the benefits dramatically. The VA loan guarantee required the applicant to find a private lender willing to lend, thereby creating an additional obstacle for Black prospective homebuyers. As the VA neglected to track their loans by the applicant's race, it is unclear how many Black veterans obtained one. In 1947, *Ebony* magazine surveyed thirteen Mississippi cities to discover only two out of 3,229 VA loans went to Black veterans (Onkst, 1998). In 1955, a VA administrator told a NAACP official that it was his "educated guess that less than 30,000 colored veterans have benefited from the provisions of the GI loan program" (Cohen, 2003, p. 171). Once again, the benefits of federal generosity shower White households almost exclusively.

The 1950 US Census offers some insight into how dramatically these two federal programs skewed homeownership during this period. Although comprising more than 10 percent of the population and 13 percent of veterans, just 2 percent of both the VA-guaranteed and FHA-guaranteed loans were held by "non-whites."[10] The median interest rate on these two loans were 4 and 4.5 percent, respectively. Those forced to borrow using other mortgage options typically paid 5 percent interest, although some paid up to 8 percent or higher (US Census Bureau, 1952). Such disparate treatment was perfectly legal. Not until President Kennedy's 1962 Executive Order entitled "Equal Opportunity on Housing" would such blatant

[10] According to the 1952 Census of Housing, "non-white" included Negroes, Indians, Japanese, and other non-White populations. Persons of Mexican birth were included as White. African Americans comprised more than 90 percent of the "non-white" category.

discrimination be against the law. By that time, it is estimated that both the FHA and VA financed over $120 billion in home loans (Quadagno, 1994). Virtually all of this largesse went into the open hands and ultimately nest eggs of White households.

CONCLUSION

Since the nation's founding, federal wealth policies have lavished their generosity on White households. Federal support for the westward expansion of slavery, the required seizure and return of escaping freedom seekers as if they were wandering cattle, and the closure of the external slave trade all increased the wealth of White slaveholders, perhaps by twentyfold over a half century. All of this wealth was taken from those enslaved. As the western lands were seized from their Indian residents, homesteading laws aimed at White immigrants offered the land under increasingly generous terms. Many of these early settlers obtained their initial land stake through illegal squatting. As the federal government opened hundreds of millions of acres to White homesteaders – up to 160 acres at no cost – it denied extending forty acres and a mule to the freedmen and their families. In the nineteenth century, property ownership of land and human chattels were the primary ways that households gained economic security and an asset base for increased wealth accumulation. These policies clearly favored White beneficiaries and enabled them to create the means for wealth accumulation within and across generations (Shapiro, 2017).

By the twentieth century, education and homeownership assumed greater significance as sources of household wealth and financial security. Federal acquiescence of, if not support for, segregated education allowed the racial education gap to persist and grow. Given the green light by the Supreme Court, local school boards realized they could ignore the educational needs of their Black children if they gave reasons other than overt racial animus. Despite surveys that revealed greater interest among Black GIs for postwar education, Jim Crow laws and de facto segregation in the North severely restricted their access to any educational or vocational assistance. Over the same period, federal intervention in the mortgage industry reinforced existing patterns of residential segregation. The extremely favorable terms pioneered by the FHA met the needs of White homebuyers at the same time they neglected those of prospective Black homeowners. Largely shunned from buying in White neighborhoods, Black households found it virtually impossible to obtain an FHA loan in the neighborhoods they were permitted to buy. White veterans were given almost exclusive access to the generous VA/FHA mortgage and the resultant benefits of homeownership.

Gaining a high school and later a college diploma along with buying a home offered millions of White households the opportunity to gain middle-class status. With their education, they could land jobs that paid adequate wages and were resistant to frequent bouts of unemployment. The steady income enabled them to generate savings that provided a financial cushion and a source of help to their children. Many obtained jobs with a retirement plan that gave them another source of assisted savings. Buying a home with a fully amortizing loan enabled younger householders to attain residential stability and create a retirement nest egg. During periods of rising property values, homeownership brought the benefits of asset appreciation to many households for the first time. This assistance enabled many more households to overcome the wealth thresholds discussed in Chapter 2 and access the privileges of wealth. However, these avenues to wealth accumulation were open almost exclusively to White households.

What is also notable are the arguments used to explain the disparities in each of these federal initiatives. In this regard, chattel slavery falls into its own category. Many rationalized it by arguing it as natural, even biblically sanctioned, that the enslaved were not fully human, or that it benefited the "contented slave." Homesteading was open to all citizens and those seeking citizenship without mention of race. Yet, most states limited the rights of even free Blacks while the federal government only allowed White males the option of seeking naturalized citizenship.[11] Regarding disparate educational opportunities, the Supreme Court in *Cumming v. Richmond County* argued that the non-provisioning of secondary education to Black schoolchildren was acceptable since it was due simply to economics and not to any racial hostility. Although this rationale offers a fig leaf of acceptability, it really makes no sense. Lastly, the redlining practices of the federal government were defended again on economic grounds and not racial animus. Amidst a financial crisis, stabilizing home values is certainly a desirable outcome. Yet, requiring strict racial segregation based only on the academic argument that the "natural outcome" of racially mixed neighborhoods is collapsing home values creates an unconvincing camouflage. Each case illustrates the need to offer a rationale that deflects from the real outcome of these programs – targeting the benefits to Whites in ways that make them look earned.

[11] In *Dred Scott v. Sandford (1857)*, the Supreme Court argued that even free Blacks could not aspire to being citizens.

The Civil Rights legislation of the 1960s effectively placed all of these arguments to justify preferential treatment of Whites outside the law. Surprisingly, these legal changes have not ended the federal government practice of targeting benefits to Whites in ways that make them appear earned. Just as the federal government offered free land and attractive mortgages almost exclusively to White households in the past, it continues to shower benefits disproportionately today. Currently, the federal government uses the tax code to shower over $1 trillion annually to households seeking to build wealth. Most of this largesse goes to White households and it all appears *earned*. Explaining how this works is the focus of Chapter 4.

4

Revealing Tax Expenditures

EARLY WARNINGS

In 1967, Assistant Treasury Secretary Stanley Surrey spoke before The Money Marketeers, a New York University forum whose members include many Wall Street professionals and hedge fund managers. His talk that day brought unwanted attention to a largely invisible topic – using the federal tax code to make social policy. He framed this use of the tax code as creating "special preferences … that are departures from the normal tax structure designed to favor a particular industry, activity or class of persons" (Surrey, 1976a, p. 53). He insisted they should be viewed as *expenditures* as they represented "spending for the benefitted activities or groups through the tax system rather than through direct government grants, loans, or other kinds of government assistance" (Surrey, 1976a, p. 53). As such, they represent a policy choice. The federal government can appropriate funds for the construction of affordable housing, or it can offer tax deductions to businesses willing to do so. He noted that while the costs associated with the former are measurable, transparent, and easily tracked, the costs of tax policy lay hidden and elude elementary budget controls. Leveraging his position in the Treasury Department, Secretary Surrey gave public expression to this concept of "tax expenditures." That day, he lobbied passionately for a full accounting of each tax expenditure, arguing that only then could policymakers formulate informed choices on best practices. No doubt he expected that such an accounting would rein in their growth.

Secretary Surrey knew full well the inherent challenges of accomplishing this task. Unlike government expenditures that carried a specific dollar amount, tax expenditures simply entail "lost" tax revenues. As he observed, some tax expenditures rest simply on a "brief and cryptic administrative ruling of the Internal Revenue Service" (Surrey, 1968, p. 323).

Unlike government programs that carry a specific line item in the federal budget, tax expenditure "trails are very often obscurely marked" (Surrey, 1968, p. 323). Due to their invisibility, they get ignored and rarely mentioned in budgetary discussions. Indeed, he characterized them as the *back door* to the federal Treasury.

Moreover, he explained how attractive this back door has become. Any direct expenditure program comes with a price tag, forcing it to compete with other pressing needs for scarce public dollars. Congress often sets spending targets that ensure this competition is fierce. Finding the front door to the US Treasury crowded with other supplicants, many seek the overlooked back door – using the tax code to reward certain activities or parties. Some are fooled by the perception that these adjustments to the tax code carry no cost (Wolfman, 1985). Even acknowledging an ambiguous cost exists limits any direct competition among competing interests. In sum, this lack of measurability makes closing this door more difficult and reduces any imperative to do so.

This back entrance to the Treasury carries other advantages as well. Small government conservatives are naturally attracted to the tax expenditure option. This route allows one to engage in social programming without increasing the size of government, either in dollars or personnel. New tax expenditures add no dollars to the federal budget; indeed, they consume federal tax revenues, which naturally limits other forms of federal spending. Nor is there a need for a new government agency or bureaucracy. Any administration of these tax provisions, as minimal as it is, is contained solely within the IRS. Supporters of tax expenditures argue they are simply funding private sector business or households, who know best how to spend the money. Indeed, this public aid flows directly to the recipients without oversight from public officials. Given these benefits, it is easy to understand their proliferation throughout the federal tax code.

Once established, tax expenditures evade Congressional scrutiny. Direct government expenditures generally receive regular reviews by federal agencies and Congressional committees. Tax expenditures, on the other hand, get embedded into the federal tax code, an arcane document that runs for thousands of pages. Lacking any price tag, these tax deductions are allowed to lie fallow until Congress gathers sufficient motivation and focus to engage in episodic bouts of tax reform. In this way, these expenditures are treated as distinct and separate elements of the federal budget.

Their lack of transparency raised additional concerns for Secretary Surrey. Quite often, their actual benefits were obscure. In a subsequent article, he offered a specific example. At that time, the elderly could deduct medical expenses only if they exceeded a 3 percent floor of their adjusted gross income (AGI). The 1969 budgetary discussions included a provision to eliminate this threshold. On its face, this appeared as a reasonable adjustment to help seniors. However, Secretary Surrey argued that this provision would cost the federal government about $210 million, with almost half ($93 million) going to senior households making more than $50,000 annually. A scant $8 million would aid older households earning less than $5,000 (Surrey, 1970a). Given that "(n)o direct assistance program would be structured in this upside-down and exclusionary fashion" (Surrey, 1976a, p. 54), he argued their obscurity produces perverse outcomes. Without careful and comprehensive accounting, Surrey contended we cannot know whether the tax expenditures function efficiently, nor who benefits from them. Given his audience, one might wonder what kind of reception he received that day to this latter point.

Using tax expenditures instead of direct government grants or loans to meet social goals enables the wealthy to benefit disproportionately. Progressive income tax rates make deductions far more valuable to those in higher tax brackets. Surrey argued that tax expenditures generate an "upside-down subsidy" that not only favors higher-income earners but is exclusionary as well. By their design, tax deductions benefit only those who pay income taxes. According to Surrey (1970b):

> The fact that deductions and exemptions benefit only taxpayers is, to take the large view, a product of the fact that we have only a *positive* income tax system. If we had a *negative* income tax as well, then direct expenditures would benefit those whose incomes were below the level of positive tax, and a continuum in treatment would prevail. (p. 720; italics are the author's)

Their combined obscurity and bias toward the wealthy make tax expenditures a stealth weapon for the powerful.

Both in his talk and subsequent articles, Secretary Surrey explained how tax expenditure budgeting should work. Each existing tax expenditure should receive regular scrutiny to determine whether it meets its desired public policy outcomes both effectively and efficiently as compared to a direct expenditure alternative. This inquiry should include a full accounting of its cost to the Treasury as well as an assessment of its benefits and beneficiaries. Any proposed tax expenditure should receive the same scrutiny to ensure an exhaustive and transparent discussion of its relative merits. Only then, he argued, could we expect an efficient and fair use of our limited federal dollars. Given his stature in the government, Secretary Surrey's first wish was realized in the Budget Control Act of 1974. This law called for the annual accounting of all federal tax expenditures. However, he was not successful in getting his second wish fulfilled. Although we know the extent of lost revenue created by the various tax deductions, our federal tax code is littered with tax preferences that generate uncertain benefits and support unrecognized recipients. We continue to suffer from the consequences of this incomplete implementation of Secretary Surrey's vision.

Even after his departure from the Treasury, Secretary Surrey continued to advocate for budgetary reform and greater transparency over access to the Treasury's back door. His persistent reminders regarding the lack of transparency and accountability surrounding tax expenditures certainly alerted policymakers of their vulnerability to abuse. Yet, his warnings were largely ignored. Since the enactment of the Civil Rights Act of 1964, designating preferential treatment on the basis of race would no longer be legal. However, given the tight links between race and wealth, policies that targeted the wealthy would function nearly as well as if they were designated as "Whites Only." Using tax expenditures would allow such preferential treatment to occur without the normal oversight or public attention.

CONTEMPORARY FEDERAL WEALTH POLICY

Unlike in the past, the current federal wealth policy relies on twelve tax expenditures – the very tool that Secretary Surrey warned us against two generations ago.[1] These twelve tax deductions, which totaled $1,210 billion in 2023, assist households as they seek to save current income, reap rising asset values, and transfer family wealth.[2] Although these twelve can get lost in the nearly 200 listed tax expenditures, they account for 60 percent of the total value. Given the vast disparities in household wealth, one might expect this federal assistance would target wealth-poor households. Such federal help could enable these households to accumulate assets, overcome the wealth thresholds, and access the privileges of wealth. Doing so could limit the expansion of, if not narrow, both the interracial and intraracial wealth gaps. Instead, these deductions funnel their assistance to those who *already* own property. Since White households own the bulk of American assets, these policies inevitably favor them. Although these tax policies make no overt mention of race, they carry profound racial consequences.

1 The Tax Cuts and Jobs Act of 2017 effectively combined two deductions previously separate and added a new deduction, thereby keeping the total at 12.

2 This total is based on the Joint Committee on Taxation (2019, 2022) and the US Department of Treasury (2023).

As they lay buried in the US tax code and leave few clues to their consequences, they have survived for decades despite their perverse and pernicious consequences.

While some of these tax expenditures are well known, like the home mortgage interest deduction, others reside in relative obscurity, like the estate step-up in basis exclusion. All shower their benefits on those already wealthy rather than those seeking to build wealth from scratch. Several facets of their design assure this focus. First, most of the twelve target the specific needs of the affluent, whether it is homeownership, self-employment, or retirement saving. As a rule, these tax deductions assist households who have already purchased a home or started their own business and offer nothing to those aspiring for either. The generous tax treatment given to pensions helps households who have already met their emergency savings needs and are now looking ahead to retirement. By design, they offer no assistance to those who cannot afford their own home, start their own business, or participate in a 401(k). They function like other entitlement programs, although in this case they are based on asset ownership. Given the vast racial disparities in wealth and asset ownership, these tax expenditures offer preferential treatment to White households without any mention of race.

Second, seven of these deductions lack any limit on the benefits extended. That means that wealthier households with more valuable houses, larger retirement plans, and more expansive investment portfolios can take greater advantage of the benefits offered by these deductions, all without limit. In essence, they function as entitlement programs without any caps on their generosity.

Third, their design as tax deductions rather than tax credits targets their benefits even more narrowly toward the wealthy. Tax deductions (and exclusions) simply reduce one's taxable income, while tax credits shrink one's tax liability. For example, a $1,000 tax credit lowers all taxpayer's tax liability by that amount, particularly if the tax credit is fully refundable. In this case, even those taxpayers whose tax liability is less than $1,000 would benefit as they would earn a tax refund equal to any difference. Tax deductions and exclusions function differently. The actual value of a $1,000 tax deduction depends on which tax bracket one resides in. For a household in the top tax bracket of 37 percent, a $1,000 tax deduction would save them $370, while it would be worth only $100 to another household in the 10 percent bracket. The deduction is worthless to households who do not owe any federal income taxes. This means a tax deduction is worth far more – almost four times – to the affluent household as compared to a middle-class household. As White employees continue to earn higher salaries than

Table 4.1 *Wealth-building tax expenditures*

1.	Home Mortgage Interest Deduction
2.	State and Local Tax (SALT) Deduction
3.	Imputed Rent Exclusion
4.	Home Sales Exclusion
5.	Health Insurance Exclusion
6.	Charitable Contributions Deduction
7.	Tax-Exempt Interest Exclusion
8.	Qualified Business Income Exclusion
9.	Life Insurance Exclusion
10.	Pension Exclusion
11.	Capital Gains Exclusion
12.	Estate Step-Up Exclusion

Black employees, even when one compares similar education and job experience, their higher incomes cause them to gain further preferential treatment from these tax deductions.

Lastly, several of the deductions are "below-the-line deductions," meaning the taxpayer must itemize their deductions to claim the benefit. For reasons just discussed, higher-income taxpayers have far greater reason to itemize and claim these benefits. While numerous sources have corroborated this pattern over the years, it is likely that it has skewed even further in recent years.[3] One of the provisions of the Tax Cuts and Jobs Act of 2017 (TCJA 2017) was to increase substantially the standard deduction.[4] Making this change makes it unlikely that most taxpayers will continue to itemize, leaving only those taxpayers in the highest tax brackets left to choose this option. All of these design issues cause these tax expenditures to create the "upside-down subsidy" identified by Surrey.

The twelve wealth-building tax expenditures are given in Table 4.1. The first four on the list largely target homeowners, meaning those who rent need not apply.[5] The home mortgage interest deduction, perhaps the most politically sacrosanct of the group, allows homeowners to deduct any mortgage interest they pay up to a limit of $750,000 annually (Ventry, 2010). Mortgage interest paid on a second home, as long as it is not a rental property, can be included as well. With this deduction, households can

[3] This list includes the Joint Committee on Taxation (JCT) *Tax Expenditures* reports.

[4] This law nearly doubled the standard deduction to $12,550 for single and $25,100 for married households, causing far fewer households to itemize their deductions.

[5] Renters can take the SALT deduction since it allows them to deduct state and local income tax payments.

use the tax savings to invest in other assets, including purchasing a bigger home and assuming a larger mortgage. Similarly, one important element of the SALT (state and local taxes) deduction is that homeowners can subtract any local property tax payments made on their primary or second home.[6] State and local income tax payments also can be deducted, but they are tied to household income, not homeownership. However, with the TCJA 2017, households can deduct only up to $10,000 for these tax payments. Like the home mortgage deduction, this below-the-line deduction, if itemized, can generate after-tax dollars that can be saved and invested in new assets.

The third tax expenditure linked to homeownership is the exclusion of imputed (net) rent from owner-occupied housing. This particular tax expenditure is neither well known nor fully acknowledged.[7] Like all owned assets, your home generates value, although not necessarily income, particularly if you use it as a residence instead of as rental property. A simple example illustrates the point. Consider two households, each owning identical properties. They swap houses so that each is a landlord and tenant to the other. Both households now earn rental income (as well as pay rent), which increases their tax liability. If each simply lived in their own home, they would experience the same value but avoid paying any taxes on that value or rental income. Homeownership offers the household a hidden subsidy. In some cases, owning a home enables one to reside in affluent neighborhoods capable of funding well-resourced public schools and local parks. Often these communities use exclusionary zoning to preclude renters from enjoying these amenities. Since all homeowners could choose to rent their property but do not, it suggests that most see greater value in simply occupying the residence. This deduction allows homeowners to enjoy the value gained from living in their own home without paying any taxes. The imputed rent is simply the likely rental value of the property minus any maintenance, insurance, and depreciation expenses that one would incur as a landlord.[8] As such, it is argued that the imputed rent is the bottom estimate of what the residence is worth to them (Goode, 1960). By excluding this value from one's tax liability, it raises the homeowner's after-tax income, thereby freeing cash for saving and investment.

6 Prior to 2017, the JCT reported a Home Property Tax Deduction and another catchall state and local tax deduction that included state and local income taxes and sales taxes. While local property taxes are used throughout the US, not all states have state income taxes.

7 While the US Treasury includes this as a tax expenditure, the JCT does not.

8 Mortgage interest and property taxes are already deductible even though the homeowner does not have to pay any tax on the imputed rental value.

The last of the homeownership tax expenditures functions differently than the others. When homeowners go to sell their home, just like any other property or asset, they may realize a capital gain on the sale. While such a gain would normally be treated as income and therefore subject to income taxes, the home sales exclusion allows sellers the right to keep all of the realized gain, up to a limit of $250,000 for single and $500,000 for married households. This generous exclusion is limited only to one's principal residence, placing it in an unrivaled category among household assets.

Taken together, these four tax expenditures offer homeownership an unequaled source of federal help as households strive to attain financial security. While they provide generous aid to homeowners, they do so only for those who have already attained homeownership. Given the wide disparities in homeownership rates between White and Black households, this funnels the aid to White households. Even worse, none of these tax deductions offers any direct help to those hoping to become first-time homebuyers. None provides a bridge to prospective homebuyers who have a stable and adequate income but simply lack the required down payment. This leaves many more Black households outside the generous reach of these tax exemptions. Facing substantial educational, employment, and credit market discrimination, Black households are less likely to have the income needed to qualify for home mortgages and less able to recover the centuries of lost opportunity in building wealth within their families and communities. As such, this federal largesse is skewed to wealthier households, who also tend to be White.

The fifth tax expenditure is the health insurance exclusion. Like the imputed rent exclusion, this represents a non-income benefit, although in this case it stems from one's employer. Normally, anything of value that an employee receives from their employer is considered taxable income unless specifically exempted. This deduction allows employees to exclude any employer-paid contributions or premiums to their health plan as well as any benefits they or their family members receive as they access health care. Each offers households an effective boost in their after-tax income as their employer pays some portion of their health insurance and the insurer pays part of their medical care expenses. Yet, the deduction does more than augment the household's savings. Health insurance coverage limits exposure to overwhelming medical bills that may result from catastrophic illness. It encourages access to preventative care that treats festering health concerns before they become expansive health problems. Poor health can lead to lost work time, which reduces income and may even trigger dismissal. The accompanying stress will only exacerbate the underlying health concerns.

In these ways, the provision of health insurance helps households avoid financial calamity as well as augment their savings and build wealth. This support depends on the quality and extent of coverage in a given policy.

Once again, one can find substantial disparities between health insurance coverage when comparing White and Black households. According to the American Community Survey, nearly 75 percent of non-Hispanic White households had some sort of private health insurance, while only 56 percent of Black households had private insurance, suggesting a vast difference in this benefit.[9] This disparity is reduced significantly when one considers public provision of health insurance. When one includes all forms of health coverage, the insured rate rises to 94 percent for non-Hispanic Whites and 90 percent for Blacks. As such, Medicare, Medicaid, and CHAMPVA (Civilian Health and Medical Program of the Department of Veterans Affairs) do much to reduce the health insurance coverage gap. While the above statistics tell us the coverage rates, they do not convey anything regarding the extent or quality of that coverage.

Some might question why the next tax expenditure, the charitable giving deduction, is included in this list of wealth-building policies. Like the home mortgage interest and the SALT deductions, it exempts specific household expenditures that are often cash outlays. Thus, it offers only marginal assistance in stretching after-tax income and allowing more savings. Further, Americans are known as generous givers to charity. Evidence shows that charitable giving – as a share of one's income – is greater among low-income households than more affluent households (Lindsey, 2002). This disparate giving occurs even as this deduction requires tax itemizing, a choice that makes sense only to affluent taxpayers. Even still, the largest share of this exemption benefits wealthier households who offer large gifts. As a limit, Congress has capped any deduction for cash gifts at 60 percent of the household's AGI. However, this cap is porous as any remaining gift can be carried forward to the following five tax years.

It is the tax treatment of noncash gifts that gives the strongest argument for inclusion here. Early on, the Treasury Department ruled that noncash gifts to qualified charities should be valued at the time of the gift. Although this ruling seems quite reasonable, it actually makes little "tax sense." Income earned as assets appreciate is only considered – tax wise – when the asset is sold and the gain is realized. This ruling exempts the charitable

[9] According to the Census of Health Insurance Coverage in the United States (Keisler-Starkey & Bunch, 2020), private insurance includes employer and union-sponsored health coverage as well as private coverage purchased independently or TRICARE.

giver from any capital gains liability and shields current income at the same time. A simple example can illustrate the point. Suppose I buy stock valued at $10 per share that subsequently increases to $110 per share. With my donation, I avoid any capital gains tax (20% × $100) and reduce my current income tax liability by the value of the gift and tax bracket ($110 × 37%). Stock that cost me $10 per share is now generating a tax saving of $57 per share. As a bonus, my name is immortalized on some building as a generous philanthropist. Similar to the above, this deduction faces a temporary limit of 30 percent of the donor's AGI; any remainder can be applied in future years. As White households have more generational wealth to give, they benefit disproportionately from this deduction as well.

The next two tax expenditures, the exclusions of tax-exempt bond interest and qualified business income, both allow households to shield specific forms of income from the IRS. Tax-exempt bonds are simply bonds issued by nonfederal governmental agencies that are exempted from federal income taxation. Anyone can purchase these bonds, but only a select few do. Their tax-exempt status allows them to offer lower yields to investors relative to other bonds carrying similar risk. Only high-income households who face the highest tax rates find their tax-exempt status worth the lower yield. No racial barriers preclude Black households from purchasing these bonds; the deeper pockets of income and wealth held by Whites simply make them more appealing to White investors.

The qualified business income exclusion represents the newest addition to the lineup of wealth-building federal tax expenditures. Created as part of the TCJA 2017, it allows owners of "pass-through" businesses the opportunity to exclude 20 percent of their business earnings from personal income taxation. "Pass-through" businesses are those not subject to corporate income taxes; their earnings "pass through" to be taxed as the personal income of their owners. They include the vast majority of businesses, including those organized as sole proprietorships, partnerships, S-corporations, and limited liability companies (LLCs). For businesses that ply a "specified service trade or business," there is an income limit ($213,300 for single and $426,600 for married households) after which the exclusion disappears.[10] However, certain types of small businesses can avoid this limitation and shield 20 percent of their business's net income without limit.[11]

[10] This limit includes most doctors, lawyers, financial planners, and other professionals that earn pass-through income.

[11] Dividends from real estate investment trusts (REITs) and income from publicly traded partnerships, which are often used in the oil and gas industry, effectively have no limits.

Self-employment levels among Black adults have persistently lagged behind the rates among Whites. An extensive literature has grown to examine and explain this self-employment gap.[12] The explanations offered are disparities in public education resources for White and Black students, limited family resources to fund post-secondary education, reduced access to business start-up and venture capital funds, and White reluctance to patronize Black-owned businesses. The dearth of Black-owned businesses means fewer Black children gain exposure to entrepreneurial ventures or the opportunity to inherit a family business. Past episodes of White racial violence targeting Black-owned businesses undoubtedly has dampened enthusiasm for this avenue of wealth accumulation within the Black community. For all of these reasons, it is likely that the self-employment gap will continue and that this tax exclusion will continue to benefit White households preferentially.

The next two tax expenditures, the life insurance and pension exclusions, assist households trying to save for the future. Their design favors households who have met their "rainy day saving" needs and now are planning for retirement, legacy gifts, or death. To understand the life insurance exclusion, one needs to understand the basics of the life insurance industry. Term life insurance policies require households to pay regular premiums over a specific term for a guaranteed benefit if death occurs. Once the term ends, the customer must renew the policy to retain the benefit. To earn a profit, insurance companies must invest the premiums at sufficient rates of return to pay any death benefits and cover their administrative expenses. This process of investing customer premiums is called "inside buildup." Neither the gains earned during "inside buildup" nor any payment of death benefits are subject to taxation in order to encourage households to protect themselves when death occurs.

This favorable tax treatment gives life insurance firms an advantage over banks and other financial institutions who profit from household savings. Recognizing this advantage, life insurers designed "whole life" insurance policies that enable their customers to make regular payments into funds that use this inside buildup to generate tax-free benefits paid in the event of death. Policyholders have the option to redeem their cash balances prematurely, making them similar to a savings fund. The difference is that income earned in normal savings accounts is taxable, while

[12] The interested reader may want to consult Borjas and Bronars (1989); Bates (1997); Blanchflower et al. (2003); Cavalluzzo and Wolken (2005); Henderson et al. (2015); Kopkin (2017).

the income earned in life insurance policies is tax-free. As the benefits paid out upon the death of the policyholder are not subject to taxation, life insurance policies provide a tax-free saving vehicle for the policyholder and any beneficiaries.[13]

Historically, the life insurance industry has focused on middle-class Americans as its primary market. This explains why the disparity between White and Black households' use of life insurance policies is smaller than many of the gaps already discussed.[14] Yet, simply counting policies does not capture the full reality. The size of the policies determines the share of benefits gained from this tax expenditure. Unsurprisingly, affluent households generally carry larger policies. As a recent Wall Street Journal article noted, the associated tax benefits are causing wealthy households to revisit life insurance as a way to transfer their wealth to their heirs and avoid paying taxes (Maremont & Scism, 2010). Tax-free inside buildup allows them to invest payments now that will yield greater benefits upon their death without anyone paying any income taxes.[15]

Pension assets function similarly to life insurance assets, with one exception: these savings are focused on retirement rather than death. Historically, most employer-sponsored pension plans were *defined benefit* plans that function somewhat like term life insurance policies. After working for one company most of your career, you would become eligible for a retirement pension that would rise with years of service and peak salary. Your employer would have the responsibility of putting away funds annually and use inside buildup to meet future pension obligations. To encourage saving for retirement, the IRS gave the same preferential treatment to inside buildup by shielding any income or capital gain from being taxed. For those not eligible for employer pension plans, Congress created 401(k) plans, so named after their legislative code. In this case, households could deposit tax-deductible funds up to some limit that would then benefit from tax-free inside buildup. Only when the funds were withdrawn after age fifty-nine and a half would the beneficiary pay any income tax.[16] Among the highly paid, they would likely face lower tax rates during retirement, thereby

13 In the case of beneficiaries that are young children, some policies may pay out the proceeds over time. Any interest generated during this interval is taxable.

14 According to the 2022 SCF, a slightly greater percentage of Black households have life insurance policies than do White households. Similar results are reported in recent surveys.

15 The benefits may be subject to estate tax if the estate exceeds the exemption level.

16 Roth IRAs (Individual Retirement Accounts) allow households to deposit after-tax funds that then along with any appreciation become tax-free after age fifty-nine and a half.

reducing even further their future tax liability. This favorable tax treatment created highly attractive vehicles for retirement saving, yet their substantial penalties for early withdrawal limited their appeal only to households who had their emergency saving needs already met.

On its face, it appears this favorable treatment only allows participants the benefits of tax deferral as they must pay taxes eventually. This is an attractive benefit in itself. Yet, this arrangement also enables participants to save tax-free. Suppose I face a 30 percent tax bracket. If my deposits to the 401(k) are not tax deductible, then I lose $100 in current income for every $70 I deposit. Tax deductibility means I get to deposit the full $100, essentially allowing me to use the taxpayers' money to make money. Eventually, I will pay taxes on the extra $30 and any interest it earns, but just a portion, allowing the bulk to pass through tax-free. That I will likely experience a lower post-retirement income tax bracket simply sweetens the deal. Effectively, the federal government is matching savers' contributions with public contributions in the form of lost tax revenues and allowing the recipient to leverage this assistance for their own gain.

The attractiveness of these 401(k)-type funds encouraged employers to shift their pension plans to *defined contribution* plans. In these plans, employers administer a 401(k)-type plan and match employee contributions by some chosen rate. No longer does the employee have a guaranteed pension, but rather contributes to a fund that can move from job to job, once vesting is achieved.

This change relieves employers of any market risk that might short-change the inside buildup needed to meet future pension benefits. Instead, the employee carries the risk on whether and how much to divert from their current salary toward future benefits. This risk imposes the heaviest burden on lower-wage earners since their pay cannot adequately meet both current and future needs. As employers have shifted away from *defined benefit* toward *defined contribution* plans, it has increasingly skewed the benefits of employer pensions. Higher salaried workers find it easier to divert current income and therefore claim the full benefits of any employer match. Once again, this would work against Black households who experience wage and salary discrimination from multiple sources.

The remaining two tax expenditures allow households to exclude income that results from household assets that increase in value. The capital gains exclusion lowers the tax rate on income earned from asset appreciation below that on wage income. Currently, the exclusion limits any taxes paid on capital gains to between 0 and 20 percent, depending on the taxpayers' ordinary income tax bracket.[17] Those in the top tax bracket – 37 percent – pay only 20 percent on their realized gains, thereby receiving an almost 50 percent break on their tax liability. Households in lower tax brackets do get a break as well, but the benefit is usually smaller. As the wealthy hold most of the high-risk investments like commercial real estate, stocks, and venture capital, which offer the greatest potential for capital gains, the bulk of benefits generated by this exclusion funnel primarily to them. Again, this preferential treatment favors White households.

This exclusion faces a real challenge in justifying its existence in the tax code. Many have questioned why income earned by one's effort or talents at work is taxed more heavily than income generated by rising asset values. Supporters of the exclusion contend that capital gains earned over long periods are often exaggerated by inflation and therefore deserve preferential tax treatment. As the tax is assessed only when the gains are realized by the asset sale, it can generate a rather large tax liability, although it is accompanied by an even larger income gain. Lastly, advocates contend the preferential treatment encourages greater turnover of asset ownership, which promotes increased flexibility and resiliency in the economy. Likely the most important reason is how valuable the exclusion is to those who earn the bulk of their income from capital assets.

The estate step-up in basis also relates to the treatment of capital gains, but as they impact family wealth and inheritance. Specifically, this tax exemption considers the treatment of unrealized capital gains upon the death of the asset owner. Under the exclusion, the tax basis of all assets in the estate are "stepped up" to their current market value. This adjustment in tax basis has two primary consequences. It effectively shields the deceased's unrealized capital gains from any income tax liability. As such, it encourages older asset owners to hold on to their investments knowing they will elude any income tax liability. This is the very behavior that the supporters of the capital gains exclusion argue should be avoided.[18] According to Secretary Surrey, this provision qualifies as the "most serious defect in the federal tax structure today" (Federal Estate and Gift Taxes, 1976, p. 499). To be fair, the step-up provision makes these long-held assets and their unrealized gains fully liable to the estate tax. This argument carries merit when the estate tax is strict and substantial but loses credibility as the estate tax is undermined.

[17] The exception are assets that are held less than one year and any capital gains that would qualify for the home sales exclusion.

[18] Curiously, very few of those who strongly support the capital gains exclusion advocate for the elimination of the estate step-up provision.

In this way, the estate step-up in basis places tremendous pressure on the federal estate tax as the remaining bulwark against simply allowing family wealth to be transferred across generations without any tax liability.

It is not hard to fathom who benefits the most from this tax exclusion. As explained in Chapter 3, the history of our federal wealth programs has enabled White households to gain overwhelming advantage in asset ownership. The nineteenth-century land policies offered White colonial settlers numerous opportunities to own land. During the twentieth century, preferential mortgage lending and zoning enabled their descendants to purchase homes in highly desired neighborhoods. Over decades, these properties have appreciated substantially, allowing White households to benefit disproportionately from the estate step-up exclusion. Although this provision does swell White estates, their ability to transfer this wealth across generations will depend on the effectiveness of the federal estate tax. Further investigation of this issue must await the next chapter.

EXAMINING THEIR IMPACT

Back in the 1970s, Secretary Surrey worried about the future consequences of federal tax expenditures that were subject to limited fiscal oversight. He recognized how their design thwarted normal budgetary controls as they resembled normal entitlements but without any budgetary limit. To emphasize his point, he quoted the Congressional Budget Office argument, which explained, "A tax expenditure is analogous to an entitlement program on the spending side of the budget; the amount expended is not subject to any legislated limit but is dependent solely upon taxpayer response to the particular provision. In this respect, tax expenditures closely resemble spending programs that have no ceiling" (Surrey & McDaniel, 1978). In contrast to many entitlement programs, these tax expenditures could be expected to expand as the country experienced economic growth and increased prosperity. Undoubtedly, Secretary Surrey hoped that the annual accounting of the tax expenditures, initiated by the Congressional Budget Act of 1974, would offer ample restraints to their expansion. Yet, as others have noted, these tax expenditures rarely get included when the debate on entitlement reform is raised (Hungerford, 2006).

Thanks to Secretary Surrey's influence, we can track the growth of these tax expenditures since 1975. Figure 4.1 illustrates their advance over time. One curve illustrates the growth of the full dozen twelve tax expenditures in constant 2022 dollars. It shows a fivefold increase in benefits. Some of

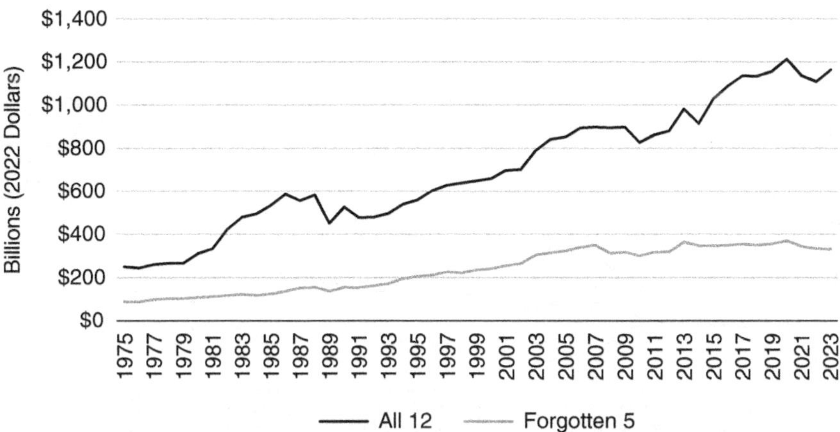

Figure 4.1 Tax expenditure benefits over time
Source: Author's calculations; Joint Tax Committee Tax Expenditures; US Treasury Tax Expenditures

this increase is due to Congressional tinkering as lawmakers have made various changes, some modest and others substantial. Five of the twelve tax expenditures, labeled the Forgotten 5, have avoided Congressional scrutiny and remained largely unchanged through the period.[19] Even these have witnessed a fourfold increase in their generosity. The explanation is simple. As households accumulate more wealth, they are better able to leverage even greater assistance from these tax breaks. It is particularly telling that none of these five tax expenditures comes with a limit or cap on their benefits.

One can compare the growth of these tax expenditures with that of federal direct expenditures themselves. This comparison is given in Figure 4.2. All three variables are indexed to their 1975 levels to provide a clear comparison. Both the Forgotten 5 as well as all twelve tax expenditures grew at a more rapid pace than did federal expenditures over the same period. Only the dramatic and unprecedented increase in spending due to COVID-19 in 2020 sharply narrowed the gap. As Secretary Surrey warned, these tax expenditures have functioned to keep the back door to the US Treasury wide open to some.

[19] The Forgotten 5 are the health insurance, life insurance, and charitable giving deductions as well as the tax-exempt bond interest and estate step-up in basis exclusions. The estate step-up in basis exclusion was rescinded in 1976 but then restored before any change was allowed to occur. All have been affected by changes in other parts of the tax code, most importantly revisions to the normal-income tax brackets.

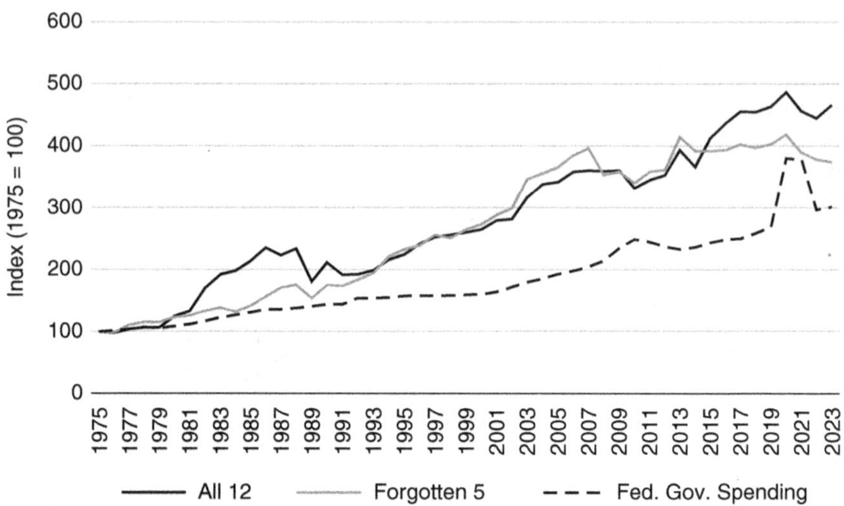

Figure 4.2 Tax expenditures versus federal expenditures growth
Source: Author's calculations; Federal Reserve Economic Data; Joint Tax Committee Tax Expenditures; US Treasury Tax Expenditures

Secretary Surrey's second major concern with the growth of tax expenditures is that they mask their distributional effects. In 1978 he wrote, with Professor McDaniel:

Not only are the tax expenditure provisions the primary cause of tax inequity, but it seems safe to say that the provisions do not even achieve what most Americans would perceive to be a fair distribution of funds, measured by criteria applied to direct spending programs. Major strides toward tax equity – horizontal and vertical – could be achieved by eliminating all the tax expenditures from the Internal Revenue Code. (Surrey & McDaniel, 1978, p. 255)

As compared to direct government expenditures, it is much more difficult to "follow the money" and see who benefits from the program. Nonetheless, it can be done. Surrey and McDaniel (1978) did so back then. They explained:

In fiscal 1977, the top 1.4 percent of taxpayers, with "expanded gross income" of $50,000 or more, received 31.3 percent of the Treasury "tax checks" delivered through the tax expenditure mechanism – over $26 billion out of a total of almost $84 billion spent. On the average, taxpaying units in this select group received, in effect, federal subsidies of $71,429. The 49,000 taxpayers with incomes above $200,000, representing 5/100 of 1 percent of total returns, on the average received federal tax subsidies of $535,653. Tax sheltered individuals live in stately mansions! (pp. 254–255)

Despite the clear evidence of these tax expenditures' "upside-down subsidy," Congress never found the motivation to rouse itself to remedy these perverse outcomes.

While it remains challenging to follow their trail of benefits, it is possible to do so today not only on the basis of household income or wealth, but also race. Only households with mortgages on their primary residences are eligible for the home mortgage interest deduction. Similarly, only households with retirement funds, whether employer-sponsored or 401(k) funds, will benefit from the preferential tax treatment afforded retirement assets. Fully ten of the twelve tax expenditures require some form of asset ownership to be eligible for the tax expenditure.[20] The remaining two, charitable contributions and SALT deductions, reflect levels of philanthropy and household income.[21] By collecting data on these and other key variables, one can estimate the distribution of benefits from these tax expenditures.

Fortunately, such information is readily available. Every three years, the Federal Reserve oversees the SCF, in which they survey roughly 5,000 households. In addition to selecting households randomly, the SCF uses tax records to generate an oversample of wealthy households to ensure adequate representation of the richest households, ones that are often missed by other surveys.[22] Due to this targeting, most view it as providing the most accurate reflection of wealth distribution in the US. Sampling weights are provided, allowing one to make broader generalizations about US society. Since the primary objective of the SCF is to understand the composition and distribution of household wealth, it queries households about their assets, debts, and inheritances using a unique range and depth of questions. For example, the survey asks households how much income they earned the previous year from tax-exempt bonds or from realized capital gains, whether from the sale of their home or other assets. These answers help to discern which households benefit from the various tax deductions and by how much. Similarly, the survey asks about each household's pension assets, real estate values, self-employment income, and unrealized capital gains. Each of these questions determines whether households are eligible for the pension deduction, imputed rent, qualified business income, and estate step-up in basis, if in the latter case they were to die suddenly. Further, the survey asks whether households itemized deductions on their

[20] This includes having health insurance coverage as a form of "asset ownership."

[21] The SALT Deduction does include deductions for residential property taxes.

[22] To protect privacy, the SCF avoids surveying those among the Forbes 400 wealthiest households.

Table 4.2 *Tax expenditure benefits*

Wealth-Building Tax Expenditures	2022 *Benefit ($ billions)*	2022 *% Share to Top Wealth Quintile*
1. Home Mortgage	36.1	68
2. SALT Exclusion	25.1	55
3. Imputed Rent Exclusion	134.2	81
4. Home Sales Exclusion	39.6	69
5. Health Insurance Exclusion	199.3	32
6. Charitable Contributions	46.6	90
7. Tax-Exempt Bonds	24.0	100
8. Qualified Business Income	55.8	88
9. Life Insurance Exclusion	19.2	86
10. Pension Exclusion	331.0	87
11. Capital Gains Exclusion	151.4	95
12. Estate Step-Up in Basis Exclusion	45.4	99

Source: Author's calculations; Federal Reserve Board, 2022; Survey of Consumer Finances; Joint Committee on Taxation *Tax Expenditures*; US Treasury *Tax Expenditures.*

taxes; this reveals whether they took advantage of any "below-the-line" deductions. By pairing information between the SCF and the Treasury/Joint Committee on Taxation (JCT) estimates, one can calculate how the benefits of the tax expenditures are distributed across American households.[23]

Table 4.2 shares the estimated cost of each deduction as well as what share goes to the wealthiest 20 percent of households. This latter measure indicates the preferential treatment these programs provide our most affluent citizens. As you can see, nine of the deductions target more than *four-fifths* of their benefits to the wealthiest *one-fifth* of American households. Three of them, including the exclusions on tax-exempt bond income, capital gains, and estate step-up in basis, shower virtually all of their benefits upon the richest households. Because homeownership is more widespread than the ownership of high-risk investments, the deductions related to homeownership are slightly less focused on the wealthy. Among the twelve, the Health Insurance Exclusion stands out as an anomaly. This is due to the widespread, although not yet universal, health insurance coverage now available. It also results from limited evidence – the estimates here are based simply upon whether households have health insurance coverage and do not reflect the quality of that coverage. Clearly, some households

[23] A fuller explanation of the methods used can be found in the Appendix.

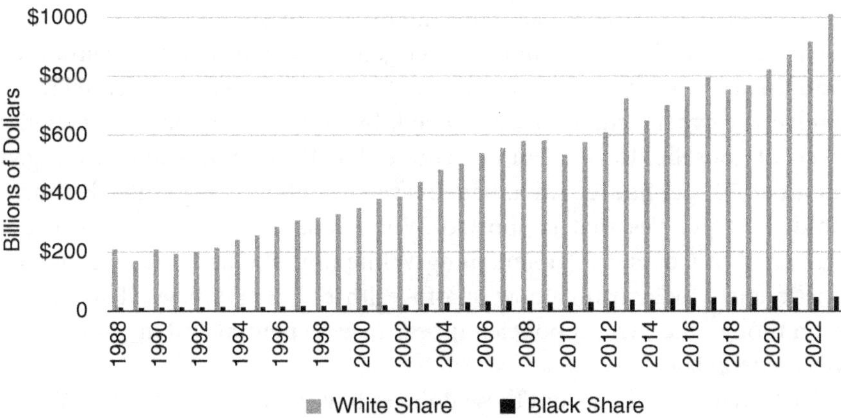

Figure 4.3 Relative shares of tax expenditures, 1988–2022
Source: Author's calculations; Federal Reserve Board, Survey of Consumer Finances; Joint Tax Committee Tax Expenditures; US Treasury Tax Expenditures

have health insurance that covers more medical procedures, offers greater protection, and reduces out-of-pocket payments. Undoubtedly, the affluent benefit disproportionately from these higher-quality plans.

Since White households own the bulk of household assets, earn higher incomes, and have greater access to health insurance coverage, these policies inevitably favor them. Although these tax expenditures say nothing about race, they carry profound racial consequences. I illustrate this by showing the relative shares received by White and Black households over time. To do this I pair the triennial SCF surveys with the annual government estimates of how much each tax expenditure costs the Treasury. In largely their current form, the SCFs go back to 1989. To capture the benefits provided in those years between each SCF, I simply use the closest survey year. Thus, I use the 1989 SCF to estimate the benefits for both 1988 and 1990 and the following 1992 survey to examine 1991 through 1993. Since asset ownership and wealth shares remain stable from year to year, this step seems reasonable.

I show these results in Figure 4.3. As you can see, the share of tax benefits going to White households far exceeds that received by Black households. Part of this disproportionate share results from the majority status of White households within the survey population and in society at large. Yet, the share going to White households outstrips, by a substantial margin, what they might benefit if the tax benefits were shared on a proportional basis reflective of population shares. Unfortunately, the figure does not illustrate this clearly. What it does show is the trends over time. While both Black and White households benefit increasingly from the tax expenditures over time, Whites experience far larger increases. Because White households have had unrivaled opportunities over generations to acquire wealth, they find themselves better able to leverage the opportunities provided by these twelve tax expenditures today. Indeed, by simply averaging the benefits over all households, one can determine that White households averaged about $8,741 per household in benefits versus only $2,396 per Black household. Past policies that supported White wealth acquisition, like those discussed in Chapter 3, are enabling White households to benefit disproportionately today from a new set of wealth-building policies. This occurs even though the current policies appear racially neutral and in compliance with federal law.

To understand the extent these policies have fueled the growth in White wealth and widened the racial wealth gap, I estimate their impact over the years. Initially, I simply total the annual assistance going to White households from 1988 to 2022. This amount totals $17.2 trillion, a sizable source of help. Yet, this figure fails to capture the full impact of these tax expenditures. Presumably, households take these annual savings and invest the funds, whether in savings accounts, stock funds, or new business ventures. To assess how much wealth these investments could generate today, I estimate three scenarios. First, I assume households save and invest the benefits at a modest 3 percent return over inflation. This represents a modest return and is widely used as a conservative baseline. Second, I assume households take the savings from one year and invest them in the stock market at the start of the following year. The funds are invested in an S&P 500 index fund, which entails no special financial knowledge nor undue risk-taking. I then calculate the value of these funds in 2022 using the S&P 500 Price Index. Lastly, I follow the same steps as above but use in this case the S&P 500 Total Return Index to calculate the current value of these funds. Unlike the normal price index, the total return index assumes that stock dividends earned over the period are simply reinvested into the fund. Using the standard price index ignores these dividends that might be spent or reinvested elsewhere.

The key results are presented in Figure 4.4. According to the SCF, White household wealth grew by $103 trillion between 1989 and 2022. Although this figure is in current dollars and so includes the impact of inflation, this increase reflects a seven-fold increase in White household wealth over the period.[24] Since 1988, the dozen federal tax expenditures

[24] White wealth increased from $16 trillion in 1989 to $119.5 trillion in 2022. Over the same period, Black household wealth increased from $492 billion to $3.5 trillion.

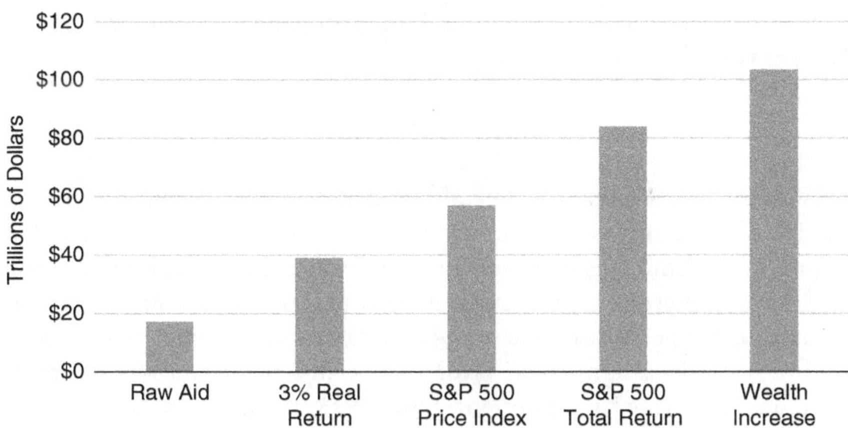

Figure 4.4 Federal help to White households, 1988–2022
Source: Author's calculations; Federal Reserve Board, Survey of Consumer Finances; Joint Tax Committee Tax Expenditures; US Treasury Tax Expenditures

funneled about $17.2 trillion, or about 17% of that increase. Assuming these benefits are invested and earn a 3 percent real rate of return, they could account for $39 trillion of the increase in White household wealth. Using the S&P 500 Price Index, the value of these past tax expenditures now can account for $57 trillion, or over half of the increase in White wealth holdings. Taking the S&P 500 Total Return Index, the value of these past forms of federal generosity could yield $84 trillion, or over 81 percent of the expansion of White wealth.

Two issues may vex certain readers. The latter estimate assumes that households benefiting from the federal tax expenditures do not consume any of their rising fortune. This is unrealistic as economists have long documented the wealth effect, a key component discussed previously in the LCH model (Cooper & Dynan, 2016). Using the S&P 500 Total Return Index may overstate the accumulated wealth effect of the federal tax deductions. Rather, it may provide an accurate estimate of the total value of these deductions to households as they choose to spend some of their good fortune on increasing their material well-being. Thus, the two S&P 500 estimates should offer good bookend estimates of the actual impact of these tax policies. Of course, not all households that benefited from federal largesse in 1989 are still alive today. In that case, I have simply assumed that whatever gains they received were passed along to their heirs. In reality, some of these benefits may have been diverted to the Treasury as a result of the federal wealth transfer tax system. As such, these estimates should be viewed as gross assistance figures. I discuss the role of the federal wealth taxes in Chapter 5 to generate a net figure.

CONCLUSION

Fifty years ago, Secretary Surrey alerted lawmakers and policymakers to the insidious nature of federal tax expenditures. He warned their veiled nature would limit effective oversight and make them susceptible to abuse by powerful interests. Any increase in their use would leave no increase in government expenditures, but simply an inconspicuous decline in federal revenues. Their design would favor the wealthy without leaving a trace. Time has confirmed his foresight. Since 1975, these dozen expenditures have risen much faster in cost than the growth of federal expenditures. Lobbyists and lawmakers have found the Treasury's back door far easier to open. Even as these expenditures have ballooned in cost to the taxpayer, their perverse favoritism has remained largely unacknowledged – until now. While several studies have examined the impact of tax expenditures on households based on their income, only two have studied their impact based on household wealth.[25] This study attempts to remedy this neglect.

It is likely that Secretary Surrey never considered how the unsupervised rise in federal tax revenues might impact the racial wealth gap. Nowhere does he appear to address this issue. However, it represents a natural consequence of his concern that powerful lobbies would feast at the Treasury's back door. One cannot discount that race had much to do with Surrey's influential voice being ignored. Just years earlier, federal civil rights laws had dismantled the legal basis of racial segregation and stratification. The elimination of these racialized structures surely generated uneasiness among Whites. Already by the mid-1970s there was fierce pushback to the modest federal efforts at affirmative action that simply *encouraged* employers and universities to admit more qualified non-Whites. Worried by the shifting racial landscape, some considered whether new structures could be created to retain White preferences. In this environment, one can understand an increased interest in using federal tax policy as the vehicle to preserve economic stratification.

As this chapter documents, these tax expenditures have demonstrated remarkable efficacy in promoting White supremacy without raising notice. This is key. The shroud over their consequences noted by Secretary Surrey explains much of their appeal. Yet, even when this cover is removed, they

[25] Two exceptions are Williams (2016, 2022).

retain an effective defense. None of these tax deductions make any mention of race. Instead, they target asset ownership, which is viewed as a reward of hard work and symbol of success. White households able to leverage these tax deductions to their advantage do so not because of their race, but because of their work ethic and fiscal discipline. No undue favoritism appears to exist here. These tax policies are simply rewarding those who apparently have demonstrated their worth. That this argument ignores any historical or institutional context is conveniently overlooked.

Despite the elimination of de jure segregation policies over a half century ago, the racial wealth gap has widened substantially over the intervening period. Earlier chapters examined the possibility that persistent discrimination in education and business as well as labor, housing, and credit markets have contributed significantly to this disturbing trend. As the evidence in this chapter demonstrates, the twelve federal tax expenditures offer an additional explanation for the expansion of the racial wealth gap. The extent of wealth that these dozen programs have funneled into the hands of White households must be seen as a willing accomplice to the widening disparities. Operating under the radar, these programs are ensuring that the wealth advantages extended to White Americans over the past two centuries will persist and expand during the twenty-first century. It is a train that continues to pick up speed without any premonition of the disturbing consequences that lie ahead.

There exists one brake to this system that requires our consideration. In addition to these tax expenditures, federal wealth policy includes a wealth transfer tax system that aspires to raise federal revenues and limit the intergenerational transfer of wealth. The estate, gift, and generation-skipping trust taxes that comprise this system could mitigate the problems just discussed. They could function to limit severely the transfer of wealth from one generation to the next, thereby curbing the runaway wealth trends. Examining these taxes and their current level of effectiveness is the focus of Chapter 5.

5

Inspecting the Leaky Bucket

TRIALS OF THE RICH

"Imagine Jeff Bezos' current $165 billion fortune completely gone in 120 years … or sooner," warns one website.[1] According to the blog post entitled *Shirtsleeves to Shirtsleeves*, only 10 percent of affluent wealth makes it past the third generation. This title refers to the proverb, thought to be coined by steelmaker Andrew Carnegie, which states: "Shirtsleeves to shirtsleeves in three generations." This appears to be an Americanized version of the old English maxim "there's nobbut three generations atween clogs and clogs." In Italian, it is expressed as "*dalle stalle alle stelle alle stalle* (from stalls to stars to stalls) and in Spanish "*quien no lo tiene lo hance; y quien lo tiene, lo deshance*" (who does not have it, does it; and who has it, misuses it). Nonwestern cultures have their versions as well. In Chinese, the proverb is "*fu bu guo san dai*," which translates "wealth never survives three generations," while the Japanese express it as "*sandai de ie wa tsubureru*," which roughly states "the third generation ruins the house." The existence of this adage across very different cultures indicates the substantial challenges families face in trying to create dynastic wealth. The Scottish saw offers some explanation for the challenges facing the rich: "The father buys, the son builds, the grandson sells, and his son begs." Who thought being fabulously wealthy would bring its own problems?

An oft-cited research study seems to give strong support to this view. Based on interviews with 3,250 affluent families conducted over a twenty-year period, the Williams Group (no relation) found that 70 percent of families squander their wealth by the third generation (Williams & Preisser, 2005). According to another article, evidence from other countries suggests

[1] From the Boyd Wealth Management blog *Shirtsleeves to Shirtsleeves* (2019).

the rate is closer to 90 percent (Castoro, 2015). It seems that creating a family dynasty, even among the very wealthy, is much harder than we imagine. The Vanderbilt family often serves as a cautionary tale. Getting fabulously rich from an empire based on the New York Central railroad, Cornelius "Commodore" Vanderbilt died in 1877 leaving a fortune estimated at $100 million. True to form, his son, William Henry Vanderbilt, added to his legacy and augmented the family wealth. Subsequent generations spent their time building art collections and stately mansions and otherwise engaging in conspicuous consumption. Heiress Gloria Vanderbilt famously told her son, Anderson Cooper, that there would be no trust fund, although he did apparently receive $1.5 million upon her death. This story of the "fall" of the Vanderbilt family serves the wealth management industry as a useful moral lesson. I doubt whether Anderson Cooper considers himself a victim, nor would most of us be disappointed with an inheritance of that size.

THE MARS CANDY DYNASTY

Milky Way. Snickers. 3 Musketeers. M&Ms. These iconic candies have broken the dynasty challenge and created one of our country's wealthiest families over the past century. Through four generations, the Mars family has continued to accumulate vast sums of wealth at breakneck pace, despite being riven by intense family conflict. Known for its jealously guarded privacy and limited public exposure – the company neglected to even comment on the death of its long-time CEO, Forrest Mars Jr. – Mars, Incorporated offers us a cautionary tale and worrisome harbinger of what we can expect in the future.

As a child with mild polio, Frank Mars learned how to hand-dip chocolate candy from his mother. Struggling to make a living as a candy salesman, Frank saw his marriage end as Ethel grew impatient with his inability to make a decent living and left with their son, Forrest. Soon after, Frank remarried – another Ethel, as it turns out – and started the Mars Candy Factory in 1911 in Tacoma, Washington. Although this initial effort failed, he relocated back to Minneapolis, Minnesota, and started a new chocolate company, this time making candy bars. According to legend, Frank's estranged son Forrest urged him to create a chocolate malted drink in a candy bar.[2] Soon after, Frank developed the Milky Way bar and sales took off. Within five years, the Mars Company was selling over $20 million in

[2] Later in life, Forrest Sr. gave the credit to Thomas Dattolo, a long-term employee and skilled candy maker.

gross sales ($301 million today) and becoming a major player in the country's growing obsession with candy. In 1930, the company introduced the Snickers bar, and two years later the 3 Musketeers. Even Frank's untimely death at age fifty in 1934 did not stop the expansion of the company as it continued to create popular new products like the Mars Almond bar that gave comfort to a nation experiencing depression and then war.

Although Forrest was the logical choice to lead the company, family conflicts dictated a different decision. Two years earlier, Forrest had demanded one-third ownership of the family business only to get rebuffed by Frank. Apparently told by Frank to start his own candy business somewhere else, Forrest left for England with $50,000 in cash and the rights to make the Milky Way bar. There, he created a separate company, altered the family recipe in response to English tastes and renamed it the "Mars Bar." Every bit as successful as the Milky Way bar back home, Forrest used it to create an independent empire of his own. Too busy to fly home to attend his father's funeral, he learned that ownership of the flagship company would pass to Forrest's half-sister Patricia.

Although fuming at this turn of events, Forrest applied his considerable talents to building his company into a global player. He oversaw the development of new candies, like M&Ms, which led to skyrocketing sales and profits. His perceptive business sense caused him to diversify the company's product mix to meet the changing needs of American households. Working with partners, he developed products that would limit time in the kitchen (Uncle Ben's) and meet the changing attitudes toward household pets (Whiskas Cat Food). By the 1960s, Forrest's independent company, known as Food Manufacturers, Inc., had outgrown the original Mars, Inc. Yet, he still had his eyes on what he saw as his birthright. Finally, in 1964 Forrest bought enough outstanding shares to take control over both companies and merge them, using the Mars, Inc. name. Family conflict meant that Forrest bought, not inherited, the family business.

Now in control over the whole enterprise, Forrest Sr. brought his three children, sons Forrest Jr. and John and daughter Jacqueline, into major management roles. Forrest Sr. continued the company's expansion as it exploited new markets and diversified into new product areas. Expanding further into the growing pet food market, he bought the Kal Kan brand and developed the Mars Electronics division that produced sophisticated vending machines. By the 1970s Mars had overtaken Hershey's as the largest American manufacturer of chocolates.

Besides peerless business acumen, Forrest Sr. brought a demanding attention to detail, an explosive anger, and a primal fear of any public exposure. Early on, he explained his plans for the company. In a meeting with top executives, he announced:

> "I'm a religious man," he told the crowd. Then, after a long pause, he sank to his knees. "I pray for Milky Way," he said. "I pray for Snickers …" No one in the room dared move. These products, Forrest explained, were to consume the executives' every moment. "That's what the consumer buys," he said. "And that's what creates profit. And profit is our single objective." (Brenner, 1992, para. 43)

In that relentless drive for profit, he demanded that each candy bar meet exacting standards and corporate facilities remain spotlessly clean and spartan. Seeing one senior executive's desk piled with papers, he reportedly hurled them off to make a point. Given his own frosty relationship with his father, one might expect Forrest Sr. to cultivate better relationships with his sons. Not so. Repeatedly, he berated both sons in public over the smallest of details. Senior executives suggested that his sons remained haunted by their father's demanding expectations and public rebuking. Distrustful of others, he ended factory tours and media events and created a culture of corporate secrecy that remains today. Retiring in 1973, Forrest Sr. was among the fourteen billionaires listed in the earliest listing of Forbes 400 Wealthiest Americans (Southern Illinoian, 1983, p. 19). Even then, he used a series of trusts to transfer ownership to his three children, but prohibited sale of the company during his lifetime (Hays, 1999).

Forrest Jr. and John took over the company as the third generation of family leadership.[3] They continued the tradition of developing new products, like Skittles and Twix, and buying established brands like William Wrigley Jr. Company, Dove Bars, IAMs, and Banfield Pet Hospitals. Only as this third generation of Mars family members have reached retirement has the family turned to outsiders to manage the firm. Today, none of the Mars family serves as part of the top corporate leadership. Yet, the Mars family retains tight control, as Mars Inc. remains a privately held company that is exclusively owned by family members. In 2023, Mars Inc. ranked the fourth-largest privately held firm in the country, with estimated sales of $47 billion and 140,000 employees (Forbes Magazine, 2023). Members of the fourth generation of the Mars clan have served as chair of the Board of Directors, including Pamela Mars (2004–2008), Victoria Mars (2014–17), Stephen Badger (2008–14 and 2017–20), and Frank E. Mars (2020–23).[4]

[3] Daughter Jacqueline Mars also worked for the company for almost twenty years in various managerial roles.

[4] Currently, the chair is occupied by John F. Mars, the remaining son of Forrest Sr.

One can see the dynastic nature by examining the family wealth over time. A recent Institute of Policy Studies (IPS) report (Collins et al., 2021) documented the Mars family wealth rising from $2.6 billion in 1983 to $94 trillion in 2020 (both figures are in 2020 constant dollars). One can also view this by comparing the reported wealth of key family members over time. In 1985, Forbes reported the wealth of Forrest Sr., Forrest Jr., and John as $875 million each ($2.1 billion in present-day dollars). This suggests that each held one-third of the company shares. After the death of Forrest Sr. in 1999, each of the three children had shares valued at $9 billion. In 2023, after the death of Forrest Jr. in 2016, the two remaining siblings have an estimated value of $39 billion each, while the four daughters of Forrest Jr. each have shares of the company worth $9.7 billion. There is not much evidence that this wealth is being dissipated rapidly.

Like many wealthy families, the Mars family has endowed charitable foundations over the years to help with selected causes and missions. According to the IPS report already cited, they have funded four different foundations, whose assets top $48 million in 2018. Perhaps it is no surprise given the company's focus on privacy and lack of public media that their philanthropy is quite modest as compared to other similarly situated family dynasties. They focus on supporting efforts in oral education and care, wildlife protection, climate change, and sustainability efforts, as well as promoting arts and culture.

During the Obama Administration, the Mars family, along with eight other billionaire families, lobbied extensively to eliminate the estate tax. According to a Public Citizen (2015) report, the Mars family spent $3.5 million supporting efforts for its repeal. The report estimated that repeal of the estate tax could save the family upwards of $24 billion. Seven other billionaire families chipped in another $7 million in the effort. Given the magnitude of their wealth and the absence of limits on campaign donations, they have substantial means to influence public policy as they see fit. Clearly, they see fit to use their resources to influence policy that meets their self-interests.

FEDERAL WEALTH TRANSFER TAXES

The source of the Mars family ire, the federal wealth transfer tax system, includes three different taxes: the estate, gift, and generation-skipping transfer (GST) taxes. Generally speaking, these taxes serve four main purposes (Joulfaian, 1998). First, they serve as a source of federal tax revenue to fund needed government expenditures. Several times during our nation's history, the federal government has enacted a wealth transfer tax to finance vital government spending, usually during times of war. Our modern estate tax, just over one century old, owes its enactment largely due to fears of entering World War I.[5] Second, these taxes are seen as providing important backstops to a leaky income tax system. Certain forms of income, particularly those favored by the wealthy, elude the federal income tax system. Unrealized capital gains and the estate step-up basis provision discussed in Chapter 4 are two examples of income that evade the IRS. The wealth transfer taxes offer a second opportunity to ensure these sources of income do get taxed. Third, these taxes function to limit the growth of large family transfers that might fund dynastic wealth, like with the Mars family. Large inheritances threaten democratic institutions, undermine meritocracy, and fuel economic stratification. Lastly, these taxes are designed to tax the transfer of wealth from each generation to the next. One can argue whether wealth accumulated within a generation is *earned* or not; no similar argument surrounds the transfer of wealth across generations. Well-designed wealth transfer taxes could satisfy each of these objectives as well as restrain the perpetuation of White supremacy into the future.

The estate tax represents the cornerstone of the federal wealth transfer tax system.[6] Upon death, the gross estate of the deceased is calculated. This includes the fair market value of all directly held property as well as any assets in which the deceased kept a partial interest. Life insurance proceeds owned by the deceased are included as well as certain gifts made during the three years prior to death.[7] Only those estates whose gross value exceeds the estate tax threshold must file a tax return. In recent decades, Congress has repeatedly raised this threshold, thereby allowing more family wealth to transfer across generations untouched by the IRS. In 2017, Congress doubled the threshold to over $11 million.[8] By 2021, the most recent year the evidence is available, only 6,158 estates were filed with the IRS out of 3.3 million deaths, a rate of less than two-tenths of 1 percent.[9] As a source of tax

[5] This is the subject of Chapter 8.

[6] Estate taxes are distinguished from inheritance taxes by the point of assessment. Inheritance taxes are assessed against receipts gifted to recipients, while estate taxes assess the estate before it is transferred.

[7] Life insurance proceeds on policies owned by others are not included in the gross estate. Given the previous chapter, one might think this is an error. Life insurance benefits are excluded from the deceased's income tax, but not necessarily the estate tax.

[8] Under current law, the estate tax threshold is adjusted automatically for inflation. In 2024, the exemption threshold was $13.61 million.

[9] The interested reader can find this evidence at Internal Revenue Service. (n.d.). *Estate Tax Filing Year Tables* and Xu et al. (2022).

collection, the estate tax has become more fictional than real. Nonetheless, these relatively few estates still represented a sizable target as they reported a collective net worth of $182 billion.

Even those required to file need not pay any tax since it is assessed only after certain deductions and credits are subtracted. Any transfers of assets to the deceased's spouse or to qualified charities are *fully deducted.* Payments toward state estate tax bills, funeral expenses, and executor's fees are treated similarly. Lastly, the estate tax threshold, now reaching $13.61 million in 2024, is deducted before any tax is considered. For married decedents, this threshold can be doubled. Only those estates that survive all of these deductions will carry a tax liability.

Under current law, the remainder is assessed at a uniform rate of 40 percent. Even then, the actual tax liability is reduced if the deceased paid any gift taxes over their lifetime or is liable for any foreign estate tax. Given all of these deductions and credits, the effective estate tax has been falling in recent years and is routinely below 20 percent (Internal Revenue Service, n.d., *Taxable Estate Tax Returns*).

Critics of the estate tax contend it can force the sale of a closely held business or family farm that lacks adequate cash to pay the tax. Despite scant evidence that this problem exists, its threat has produced substantial remedies. Family-held businesses can request a waiver from current market valuation and instead receive a valuation based on current use. For example, the family farm might be worth more if the land is sold for development instead of continuing as a working farm. Current use valuation can lower the estate tax bill and limit the need for selling the farm. Further, the estate can gain a fourteen-year waiver that defers actual payment of the tax. Each of these preferential provisions offers further assurance against any forced liquidation of small family enterprises, ones that are likely to be disproportionately White.

An estate tax, standing alone, would make it a wholly voluntary tax. In anticipation of death, wealthy households could transfer their assets as inter vivos gifts. Many did exactly that before the enactment of the federal gift tax. In its current form, the federal gift tax is a separate tax that includes both annual and lifetime thresholds. In 2024, the annual threshold is $18,000 per recipient. Gifts below this threshold need not be reported, nor are they subject to any tax. Gifts above this amount must be reported and count against the lifetime threshold, which is currently equal to the estate tax threshold.[10] Therefore, large gifts made above the threshold

[10] Gifts paid directly to educational or medical facilities on behalf of an heir are exempt as well.

reduce one's estate tax exemption by a comparable amount. In this way, the gift and estate taxes are *unified*.

Despite this unity, these two taxes retain important discrepancies. Inter vivos gifts of noncash assets do not receive the same step-up valuation that these assets would receive if part of an estate. Instead, such gifts come with a *carryover basis*; this makes the recipient responsible for any unrealized capital gains and liable once the asset is sold. This distinction encourages donors to retain these assets rather than transfer them while living. On the other hand, the gift tax is assessed on a *tax-exclusive* basis, while the estate tax is assessed as *tax inclusive*. This means that gift tax is assessed only on what the recipient actually receives, while the estate tax is based on the whole transfer. A simple example can clarify this distinction. A 40 percent assessment on a $100,000 net estate would leave the heir $60,000. Assessing the same 40 percent on a gift of $100,000 would give the recipient $71,429 and create a tax liability of $28,571. The latter figure represents 40 percent of what the recipient actually gets.[11] These two arcane differences in tax treatment demonstrate how provisions in the tax code, once embedded, resist subsequent scrutiny or remedy. These differences certainly influence which and when assets are transferred across generations.

Despite their common front, clever tax attorneys have designed ways for the rich to avoid paying these taxes. One common way is to create a generation-skipping trust. Under this arrangement, the donor places assets in a trust account in which the beneficiary is at least two generations away, say one's grandchildren. The trust is designed so that any income earned supports the skipped generation, perhaps the donor's kids.[12] Once all of the designated members of the skipped generation die, the trust fund reverts to the third-generation beneficiaries. Any assets placed in a generation-skipping trust are subject either to the gift or estate tax, but they avoid any tax on the second intergenerational transfer. Consider the circumstances in which the wealthy grandparent transfers wealth to their children and they eventually pass along wealth to the third generation. Each transfer is subject to taxation. Thus, the generation-skipping trust offers donors an effective vehicle to create a family dynasty, at least for two or three generations. These trusts carry the added benefit of allowing the donor to name the specific circumstances under which any trust distributions can occur.

[11] Tax-inclusive basis means the beneficiary will receive an amount equal to (1 – tax rate) × Estate. Tax-exclusive basis is calculated as equal to the Gift ÷ (1 + tax rate).

[12] In the case of beneficiaries who are non-descendants, the beneficiaries need to be twenty-five years or more younger than the donor.

Historically, limits were placed on such "dead hand control" of past donors by an English common law doctrine known as the *rule against perpetuities*. This rule generally limited the duration of trusts to the lifetime of any person already alive at the time the trust is created.[13]

To close this tax loophole, Congress enacted a third wealth transfer tax, the GST tax, the aim of which is to ensure wealth is taxed each time it is transferred from one generation to the next. It does this by subjecting the assets to taxation as the trust is created, and again when the assets are distributed to remote beneficiaries. For example, I might create a trust that will ultimately benefit my great-grandchildren. This trust provides some income to my children and their children during their lifetimes, given specific instructions I determine. With the passing of all my children, the trust is assessed at the top estate tax rate. The same happens again with the passing of all of my grandchildren and then great-grandchildren. At that point, the trust is dissolved. With each intergenerational transfer, the trust is subject to the top estate tax rate. In this way, the GST tax provides a backstop to those trying to avoid estate or gift taxes. While this may sound simple enough, the actual tax code provisions are quite dense and complex.

EVALUATING THE SYSTEM'S EFFECTIVENESS

It makes sense to evaluate how well the three taxes are meeting their goals. Recall that the first objective considers the extent these taxes contribute to the US Treasury. Figure 5.1 addresses this issue. The black line tracks the actual revenues raised by the taxes in 2022 constant dollars.

These taxes increased substantially during the boom years after World War II as well as the last two decades of the twentieth century. Both periods show their revenue potential during times of prosperity and wealth expansion. Recently, they have dwindled as a source of funds in a time when federal budgeting cries for additional revenue. The second, gray line tracks their share of federal revenues. Interestingly, after peaking at nearly 10 percent of federal revenues toward the end of the Great Depression, they have borne a decreasing share of the tax burden ever since. Initially, this declining share was the result of an expanding use of the federal income tax. More recently, it is the result of changes to the estate and gift taxes. Currently, they fund less than 1 percent of federal revenues, a minuscule share.

[13] This limit stems from the fact that the wealthy donor may know something about the character of heirs that are alive, but nothing about those still unborn.

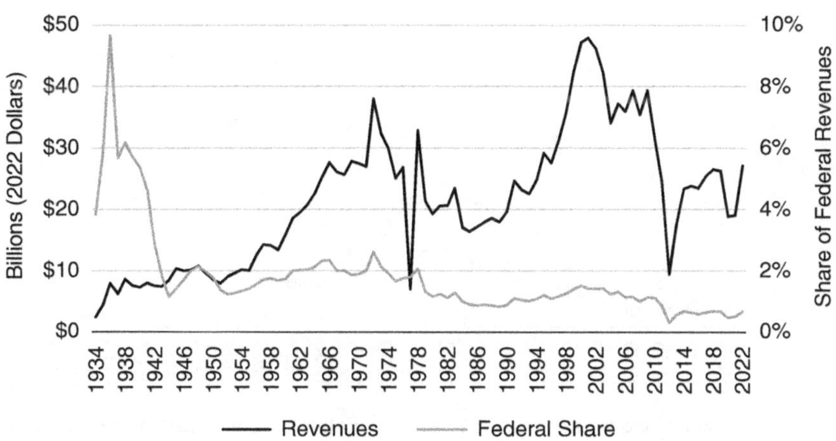

Figure 5.1 Wealth transfer taxes as revenue source
Source: Author's calculations; Joulfaian (1998); Office of Management and Budget, Historical Tables 2.1, 2.5

Another important goal of the wealth transfer taxes is that they capture income that may get missed by the federal income tax. Two important leaks are tax-exempt bond income and any unrealized capital gains due to their step-up treatment at death. The fungibility of income and wealth pose challenges to making this assessment. However, an untaxed income source will show up as increased wealth in one form or another. If these wealth transfer taxes serve as effective backstops, then periods of increasing wealth should lead to proportionate increases in their tax collections.

The evidence provided in Figure 5.2 sheds some light. Using 1933 as the base year, it tracks aggregate household wealth, gross (taxable) estate values, and estate tax revenues over eighty years. As the figure illustrates, household wealth has grown dramatically over the period, increasing fifteen times in real terms. The remaining two figures follow somewhat different paths, at least recently. Taxable estate measures how much estate wealth is subject to taxation given the existing tax rules. Through the immediate post-World War II period, the gross estates rose faster than total household wealth, suggesting the tax was functioning effectively. Rising tax revenues offer further proof that the estate tax in particular was capturing some of the increased wealth during this period.[14] Yet, tax policy changes in 1976 raised the estate tax threshold, causing less estate wealth to be subject to

[14] The estate tax collects the overwhelming share of taxes collected by the three taxes.

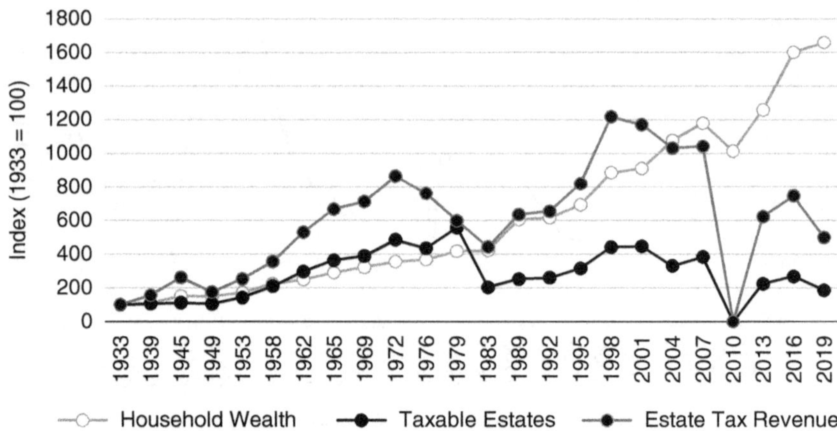

Figure 5.2 Household wealth and estate tax trends
Source: Author's calculations; Federal Reserve Board, Survey of Consumer Finances; Internal Revenue Service (n.d.) Taxable Estate Returns; Wolff (2018), p. 558

taxation. Congress has raised the threshold several times since, which has decoupled tax collections from the expansion of household wealth. Since the estate tax does exact a progressive toll on those estates with a tax liability, the estate tax revenues have generally outpaced the increase in taxable estates. Whatever effectiveness the estate tax demonstrated early on as a backstop to the federal income tax has dissipated in recent decades. Both the details and underlying reasons for these policy changes are discussed in Chapter 7.

We can understand best how poorly all three taxes are functioning by examining data from a recent year. Estate and gift tax filings in 2020 for wealth transfers that largely occurred during 2019 are provided in Table 5.1. Out of the roughly 2.8 million adult Americans who died in 2019, only 3,441 had estates large enough – those above $11.4 million – to file Form 706.[15] Although the gross value of those few estates exceeded $122 billion after deductions made for bequests to surviving spouses, gifts to charitable organizations, and payment of administrative fees, $48 billion was left to various individuals. Of this, just over $9 billion was paid to the Treasury, well below the supposed 40 percent tax rate. In contrast to the estate tax, the filing thresholds for the gift tax are much lower, causing far more filers. In 2019, only those households who made gifts exceeding $15,000 to

[15] Some estates that have used their lifetime exemption through earlier gifts may be required to file even if their gross estate is below the legal exemption.

Table 5.1 *Effectiveness of estate and gift taxes, 2019–20*

	Estate Tax	Gift Tax
Number of Tax Filers	3,441	174,076
Number Who Paid Taxes	1,275	516
Percent Who Paid Taxes	37%	0.3%
Gross Wealth Transfer (mill.)	$122,255	$75,239
Net Wealth Transfer (mill.)	$48,334	$65,706
Taxes Paid (mill.)	$9,334	$403
Percent of Wealth Transfer	19%	0.6%

Source: Author's calculations; IRS Estate Tax Data Tables Filing Years, Table 1; IRS Statistics of Income Tax Stats Gift Tax Statistics, Table 1

any recipient were required to report the payment.[16] Their reported gifts exceeded $75 billion, although some went to spouses and charitable organizations, leaving nearly $66 billion to remaining family members. Despite this vast transfer of wealth, a scant 516 households paid just $403 million in gift taxes, at rate well below 1 percent. Between the two taxes, over $100 billion dollars was reportedly transferred in 2019; less than $10 billion was paid in either tax. With all of the exemptions and deductions currently allowed, these taxes are incapable of providing an effective backstop to the federal income tax.

On paper, the estate and gift taxes appear progressive. Only the largest estates are subject to any tax liability, and at an aggressive 40 percent tax rate. Perhaps the taxes limit the growing concentration of wealth as they capture substantial portions of the very largest wealth transfers.

Yet, a particularly egregious example shows that massive loopholes exist even here. To resolve a contentious budgetary impasse, Congress *temporarily* raised the gift exemption from $1 million in 2010 to over $5 million in 2012. Worried that this threshold would revert back the following year, households responded with an unprecedented cascade of gifts. That year, over 100,000 households reported gifts exceeding $1 million, with an average gift of over $3 million. Collectively, they gave over $350 billion to recipients of their choosing. Due to the generous loopholes, most of this wealth transfer went untouched by the IRS. Fewer than 4 percent of these large donors paid any tax on their gift and together they paid slightly above 1 percent in tax. Since then, the gift (and estate) threshold has been doubled

16 Households that want to split their gifts are required to report all gifts, no matter their size.

Table 5.2 *Intergenerational giving and attitudes, 2022*

	Black Households	White Households
Have Inherited	10%	29%
Average Inheritance	$76,328	$324,762
Share of Total Inherited	1%	93%
Expect to Inherit	8%	17%
Average Gift Expected	$442,689	$1,073,394
Share of Expected Gifts	3%	90%
Leaving a Legacy Important	68%	51%
Leaving a Legacy Likely	64%	61%
Support to Others	20%	13%
Support to Next Generation	10%	8%

Source: Author's calculations; Federal Reserve Board Survey of Consumer Finances, 2022

again, indicating a further erosion of its effectiveness. At this point, only those households in the top 1 percent need to worry about estate planning.[17]

Amazingly, the IRS does not report its tax data on the basis of race. Thus, we cannot know for certain how much these rules favor White households and their efforts to transfer wealth to the next generation. However, we can retrieve gift and inheritance evidence from another source to gain insight, and this evidence is reported in Table 5.2. According to the SCF, White households are nearly three times more likely to report having received some past gift or inheritance than Black households. White inheritances average more than four times those received by Black households, enabling Whites to capture 93 percent versus 1 percent of the reported gifts and inheritances. This pattern confirms that the large leaks in our wealth transfer tax system redound mostly to the benefit of White households and their beneficiaries. As these figures are simply raw numbers, they do not reflect how gifts received years ago may have been used to benefit the recipients today.[18] The disparities do not end here. The SCF asks households whether they expect to receive a future gift or inheritance, as well as its size. One may question the accuracy of these answers. However, White households report twice the optimism of Black households about receiving a future inheritance and expect such transfers to be, on average, more than twice as

17 According to the 2022 SCF, only the top 1 percent of households held more than the estate tax exemption threshold of $12.06 million.

18 These estimates rely on self-reporting, a source that is susceptible to significant recall bias. As such, we should view these totals as lower-bound estimates.

large. If their expectations are realized, they stand to gain another 90-plus percent share of future wealth transfers.

Some might wonder if these differences in intergenerational giving reflect different cultural attitudes between White and Black households toward such transfers. Again, the SCF offers some insight here. Black households attach a greater importance to leaving a legacy and report a greater likelihood of doing so than do White households. Perhaps their disadvantaged position offers Black households a clearer understanding of the importance of leaving a legacy. Moreover, Black households back up their beliefs with action. More Black households offer support to other family members than do White households, at 20 and 13 percent, respectively. Much of this family support goes to siblings, parents, and grandparents who are likely in some distress. Even still, slightly more Black households report supporting the next generation than do White households, by a 10 to 8 percent margin. Of course, the amounts that are transferred are much smaller among Black family members than among Whites.

While the estimates given above reflect reported gifts and inheritances received by households *over their lifetimes*, answers to the SCF can also be used to estimate the annual transfers of wealth. In 2019, the total reported transfers are approximately $431 billion. We already know from the IRS 2020 tax filings – the year that most of these transfers would get reported – that the estate and gift tax collections were only $9.7 billion. Just 2 percent of the estimated wealth transfer was captured by our federal wealth transfer taxes while the remaining 98 percent went to the selected recipients unscathed. This damning evidence demonstrates how our leaky tax system is functioning to support and perpetuate White wealth and thereby White supremacy.

The last objective of the wealth transfer taxes is ensuring that wealth is subject to taxation each time it is transferred across generations. On this point, the current system is woefully ineffective.

As it created the GST tax to close one loophole, Congress created a larger problem. To limit opposition to the new tax, Congress offered a generous exemption of $1 million.[19] Unlike the exemptions on the estate and gift tax, this exemption shielded these trust assets from taxation for the duration of the trust no matter how much these assets appreciate (Dukeminier & Krier, 2002). Congress neglected to place a limit on their duration, instead relying on state law and their adherence to the rule against perpetuities. This omission along with the generous exemption created a loophole that has since been busted wide open.

[19] Of course, this could be doubled by one's spouse.

Back in 1986, three states – Idaho, Wisconsin, and South Dakota – had already eliminated any rule against perpetuities. At the time, this seemed to matter little. One could set up a trust that might last for many generations, but there was little reason to do so.[20] The creation of the GST tax exemption changed all that. Now one could place $1 million (or $2 million with a cooperative spouse) into a trust designed to support future generations fully exempt from any future taxation. One could construct the trust so that it balanced income support for living descendants with the need to grow the corpus to benefit future beneficiaries. Observers began to call these innovative trusts *perpetual* or *dynasty trusts*.

The race began. Bank trust departments and estate tax attorneys saw that increasing numbers of their potential clients were contacting competitors in states that lacked any limits on the trusts' duration. South Dakota was particularly well positioned given its added appeal of having no state income tax. Larger banks simply opened offices in one of the nonregulating states. Quickly, state officials recognized the lost employment, fees, and taxes that would result if the lucrative wealth management industry relocated elsewhere. State after state amended their long-standing rule against perpetuities. Today, at least three states (Colorado, Wyoming, and Utah) allow trusts that last one thousand years, while another eighteen along with the District of Columbia impose no limit on their duration (Waggoner, 2014). Others like Arizona (500 years), Nevada (365 years), and both Florida and Tennessee (360 years) have taken more modest approaches.

Not to be outdone by the states, Congress had added its own fuel to the dynasty trust frenzy. In 2001, it raised the GST tax exemption to make it equivalent to the estate and gift tax exemptions.

Since then, Congress has continued to increase the unified exemption for all three taxes until they now (in 2024) equal $13.61 million. What this means is that a wealthy donor can fund a dynasty trust by this amount (or double with the assent of their spouse) with the expectation that it will be untouched by the IRS for generations to come. This offers the wealthy an effective tool in overcoming the challenge of extending their wealth and power over more than three generations. With the help of skilled estate tax attorneys, one can create a dynasty trust that can last in perpetuity. Trust fund income can be used to ensure that each generation receives adequate support for educational, health, and livelihood needs as well as some substantial payment once each child reaches maturity. Further funds can be dispensed to provide investments in business or career development

[20] A relatively low tax exemption limited the tax value of such a trust.

as well as generous annuities during retirement. At the same time, prudent investment can assure the trust fund assets continue to appreciate, thereby meeting the needs of a growing number of descendants. One can easily manage the potential conflict between supporting current versus future beneficiaries by funding these trusts with assets capable of rapid appreciation.

A simple simulation example can demonstrate the potency and durability of such a dynastic system. Assume two parents who collectively fund their trust with $25.84 million and use their entire exemption allowed in 2023 to shield the fund fully. This couple has two children who each have two children of their own and so forth across subsequent generations. At age twenty-six, each descendant becomes a direct beneficiary and gives birth to two more children. After the first generation, each descendant gains annual income from the trust at age twenty-six and does so for fifty years until their death at age seventy-five. The trust assets are assumed to appreciate at a 6 percent real rate, with two percent of that growth being used to fund current beneficiaries. At the outset, the donors' children receive $91,000 *annually*, an amount that slowly increases to $228,000 by the year of their death.[21] Even with these annual payouts to each beneficiary, subsequent generations receive higher annual payments and greater total benefits from the trust, as illustrated in Figure 5.3.[22] Summing the annual payments shows the trust is capable of offering multimillion-dollar payouts to future beneficiaries and does so at an increasing rate, as shown in Table 5.3. Despite making these generous payments, the trust fund would exceed $1 trillion a hundred years from now, even without the help of inflation. The addition of inflation would not change the dynamics of this simulation, but simply inflate the numbers over time.

The emergence of these dynasty trusts along with their appeal to the wealthy will assure their increased use going forward. They offer the rich wholly new opportunities to overcome the challenges of shirtsleeves to shirtsleeves. Certainly, they will have racial consequences as well.

The massive federal support that has funneled support to White households, both past and present, has primed their ability to take advantage of these opportunities. These dynasty trusts offer a more secure vehicle to replicate the current wealth disparities across future generations.

[21] In the simulation, they are fifty-one at the time the trust is triggered, so they *only* benefit for twenty-five years.

[22] As long as the trust can earn more than 3 percent real interest, it is capable of withstanding the Malthusian pressures of growing numbers of beneficiaries.

Table 5.3 *Expected recipient benefits*

Future Beneficiaries	No. of Beneficiaries	Recipient Benefits (millions)
1st Generation*	2	$3.341
2nd Generation	4	$8.740
3rd Generation	8	$11.200
4th Generation	16	$14.504
5th Generation	32	$18.450

* Only benefits from twenty-five annual payments.

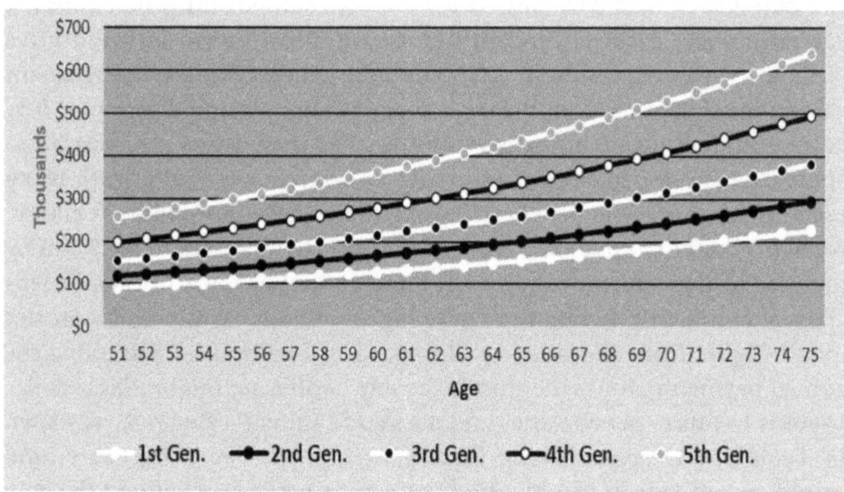

Figure 5.3 Trust fund support for future beneficiaries
Source: Author's calculations

Lucky descendants of those able to fund one of these trusts are assured a sinecure that elevates their prospects beyond measure. Their design allows the donor to limit the indolence and extravagance of descendants from undermining the family wealth. In this way, these trusts can cement a system of replication that overcomes human frailty. And unlike the vehicle the Mars family has used, the closely held family business, the dynasty trust will serve a much wider variety of wealthy donors.

IT GETS WORSE

For most of us, the current GST exemption appears more than generous. Still, for the uber rich, like the Mars family members with billions in their portfolios, this cap may not be lavish enough. Fortunately – for them – clever estate tax attorneys have developed several work-arounds to evade the exemption cap. One easy method is placing assets that are liable for rapid appreciation. In this way, the trust assets can appreciate more rapidly than the assumed 6 percent and thereby distribute greater generosity to current and future beneficiaries. However, this strategy still limits the initial trust fund deposits to levels set by the exemption. Studious estate tax attorneys have examined the dense tax statutes to find ways to bypass this limit.

Wealthy donors can exploit subtle differences in the personal income and estate tax codes by using a grantor trust, a trust account over which the donor retains control. The donor can elude the exemption by transferring assets from a closely held business. Rather than funding the trust with cash or marketable assets, the donor can place nonvoting shares of preferred stock of the family business. Since these shares are not marketable, their value is subject to wide discretion. Accounting norms allow a discount of 40 percent. This means the donor could fund the trust with stock that is actually worth $19.054 million and still meet the $13.61 million exemption. A willing spouse could double this amount. While beneficial, this method does not take full advantage of the potential loopholes.

Alternatively, the donor can "seed" the grantor trust with cash and assets worth $13.61 million. Next, the trustee who is managing the trust purchases for $100 million shares of the family business that are actually worth $166 million. To make this transaction appear as having a "business purpose," the trust offers in return an immediate cash payment of $10 million and a 10-year, interest-only promissory note that includes a prepayment clause.[23] Dividends from the stock shares can pay any interest payments. This structure along with other technical details allows the transaction to evade any wealth transfer taxes (Goodwin, 2010). Over time, any increase in the value of the family business benefits the trust. Suppose the shares double in value, the stock shares that were actually worth $166 million are now worth $332 million. The trust pays off the promissory note and keeps the difference to the benefit of future descendants without any tax liability. Again, with a willing spouse, all of these numbers can be doubled.

Another tool available to the wealthy, one that can ably complement the one just discussed, is the grantor retained annuity trust, or GRAT. In this case, the wealthy donor transfers assets to an *irrevocable trust*. This form of trust is one that the donor has no control over and cannot revoke

[23] The 10 percent ratio between cash offered and the purchased stock is typical. A lower ratio would enable an even more aggressive use of this tax-evading strategy.

without the blessings of the beneficiaries. As such, the transfer of assets to this trust is liable to the federal gift tax. However, nuances in the tax code allow one to reduce or even evade paying this tax. In exchange for the donated assets, the trust commits to make annual payments as an annuity back to the donor. The gift tax is assessed on any difference between the fair market value of the donated assets minus the expected value of the annuity payments. Over the course of the annuity period, the donated assets may appreciate in value. However, none of this appreciation is subject to the gift tax. Again, by donating assets that are liable to substantial appreciation, one can transfer wealth to one's descendants with minimal tax liability.

GRATs can be used aggressively to transfer wealth to heirs with little or no gift tax liability by designing what is called a *zeroed-out GRAT*. In this case, the annuity is designed so that its value is equal to the market value of the gift, leaving nothing to be subject to the gift tax. The IRS does have rules regarding how the present value of the annuity is determined; in early 2019 the designated discount rate was 3.4 percent (Burke, 2019). Consequently, trust assets that grew more quickly than this rate would generate a remainder after the annuity was paid off that would then go to the beneficiaries tax free. Consider an example. A donor could fund a trust with high-yielding assets with a market value of $50 million. Using the 3.4 percent discount rate and assuming a 10-year annuity, the trust would pay the donor $5,981,790 annually. If the deposited assets grew at the same 3.4 percent, then the trust remainder after the annuity is paid would be $167. That would be the amount liable for the federal gift tax. If the assets grew at 8 percent over the ten-year period, the remainder would exceed $21 million. For a tax liability of $167, one could transfer over $21 million. Unlike the dynasty trusts, there is no limit to how much wealth one can transfer using a GRAT.

However, they do come with limitations. Most importantly, GRATs cannot be used effectively with a dynasty trust. While the gift tax liability is determined at the outset when the trust annuity is started, the GST tax is assessed at the end on the remainder. Consequently, all of the potential appreciation would be assessed against the GST exemption, dollar for dollar. For this reason, GRATs are best suited to transferring wealth directly to one's children. Another problem is if the donor dies before the annuity is paid fully. In the event of death, whatever is left in the trust, including any appreciation, reverts back to the donor and becomes part of the estate. Lastly, there is always the chance that the deposited assets will underperform and not meet the 3.4 percent benchmark. In that case, there will be nothing to transfer, although the donor will still need to pay the gift tax on the $167 as well as any fees incurred in creating the GRAT.

CONCLUSION

Using a conventional viewpoint, one might conclude from the evidence that our federal wealth transfer tax system is fully dysfunctional. No matter which of the four tax system objectives one chooses, it is obvious the current tax structure is failing. Our current wealth transfer taxes function not as a leaky bucket, but one almost ready to collapse from rot. The current tax exemptions smooth the legal transfer of wealth untouched by tax authorities at levels never experienced during its century of existence. That two-parent households can transfer over $26 million before they need to consider a tax adviser is evidence of a tax that exists in name only.

Perhaps we should reconsider the conventional perspective as well. Neither rising awareness of the growing concentration of wealth nor the expansive loopholes in the tax system has stirred Congress to limit massive intergenerational transfers of wealth. Instead, Congress has repeatedly expanded the tax exemptions and increased the allure of dynasty trusts. They have remained passive in the face of clever tax attorneys who have designed ways to avoid even the modest limits on gifts and inheritances. Dynasty trusts offer an effective remedy to a problem that has bedeviled the rich across the globe and over many centuries – how to ensure their current wealth is not squandered three generations hence. Instead, these trusts ensure a rarefied lifestyle to their descendants, perhaps in perpetuity. Most of the beneficiaries of these changes are White households and their heirs.

Perhaps the current system is functioning exactly as intended. The retention of a system that operates in name only provides the fiction that family transfers are subject to some tax. This offers the appearance that larger estates carry some tax liability. The presumption that the donor pays the tax provides cover to the recipients who bear no tax liability at all.[24] Recipients of large gifts and bequests receive far more favorable tax treatment on this source of income than do struggling households who earn their income from work. All of this shrouds the reality of a porous tax system that benefits the wealthy and their beneficiaries, who happen to be mostly White. The current system seems well designed to lavish generous benefits to White households without the obvious appearance of doing so.

To be clear, all of the loopholes and tax-evading strategies discussed in this chapter are equal-opportunity providers when we consider race. Wealthy Black households are as likely to contact estate tax attorneys and

[24] The one exception is when a recipient receives an inter vivos gift of an asset that carries unrealized capital gain. In this instance, they are liable for that gain when the asset is sold.

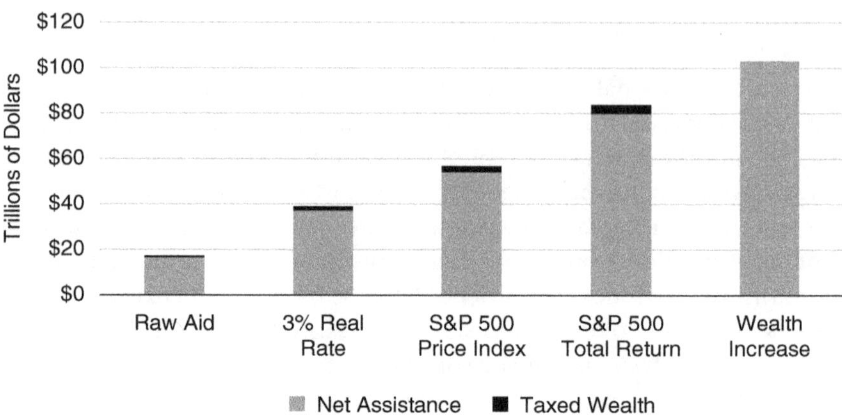

Figure 5.4 Net federal help to White households, 1988–2022
Source: Author's calculations; Federal Reserve Board, Survey of Consumer Finances; Joint Tax Committee Tax Expenditures; Office of Management and Budget, Historical Tables 2.5; US Treasury Tax Expenditures

follow their advice, perhaps even more so given the importance attached to leaving a legacy. Yet, far fewer Black households have had the opportunities to accumulate vast amounts of wealth than White households. In 2022 among households headed by someone sixty-six years or older, White households hold 92 percent of the wealth as compared to 1 percent among Black households. When we consider seniors that hold at least $10 million in net worth, the White share rises modestly to 94 percent while the Black share falls below one-half of 1 percent. Far more White households possess levels of wealth that meaningfully can fund a dynasty trust. And these trusts offer unparalleled opportunities for White wealthy households to perpetuate their advantages far into the future.

Recall from the discussion in Chapter 4 of how much the federal tax expenditures might have contributed to the growth of White wealth over the past thirty years. At that time, I cautioned patience until we could investigate the impact of the federal estate and gift taxes on the accumulation of wealth and the racial wealth gap. Given the evidence raised in this chapter, I suspect the results illustrated in Figure 5.4 evoke little surprise. This figure reproduces the results shown in Figure 4.4, including the $103 trillion increase in White wealth as well as the four estimates of federal assistance: $17, $39, $57, and $84 trillion. Recall these numbers measure the raw total of federal assistance as well as the current value if these benefits were saved and invested at a 3 percent real of return in an S&P 500 stock fund or with an S&P 500 Total Return Index. Figure 5.4 adds the effects of the federal estate and gift taxes over the same period. In each case, these taxes are subtracted out along with any "lost wealth" their loss in the past would generate today.

There is no easy way to tell who paid these taxes. Consequently, I have assumed that White households carried their full burden alone. Although this is not the case, it is not too far from the truth. As you can see, the takeaways that result from the estate and gift taxes pale in comparison to the levels of federal help. All told, the three taxes collected roughly $700 billion over the thirty-five years with an estimated "lost wealth" that ranges from around $2 to $4 trillion depending on the case. These figures simply corroborate the leaky bucket we have acknowledged throughout this chapter.

Having acknowledged the contributions of our contemporary federal wealth policies to the accumulation of wealth among White households, one might wonder about the past policies discussed in Chapter 3. What about the preferential treatment given to Whites through a century and a half of legalized slavery and Jim Crow segregation and discrimination? There exists an extensive and provocative literature in which scholars have tried to estimate the dollar value of wealth extracted from African Americans and transferred to Whites. Several studies have estimated the amount of wealth taken from the enslaved during the antebellum period.[25] Darity (2008) has estimated the lost wealth that has resulted from the unfulfilled promise of "forty acres and a mule." Chachere and Udinsky (1990) measured the lost wealth experienced by Black workers due to labor market discrimination during the Jim Crow period. As careful as these studies are, they all fall short of calculating the full measure of how past policies have affected the racial wealth gap. As an alternative, I suggest that the racial wealth gap as calculated in 1962 provides a rather simple and intuitive estimate of past federal help. At that time, White households held just over $1 trillion more wealth than did Black households. It is not far-fetched to argue that the vast bulk, if not the whole amount, is the result of the full range of preferential treatment. Since some of this treatment stems from state and local policies, one can argue that this can be considered an upper bound estimate.

Figure 5.5 considers the potential impact of this wealth advantage in 1962. It illustrates in the first column the raw numbers of both the past (the $1.04 trillion in 1962) along with the tax benefits previously discussed. It then considers the potential if that initial stake in 1962 was invested in assets that yielded a 3 percent real return. It is assumed that over time,

[25] The interested reader should review Marketti (1990), Neal (1990), Ransom and Sutch (1990), and Craemer et al. (2020).

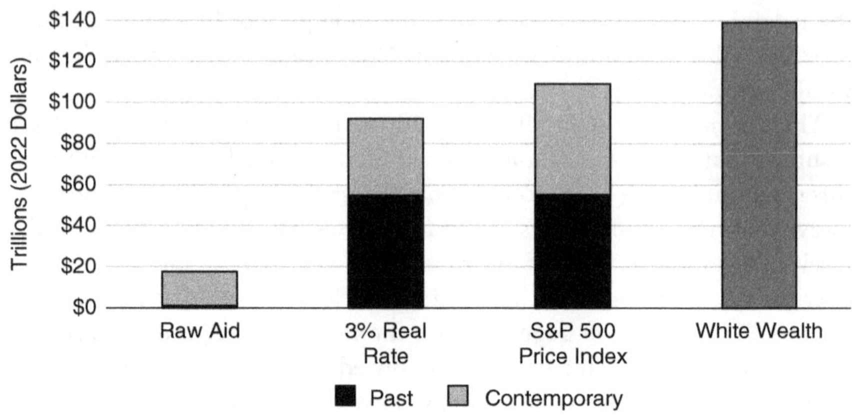

Figure 5.5 Federal contribution to White wealth
Source: Author's calculations; Federal Reserve Board, 1962 Survey of Financial Characteristics of Consumers, Survey of Consumer Finances; Joint Tax Committee Tax Expenditures; Office of Management and Budget, Historical Tables 2.5; US Treasury Tax Expenditures

households who have accumulated wealth transfer it to subsequent generations either through gifts or bequests. Estate and gift taxes are subtracted annually. The resultant figure is then added to the comparable tax benefits figure found in Figure 5.4. Similarly, it is assumed that the amount in 1962 is invested in the stock market. Each year the estate and gift taxes are taken out and adjustments made according to the lost wealth. Interestingly, both estimates generate about the same value, or $55 trillion. This represents almost 40 percent of the current level of White wealth, at $139 trillion. When combined with the contemporary help, it is clear that most of the current White wealth, as much as two-thirds to three-quarters, can be attributed to public assistance.

Despite familial dysfunction, the Mars family has become notable in their ability to sustain ever-increasing wealth transfers across four generations, averting the shirtsleeves-to-shirtsleeves outcome that has diminished so many past family dynasties. Their experience will likely become more commonplace as wealthy Whites take increased advantage of dynasty trusts and GRATs. These options will offer far more flexible vehicles than the closely held business model used by the Mars family. Moreover, the dynasty trusts may prove to be more durable and effective wealth preservation tools than any available to date. Overcoming the shirtsleeves-to-shirtsleeves challenge will simultaneously remedy a long-standing challenge to White supremacy in the past.

Over the next two chapters we will investigate how we got here with the federal wealth system we currently have. In Chapter 6, we will examine the roots of the current tax expenditures and trace their evolution over time. What were the economic and political pressures that led to their creation? Once enacted, did they remain unchanged or were they amended over time? To what extent was their evolution related to particular circumstances of our nation's racial history? In Chapter 7, we will take a similar look at the creation and evolution of the wealth transfer taxes introduced in this chapter and address similar questions. That chapter will examine how the federal wealth taxes – at one time notable achievements of an anti-elite coalition – became so diminished and undermined.

6

Exploring Past Roots

INAUSPICIOUS BEGINNINGS

During the spring and summer of 1913, Congress sprang into action with unusual agility. Earlier that year, five states in rapid succession ratified the Sixteenth Amendment, thereby removing any constitutional prohibition against an income tax. Shortly thereafter, Rep. Cordell Hull, a junior member on the Ways and Means Committee, was tasked with writing the income tax statute. Born in a log cabin, Hull was an obscure congressman from Tennessee. Yet, he was the natural choice for the job. Years earlier, he had studied tax policies adopted in other countries and was viewed as a knowledgeable and ardent advocate of a federal income tax. Without help from a legislative staff or hindrance from organized lobbies, Hull wrote a fifteen-page bill over a matter of weeks. Over the summer, Hull's draft generated modest debate, mostly around the exemption levels and tax brackets. It passed easily in the House but faced stiffer opposition in the Senate, where Democrats held a smaller margin. Under the leadership of Senate Finance Chair Furnifold Simmons (D-NC), the final bill passed with a 44–37 margin in the Senate. By early October, President Wilson signed the legislation into law. Although the current tax code runs to thousands of pages, Hull's modest draft shaped our modern income tax system.

Given the heated debates over tax policy today, it is surprising how little interest this initial bill generated. With hindsight, we recognize the pivotal role it played in shifting the source of federal funds. At the time, its birth was overshadowed by a desire to reduce federal tariffs. What we presently refer to as the Revenue Act of 1913 is truly known as the Underwood Simmons Tariff Bill of 1913. Hull's efforts did not warrant their own legislation, but were wrapped within a larger tax bill. For decades, high tariffs and excise taxes funded the federal government as they were the preferred taxes of the normally dominant Republican Party. The watershed election of 1912 swept Democrats back into power after nearly sixty years of Republican control of Washington. Much of the country, particularly in the South and West, viewed the "Republican tariffs" as regressive taxes that raised the cost of necessities and padded the profits of Eastern manufacturers. Many supported the income tax because it offered to restore federal revenues that would suffer under reduced tariffs. Hull's income tax bill was simply the tail of the wagging dog.

The tax law's modest design undermined potential opposition by those who would object to a "soak the rich" bill. The final version exempted all household incomes below $3,000 for individuals and $4,000 for married couples, levels that equal $87,797 and $117,062 today.[1] These exemption levels excluded virtually all Americans.[2] Only 4 percent of households filed, while less than 2 percent actually owed taxes. The tax rates ranged from a measly 1 percent to a top rate of 7 percent! Not until 1942, amid the need for pressing wartime expenses, would the personal income tax morph from a *class tax* to a *mass tax*. Until then, it remained the province of the rich. Despite its innocuous sting, opponents denounced it as a Trojan horse that would dominate American economic life. Some of their fears were realized just a few years later.

Given the inherent complexities of an income tax, Hull's fifteen-page bill left many key details unexplained. For instance, the Sixteenth Amendment gave Congress clear authority to tax income "from whatever source derived"; Hull offered few specifics, leaving this open for future interpretation. Some suggest he used ambiguity to gain passage for the bill, while others contend his contradictory answers to colleagues' questions reveal an incomplete consideration of key issues (Zelenak, 2018a). The tax bill did spawn the Bureau of Internal Revenue, the forerunner to the IRS. To redress the ambiguities, Bureau officials would be required to make numerous rulings that continue to influence our current tax system.

Most of the dozen tax expenditures discussed previously trace their roots back to these early years. To understand these decisions, one must acknowledge the prevailing influences that shaped them. While passage of the Sixteenth Amendment gave Congress clear authority to enact an income tax, it did not remove all clouds of constitutional illegitimacy.

1 Using Bureau of Labor Statistics (n.d.) Consumer Price Index Series, 1913–2023.

2 One consequence, whether intended or not, was that it eased the herculean task of implementing this system. Indeed, in 1914 tax filers merely filed their returns but did not actually pay taxes, presumably to ensure the system was workable.

Constitutional questions hung over many unresolved issues, causing lawmakers and Treasury officials to consider how the Supreme Court might rule. Moreover, these formative years for the income tax occurred during a period in which naked White supremacy reached an apex. Across the country, blatantly restrictive voting laws were enacted to eliminate Black political participation. An unprecedented upsurge of domestic terrorism supported these actions as lynchings averaged over 111, 79, and 57 per year in the 1890s, 1900s, and 1910s, respectively (Tuskegee University Archives Repository, n.d.). Across the country, large numbers of monuments commemorating the Confederacy and nostalgia for the "Old South" were erected. Many were built in the shadow of the local courthouse, serving as a reminder of White dominion. Both of these threads require further elaboration.

CONSTITUTIONAL CLOUDS

One primary reason delegates gathered at the Constitutional Convention in 1787 was to redress the limited powers of taxation granted to the federal government under the Articles of Confederation (Johnsen & Dellinger, 2018). To remedy this defect, Congress was given wide powers to tax the American people directly: "The Congress shall have Power To lay and collect Taxes, Duties, Imposts and Excises, to pay the Debts and provide for the common Defence and general Welfare of the United States; but all Duties, Imposts and Excises shall be uniform throughout the United States" (US Constitution, art.1, §8, cl. 3).

Seemingly, the only limitation on Congressional taxing powers is the requirement of uniform application across the states. Yet, one additional phrase did set limits: "No Capitation, or other direct, Tax shall be laid, unless in Proportion to the Census or Enumeration herein before directed to be taken" (US Constitution, art.1, §9, cl. 4).

While this restriction does not apply to *indirect taxes*, it does require that *direct taxes* be levied proportionately to state populations. During the convention debate, when delegate Rufus King asked what exactly constitutes a *direct tax*, no one answered (Farrand, 1911, p. 350). Ever since, including the recent *National Federation of Independent Business v. Sebelius (2012)* decision, the Supreme Court has wrestled – without conclusion – which taxes are *direct* and which are not. While *indirect taxes* are viewed as those that are imposed on things, like excise taxes and tariffs, there is no definitive ruling on which taxes are *direct*.

Over its first century, Congress enacted a variety of income taxes (1862, 1864, 1894) and inheritance taxes (1797, 1862, 1898). All were introduced as temporary measures to meet specific military threats or fund wartime expenses. In each case, opponents filed lawsuits that required Supreme Court rulings. The earliest decision, *Hylton v. United States* – one decided by Court members who were themselves delegates to the Constitutional Convention – concluded only poll and land taxes were direct taxes.[3] Over the next century, subsequent Court rulings adhered to *Hylton*. Not until 1895, in a surprise ruling that gave scant attention to precedent, Pollock v. Farmers' Loan and Trust invalidated the 1894 income tax by expanding the definition to include both personal property and any income generated by such property. While the Sixteenth Amendment eventually trumped *Pollock* on income sources, it did nothing to clarify which taxes are direct and which are not.

While the *Pollock* decision is not generally considered part of the Lochner era of the Supreme Court, it certainly is consistent with the very conservative views expressed by Court decisions over this period. The Lochner era refers to two generations of Court decisions in which it struck down one law after another that it viewed as infringing on individual rights, particularly those that related to freedom of contract in the marketplace. Over this period, the Court rejected laws that set maximum work hours, minimum wages, and limits on child labor. In this vein, *Pollock* concluded that federal efforts to redress natural market outcomes in income and wealth were additional examples of federal overreach. Conservative Court decisions during this period also dismantled key pieces of Reconstruction and laid the ground for legal segregation. Various Court decisions undermined the Civil Rights Act of 1875 and give legal legitimacy to the era of de jure apartheid (*Plessy v. Ferguson*, 1896; *Cumming v. Richmond*, 1899). One cannot understand the ensuing income tax policies without acknowledging the cloud that the Court cast over the Congress and its legislative actions.

WHITE DOMINION

Although a neglected history, the last three decades of the nineteenth century saw more than two dozen African Americans serve in both halls of Congress enacting legislation and representing their constituents. When George Henry White left office in March of 1901, it would be almost

3 Some believe this clause was inserted to protect slavery. Given the law treated enslaved persons as property and slaveholders were land-rich, proponents of slavery recognized their potential vulnerability to a national property tax. The reference to enumeration refers obliquely to the infamous Three Fifths Compromise.

another three decades before another Black lawmaker took the oath of office. A decade later, Congressional deliberations on the emerging income tax were lily-White affairs. Similar changes were occurring across the federal government. A consequence of Republican rule, more than 400 African Americans held white-collar Civil Service positions, with many in supervisory roles that included Whites as their subordinates. Within the Treasury Department, John Carroll Napier served as Register, causing his signature to be embossed on every dollar printed. The new Democratic Administration, including Treasury Secretary McAdoo, moved quickly to segregate the offices, toilets, and lunchrooms in order "to remove the causes of complaint and irritation where white women have been forced unnecessarily to sit at desks with colored men" (Yellin, 2013, p. 135). Black administrators with Civil Service protections were denied promotions, demoted, or reassigned to less important offices. As the department most responsible for developing tax policy, any possibility of including Black perspectives in the deliberations were being quickly eliminated.

Across the street in the White House, President Wilson carefully remained aloof of the changes occurring in his Administration. In a letter defending efforts to segregate the federal workforce, Wilson labeled them as "departmental" decisions that were beyond his responsibility but clearly beneficial to both Black and White employees (Yellin, 2013, p. 115). Two years later, Wilson ordered a private screening of *Birth of a Nation* in the White House. During his term of office, the nation experienced a spasm of racial hostility including the infamous East St. Louis and Chicago race riots, none of which generated much federal response. Just a few years later, the KKK was parading down Constitution Avenue and offering a clear signal of the racial status quo.

FIRST FRUITS OF THE FEDERAL INCOME TAX

An essential requirement of Hull's income tax bill is that it identified which sources of income were subject to taxation. Given the broad mandate provided by the Sixteenth Amendment, the law defines income expansively as "arising or accruing from all sources of income."[4] Soon thereafter, it details various sources of income including all:

> compensation for personal services, of whatever kind and in whatever form paid or from professions, vocations, and businesses, trade, commerce, or sales or dealings in property whether real or personal, growing out of the ownership, use, or interest

[4] See Underwood Simmons Tariff Act of 1913, Section II, Sub-section A, Sub-division 1.

in real or personal property, also from interest, rent, dividends, securities or the transaction of any lawful business carried on for gain or profit, or gains or profits or income derived from any source whatever including the income from, but not the value of a property acquired by gift, bequest, devise, or descent. (Underwood Simmons Tariff Act, Sec. II, Sub-sec. A, Sub-div 2)

This level of detail suggests an all-encompassing definition of income, although one that, curiously, exempts the value of property acquired by gift or bequest. After defining income in this way, the statute lists about a dozen exclusions or exemptions, some of which are of particular interest to us.

The first exclusion mentioned is life insurance benefits paid on behalf of the deceased. From discussions at the time, it is clear that lawmakers saw these payments going to widows and orphans upon the death of the primary breadwinner. They argued these payments served the public interest as they reduced demands on the public purse by impoverished families. Moreover, treating a lump sum death benefit as annual income could generate an unduly harsh tax bite. One issue left undecided by the law's brevity was how the tax authorities should treat the appreciating assets – the inside buildup – within life insurance policies.

Two other deductions specifically relate to constitutional concerns and the uneasy tensions within a federalist structure. The statute expressly allows taxpayers to deduct their state and local taxes.[5] Here we see the origins of what we now call the SALT deduction. Further, the law excludes any interest earned from state and local bonds, creating the tax-exempt bond exclusion.

Both of these exceptions stem more from constitutional concerns than protecting wealth. Ever since Supreme Court Justice John Marshall's warning that the "power to tax is the power to destroy," Congress has refrained from treading upon tax sources available to state and local governments. Wary of any perception of constitutional overreach, Congress took this warning to heart as it excluded all compensation earned by state and local government officials, all federal judges, and even the sitting President. As worries regarding Court pushback waned, Congress has rescinded many of these exclusions, although the SALT and tax-exempt bond exemptions have survived with few changes.[6]

[5] It excludes local taxes that are assessed to pay for local benefits. These could include fees charged to specific properties to pay for street and sidewalk construction as well as water and sewer hookups.

[6] The introduction of the standard deduction in 1944 along with the cap imposed by the TCJA of 2017 have limited the SALT deduction.

Although never mentioned specifically, the 1913 statute did create the home mortgage interest deduction by exempting interest paid on *any* debt. While this tax deduction has achieved sacred cow status, one scholar attributes its insertion as largely accidental as it was lumped with other forms of household debt (Ventry, 2010). Among others, Secretary Surrey contended its inclusion solved an administrative dilemma of how tax authorities might differentiate debt incurred for personal as opposed to profit-seeking reasons.[7] Back then, the home mortgage had not yet become the economic and political powerhouse of today. According to one source, mortgage debt accounted for just 11 percent of all household debt.[8] Recall that home mortgages of that era had short terms and were interest only, thereby limiting their appeal. Nonetheless, those wealthy enough to own a home and carry a mortgage became the beneficiaries of this decision. No doubt the vast majority were White.

The 1913 tax law birthed one other homeownership exemption, although neither explicitly nor immediately. A century ago, lawmakers were familiar with the concept of imputed net rental income from owner-occupied housing. Many European countries with established income tax systems included it as a source of taxable income, as did Wisconsin as part of its state income tax. While much of the debates of that time went unrecorded, it is clear that lawmakers recognized it as source of income "in whatever form" from the use of real property as well as a benefit enjoyed exclusively by homeowners.[9] Ultimately, Congress avoided the issue, leaving it in the hands of Treasury officials to decide. Initially, the tax authorities followed suit and sidestepped making a clear decision. In the instructions for the inaugural Form 1040, Treasury officials warned homeowners against deducting the rental value of their home as living expenses or counting it as income, thereby conveying their ambiguity on the matter (Zelenak, 2018a).

Including the imputed net rental income from owner-occupied housing does face unique challenges, then and now. Any new tax will inevitably generate a ready opposition. Adding a tax that is not attached to a clear income source to pay the levy will cause additional resistance. Even worse, a tax that appears to reach inside one's private home – a key bastion of the American Dream – will augment immeasurably the defiance. Given the likely resistance, a tax expert of that era, Dr. Blakey, predicted the Treasury officials would rule incorrectly and exclude this source of income because

[7] Both Surrey (1958) and Kahn (1960) make this argument.

[8] Ventry (2010) cites this figure from Klaman (1961).

[9] One can find this in the Congressional Record. See 50 Congressional Record (1913), 3848.

"an improper ruling would probably cause less protest than a proper one" (Blakey, 1914, p. 39). Even if the Treasury officials had been willing to suffer the expected rebuke, they would have to resolve the thorny administrative challenge of assessing its value to each homeowner, a task more difficult back then. Dr. Blakey (1915) concluded there were practical solutions to the measurability problem, although he advised a delay of several years given all of the issues the tax administrators were facing with the new tax. No doubt his patience would have been long exhausted as a century has passed and only once has Congress given its rescission serious concern (Ventry, 2010). Over the intervening years, rising homeownership rates among Whites and higher tax rates have stiffened opposition to ending this exemption (Brannon, 1986).

The 1913 statute was equally silent on the specific treatment of capital gains. The law defined income as "accruing from all sources in the preceding year," making clear that it should include any appreciation of property. The statute's language even suggests that any gains should be taxed regardless of whether the asset is sold and the gain is realized. What was left unmentioned is the tax treatment of capital losses. Given all of this, Treasury officials were tasked with sorting out the hoary details. Unfortunately, they did not measure up to the task. Over the next few years, Treasury officials made contradictory decisions. Several rulings said that corporations needed to adjust their book values annually and determine their net income accordingly (Blakey, 1915). Other rulings acknowledged the administrative difficulties in assessing property values annually; they allowed businesses and households to wait until the assets were sold before determining capital gains (or losses) (Blakey, 1915). One final decision limited the inclusion of capital losses to only those engaged in "trade" or business and ruled that one transaction did not make a business (Blakey, 1915). Despite these contrary rulings, a common practice emerged to view capital gains as normal income once realized. This gave property owners a tax deferral as they could defer paying any taxes until they chose to sell the asset. To be sure, low marginal tax rates limited the value of this tax deferral as well as any pressure to extend preferential treatment to capital gains. Shortly, this would change.

Fully half of our twelve federal wealth deductions can trace their origins to the 1913 law. Despite its broad definition of income, the bill excluded four sources of income and created allowable deductions for two others. While all of these exemptions redound to the benefit of the wealthy, each carried additional rationales for their inclusion. Moreover, the tax law's high exemption along with the very low marginal tax rates severely limited the value of these tax expenditures. What should not get lost is the transformative nature of the bill itself. To shift federal finance from indirect taxes on goods to a direct tax on household income represented a sea change, even if modestly inaugurated. Doing so shifted the tax burden from one inescapably regressive to one potentially progressive. Further, it created a far more elastic funding source that the federal government could tap when circumstances demanded. It would take three decades for this to occur.

STUMBLING INTO THE STEP-UP IN BASIS HOLE

Just three years later, Congress dramatically shifted the tax landscape again as it enacted the modern estate tax. While the full story of this drama is told in Chapter 7, its enactment did produce the next tax expenditure, applying the step-up in basis among estates. The reasons for treating estates in this way are obscure. Recall that the 1913 law specifically exempted gifts or bequests from being taxed as income, but not the income from such transfers. One argument is that Congress intended the language to serve as a tax deferral, but not as a tax exclusion. They expected the heirs to pay any past capital gains, but only when the assets were sold.[10] In their confusion, Treasury officials allowed unrealized gains in estates evade any income tax liability (Zelenak, 2018b). Another argument contends Treasury officials were apprehensive about how the conservative Supreme Court might rule on these issues (Kornhauser, 1985). By adopting the step-up in basis, the Treasury effectively dodged this constitutional concern. Moreover, it avoided the need to determine the cost basis of the deceased's assets, itself a knotty administrative challenge.

Given the low marginal tax rates of that time, it is likely this provision did not generate substantial interest.[11] However, the loophole's absurdity did not escape notice. At the time, bequests and gifts were treated similarly. One inquirer to a financial advice column in the *Wall Street Journal* (1920, p. 2) wrote, "It would seem that … by buying at 90, deciding to take profits at 115, it's only necessary to give the stock to your wife with instructions to sell, and the profit will remain in the family. This seems to me to so easily permit evasion of the income tax law that there must be further explanation." There was no further explanation to give. While Congress

[10] In this case, any assets in the bequest would retain their *carryover basis*, or historic cost as in the case of inter vivos gifts.

[11] The 1916 Revenue Act enacted a top estate tax rate of 10 percent. The same tax law raised the top income tax rate from 7 to 15 percent.

did close the gifts loophole shortly after, it left untouched what Secretary Surrey called "the most serious defect in the federal tax structure" (Kurtz & Surrey, 1970, p. 1381). Not until 1976 did Congress rescind this exemption. This decision generated such a withering response from tax lawyers, bankers, and accountants on behalf of their wealthy clients that it was revoked in 1980 before it could be implemented (Zelenak, 2018a). One commentator at the time called it the tax provision most treasured by the wealthy.

THE GIFT TO CHARITABLE GIVING

Finding itself now involved in World War I, Congress acknowledged the need for more revenue to pay for the wartime effort. In response, it expanded the reach and catchment of the federal income tax in dizzying fashion. First, it lowered the tax exemption from $3,000 and $4,000 to $1,000 and $2,000 for individual and married households, respectively. This change swept up more individuals as it increased the number of tax filers by tenfold over a two-year period.[12] Still, this represented a small sliver of American adults. Second, it raised the marginal tax rates throughout the income continuum. Those at the very bottom saw their tax rates increased by 2 percent while the increase grew larger as the tax became far more graduated and progressive in design. On incomes above $2 million, the rates were raised from 15 to 67 percent. No doubt this change confirmed the fears of all who opposed the tax's enactment just four years earlier.

During Senate deliberations, these higher rates triggered an amendment by Senator Hollis (D-NH) to exclude charitable donations from taxable income. Hollis contended that the higher tax rates would drain the very funds that households use to make charitable gifts, thereby undercutting giving to educational and social welfare charities. He argued that such giving relieves the government from burdens that increased hardship would entail. Making the case, he stated:

> Look at it this way: For every dollar that a man contributes for these specific charities ... the public gets 100 percent ... If it were undertaken to support such institutions through the Federal Government or local governments and the taxes were imposed for the amount ... instead of getting the full amount they would get a third or a quarter or a fifth. (55 Congressional Record, 1917, S6729)

Reportedly, Hollis's amendment was embraced by his Senate colleagues without much debate and endorsed unanimously (Duquette, 2019). Similar

[12] See the US Internal Revenue *Statistics of Income* from 1916 and 1918.

to the justification used to exclude death benefits, this argument that charitable giving is a public good that reduces the need for public provision has dominated thinking for decades (Duquette, 2019). Congress did limit the benefit as households could deduct no more than 15 percent of their taxable income.

In truth, the 15 percent cap functions more selectively than appears at first glance. Widely disparate marginal tax rates will exacerbate the "upside-down subsidy" and offer very different benefits. A dollar of philanthropy given by the wealthiest taxpayer facing the top rate would save 67 cents in taxes, while the same dollar would save the lowest-earning households 2 cents or nothing at all. This disparity only expanded with the introduction of the standard deduction (in 1944) and the requirement that taxpayers itemize to gain their tax reward. Even worse, the Treasury Department ruled that noncash gifts would be valued at their current value. Recall that this decision opened a bevy of benefits. By gifting appreciated assets to eligible charities, wealthy donors could avoid paying any capital gains tax, shield current income from the income tax, and shrink their estate to elude any estate tax. Recall from Chapter 4 that wealthy households might fare better by gifting the asset than selling it and keeping the after-tax residual. Not only did this loophole remain unchallenged for decades, but Congress periodically raised the limit on such gifts from 15 to 20 to 30 percent. In 1986, they eliminated the deduction for appreciated assets but rescinded that decision just seven years later.

PRIVILEGING CAPITAL GAINS

The top marginal tax rates of this period (77 percent in 1918 and 73 percent thereafter) placed enormous pressures on Congress to lower tax rates on capital gains. Unlike the charitable deduction, preferential treatment for capital gains took longer to emerge, largely due to the constitutional questions surrounding their taxation. In 1920, no fewer than four legal challenges were advancing toward the Supreme Court. In one case, Frederick F. Brewster had inherited a vast fortune from his father, a close associate of John D. Rockefeller and trustee of Standard Oil. In 1916, Brewster sold over $400,000 in bonds from his private investments, earning a tidy profit of $84,000 (Brown, 2022). Not seeing this capital gain as income, he neglected to report it, only to receive a tax bill from the Bureau of Internal Revenue. Although he paid the bill under protest, he then sued the tax commissioner for recovery. The suit claimed that any capital gains represented an increase in wealth and not income and therefore were still subject to the constitutional limits on *direct taxes* (E. H. S., 1921). Urged by Solicitor General William L. Frierson to resolve the issues fully, the Court coupled the four cases together informally and offered a brief, nine-page opinion that upheld the constitutionality of the tax on capital gains (Kornhauser, 1985).

The Court's decision now sent the issue of high tax rates back to Congress. By 1921, the country had endured world war and overcome the Spanish flu epidemic but was mired in a recession as the transition to peacetime was slow and uneven. Capitalizing on these problems, the Republican Party swept back into power and was looking to lower taxes and stimulate the economy. Sound familiar? Newly appointed Treasury Secretary Andrew Mellon, one of the wealthiest Americans, aimed to slash the top income tax rates and cap the capital gains rate. The House agreed to reduce the top income bracket from 73 to 50 percent and cap the capital gains rate at a lowly 12.5 percent. At this level, only households earning more than $31,000 (over $525,000 in 2023) would benefit since below that level households would face an ordinary tax rate below 12.5 percent. Looking to benefit all households, the Senate countered with a proposal that only 40 percent of any capital gains would be taxable. Ultimately, the Congress ratified the House version, thereby ensuring the preferential treatment would benefit only the rich. Even better, the law assured investors that their capital losses could be deducted from their ordinary income at normal tax rates.

Over the past century, the preferential treatment given to capital gains has fluctuated as attitudes have ebbed and flowed. Critics of the exclusion have viewed capital gains as a source of unearned income that should be taxed more heavily than wage, or earned, income. Supporters contend that high tax rates discourage the sale of appreciating assets, hinder reinvestment, and lower government revenues. The Treasury decision to require a realization event before assessing any gain as income gives asset owners tremendous discretion and leverage. Tax avoidance is easy since one simply refrains from selling the asset. Various Congresses have responded differently to these arguments over the years. Figure 6.1 depicts these changes and their impact on high-income households. It compares the top tax rate on ordinary income with the top rate on capital gains on assets held long-term. It is the gap between these lines that shows the extent of the exclusion and its value to affluent households.

Somewhat narrow in the 1920s, the gulf in tax rates widened dramatically through the middle half of the twentieth century as Congress raised the top tax rates on ordinary income to above 90 percent for almost two decades. With the declines in the ordinary tax rates in the 1960s and 1980s, the value

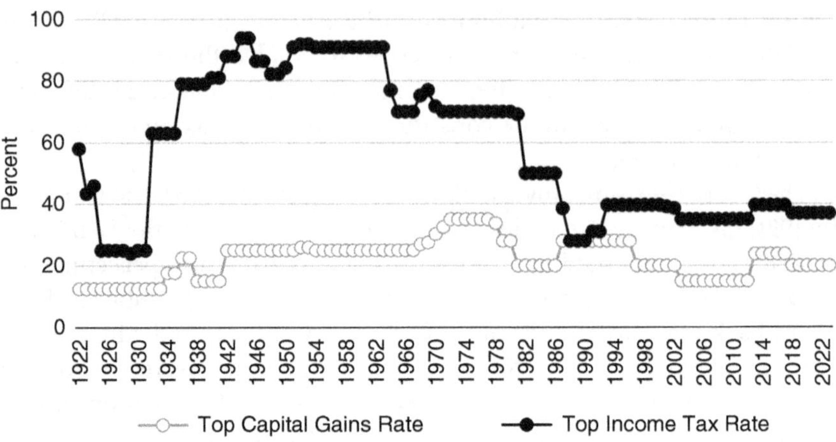

Figure 6.1 Capital gains exclusion over time
Source: Wolters Kluwer; Tax Policy Center

of the exclusion diminished even though the capital gains rates also fell. The exclusion actually disappeared as a result of the 1986 Tax Reform Act. However, it quickly reemerged in 1992 and has remained relatively consistent despite various efforts to eliminate any tax on capital gains.

It is important to acknowledge the impact of this preferential treatment accorded to capital gains during much of the twentieth century. During this period of high personal income tax rates, the low rates on capital gains gave wealthy households an easy avenue for tax avoidance. By keeping their wealth in capital assets, they protected their considerable gains. Rather than take compensation in higher salaries, executives could negotiate greater equity compensation to limit their tax liability. By shielding vast portions of their income from taxation, these households could reinvest their savings into larger stock, real estate, and business equity holdings. At the same time, our country's system of system of apartheid curtailed opportunities among Black households to do the same. Scarce educational opportunities restricted avenues into professions that might lead to higher compensation. Racial covenants, redlining practices, and "steering" by realtors severely limited the range of neighborhoods that prospective Black homebuyers might consider. Acts of racial violence often greeted Black families unwilling to stay within the prescribed boundaries. While segregation did offer modest opportunities for Black businesses to meet the needs of the Black community, the pervasiveness of White racism stunted their ability to expand their market. And when Black businesses did blossom successfully despite the odds, they often received the fury of White envy, as in the Tulsa Massacre. Whatever its form, anti-Black racism benefited White businesses that would have suffered from more robust Black competitors. These disparities persist today as White and Black households hold 85 and 2 percent of all unrealized capital gains, respectively.

FAVORING RETIREMENT SAVINGS

Much like the mortgage interest deduction, the origins of the pension deduction are obscure. Even before any preferential tax treatment, employers saw pension plans as effective recruiting tools to attract senior executives and a humane way of severing ties with them as they aged. Early on, favorable changes to the tax code made pensions more attractive, although their appeal spread slowly. Starting in 1918, several Treasury decisions ruled employer contributions to pension trusts as tax-deductible expenses (Ozanne, 1987). Nearly a decade later, a conservative majority in Congress was poised to slash income tax rates (Blakey, 1926). To this end, the Coolidge Administration introduced detailed tax proposals, none of which included pension trusts. Instead, inserted as a floor amendment that was enacted without much debate, Congress permitted pension assets to appreciate without affecting the employee's taxable income (Ozanne, 1987). To gain this preferential treatment for "inside buildup," pension plans were simply required to be available to "some or all employees." Despite this favorable treatment, it is estimated there were only 500 pensions in 1929. It is no stretch to argue that most of the covered employees were managerial and virtually all were White.

Circumstances sparked by World War II accelerated the growth of pension assets. To finance wartime expenses, Congress boosted the corporate tax to 40 percent and top individual tax rates to 94 percent. Overnight, preferential tax treatment became more meaningful. Congress also lowered the tax filing threshold; the income tax that touched only six percent of households in 1939 now required three-quarters to file just six years later (Turner, 1999). Moreover, the War Labor Board ruled that the existing wage and salary freeze did not extend to fringe benefits. Employers, desperate to fill empty jobs, could lure potential employees with more generous pension benefits. Even after the removal of wartime wage controls, the high tax rates encouraged further expansion of pension benefits in light of their preferential treatment. Employers valued the tax deductibility of any contributions while employees appreciated rising future income without incurring any immediate tax liability.

The growth in private pensions was dramatic. By 1950, nearly ten million private sector workers, about one-quarter of the total, participated in a pension plan. These numbers continued to grow until by 1980 nearly half of private sector workers were enrolled, virtually all of them in *defined benefit plans*. Congress enacted various regulations to assure the plans' financial integrity and their accessibility to more employees. Regarding the latter, plans were required to be uniformly available to 70 percent of the company's workforce, at least among selected job classifications. This latter provision generated a huge breach as many businesses relegated their Black employees to low-skilled jobs that did not come with the same level of benefits. This system of voluntary employer pensions gave the mostly White skilled workforce an important supplement to Social Security while ignoring the similar needs of most Black employees.

This outcome of stratified pension benefits has persisted despite major changes in the pension system. In 1962, Congress created Keough retirement savings plans to offer self-employed workers benefits similar to those provided to employees. Under these plans, contributions to qualified plans were tax-deductible up to a limit, asset appreciation was sheltered from taxation until withdrawn, and withdrawals could occur at age fifty-nine and a half without penalty. Soon after, Congress expanded this program to anyone when it introduced the 401(k) plans. Employers quickly saw their appeal and have since engaged in a relentless shift from the older *defined benefit plans* to these newer *defined contribution plans*.

The switch to *defined contribution plans* shifts the risks of retirement saving from the employers to *all* employees, although the burden is not equally shared. Higher-salaried workers benefit more from the employer contributions and the tax-deferred inside buildup. Their higher incomes allow them to take full advantage of any matching contributions from their employer. Shorter vesting periods and increased portability means these employees lose little as they seek better terms from other employers. As White employees earn higher salaries and receive more offers to assume managerial and professional positions, they benefit more fully from these plans. Persistent labor market discrimination limits the share of Black households who can access these opportunities. Earning lower median salaries effectively lowers the appeal of these plans to Black employees as the employer contributions are smaller and their ability to defer income more challenging. Lower levels of household and extended family wealth cause Black households to dip into these funds more frequently, despite the penalties paid. Given these disparate circumstances, it is unsurprising that White employees participate in greater numbers, carry larger account balances, and thereby benefit more fully from the federal government's generosity.

MAKING HOMEOWNERSHIP PEERLESS

On October 20, 1951, President Truman reluctantly signed HR 4473, also known as the Revenue Act of 1951. After a long and stormy session, Congress had finally passed a compromise bill that few truly supported. Following years of war and heavy tax burdens, many in Congress pushed for lower taxes on the American public. Others saw the Cold War demands and an expanding war in Korea as requiring new revenues. HR 4473 was the legislative sausage that resulted from these competing interests.

A provision of the bill, §1034, expanded the capital gains exclusion by exempting any gains made from the sale of one's principal residence. A sponsor of the change, Rep. Forand (D-RI) insisted any gains from current home sales should not be counted as income as they were caused by recent inflation. Moreover, he argued many of these sales were "involuntary" as pressing defense needs required workers to relocate across the country to take jobs in specific defense plants (Klein, 1998). Taxing these gains would hinder those unable to pay the inflated home prices in the new location even after selling their current home. No doubt, some argued this represented a threat to the country's national security interests. While many home sales were not "involuntary," supporters claimed discerning the difference posed undue administrative challenges. Consequently, the provision offered a roll-over stipulation. According to §1034, home sellers could avoid paying any capital gains if they purchased within a year another home whose purchase price exceeded their selling price. The homebuilding industry welcomed this requirement.

Curiously, this exemption immediately follows §1033 in the tax code, which describes a similar exclusion stemming from an earlier war. Under this previous provision, shipowners forced to sell their ships to the US Government during World War I received special treatment. Congress recognized that paying capital gains on these sales would penalize shipowners as they bought more expensive replacement ships after the war. While this earlier provision was created to respond to a narrow set of circumstances, it was resurrected for use in much different and broader circumstances. Trying to make the parallel fit, Rep. Forand claimed that homeowners rarely sell their homes for profit, unlike other appreciating assets, and instead do so out of necessity (97 Congressional Record, 1951, 6960). According to the House

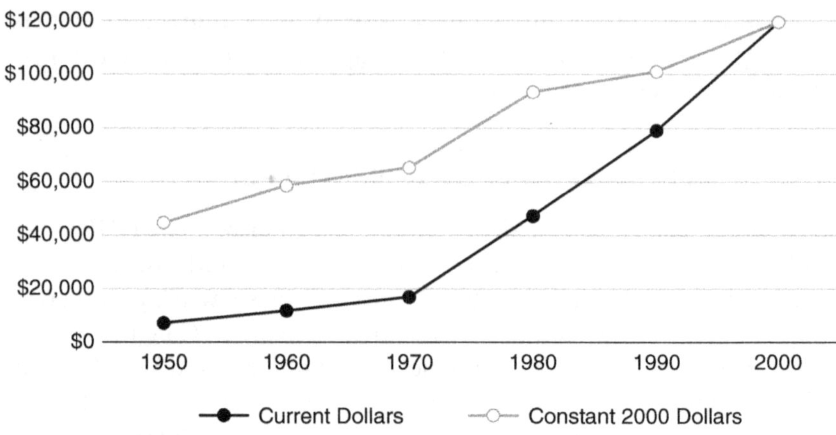

Figure 6.2 Median home values
Source: US Census Bureau, Historical Census of Housing Tables

Ways and Means Report, home sales triggered by employment changes or accommodation to a larger family "partakes of the nature of an involuntary conversion" and that these sales are "particularly numerous in periods of rapid change such as mobilization or reconversion" (H. R. Rep. No. 82-586, at 27, 1951). According to the available record, this particular provision generated scant floor debate and received bipartisan support.

For current and prospective homeowners, the homes sales exclusion could not have come at a better time. Owning one's home was portrayed as a key facet of achieving the American Dream. Federal mortgage loan guarantees and thirty-year mortgages enabled more households to make homeownership a reality. Rising homeownership rates encouraged an increase in median home prices. As Figure 6.2 illustrates, households buying a median home during the period could typically expect to earn substantial capital gains, even after inflation, if they maintained ownership for several decades. To be sure, the figures in the graph may overstate typical appreciation since new homes added to the housing stock were larger and more expensive. Nonetheless, rising new home prices would elevate the prices experienced by the older housing stock. This exclusion gave an increasing number of households their first real opportunity to accumulate wealth. Never before were so many Americans able to profit so much from financial leverage, a tool that historically had been reserved just for the rich.

While a substantial gift, the roll-over exemption only deferred one's tax liability. At some point, households would no longer want to "buy up" but instead "cash out." At that point, sellers would have a large tax liability since their historic basis would be equal to the purchase price of their first home (Kahng, 2013). To relieve this concern, Congress created in 1964 a one-time exclusion of realized gains up to $20,000 to home sellers aged sixty-five or more.[13] Supporters insisted that taxing this gain would only reduce the limited funds on which seniors must now depend. Given the modest cap, the initial design of this exemption did favor less affluent households who were selling lower-priced homes (Gravelle & Jackson, 2005). Yet, the door was now cracked. Citing the need to respond to inflation, Congress raised this limit three times over the next seventeen years to $35,000, then $100,000, and finally $125,000. In 1978, Congress lowered exclusion to those fifty-five and older. Finally, in 1997 Congress eliminated the roll-over provision and simply raised the exclusion to more generous limits of $250,000 for singles and $500,000 for married couples. These limits create a tax-free income source for all homeowners and a ready augmentation to their net worth. It represents a major form of assistance, one that is unavailable to households that rent.

It is important to recall what other circumstances are affecting homeownership as these tax changes are occurring. The same FHA and VA loan guarantees that are expanding access to many Americans include residential mortgage maps that cement racially segregated neighborhoods and exclude non-White homebuyers. New highway construction is connecting downtown to the expanding White-exclusive suburbs. Many of these highway projects entail "slum clearance," forcing Black property owners to sell their homes and businesses to accommodate the new roads. Just three years before the exclusion was enacted, the Supreme Court ruled in *Shelley v. Kraemer (1948)* that racial covenants, although not illegal in themselves, could not be subject to state enforcement. Interestingly, in that case, three of the Court justices recused themselves from the case because they owned properties that had racial covenants. Not for almost another two decades would the Fair Housing Act of 1968 finally make housing discrimination illegal. While now illegal, prospective Black homebuyers experience discrimination in multiple ways even today (Kamin, 2024). Given these circumstances, the differences in homeownership rates illustrated in Figure 6.3 should offer little surprise. Whites have been far more likely to capture the home sales exclusion's generous benefits.

[13] It is actually a very complicated calculation that requires knowing the historic cost basis as well as the selling price. First, one calculates the exclusion rate, which equals $20,000 divided by the sales price of the home. One then multiplies the exclusion rate times the realized capital gains, and that result is the size of the excluded gain from taxation.

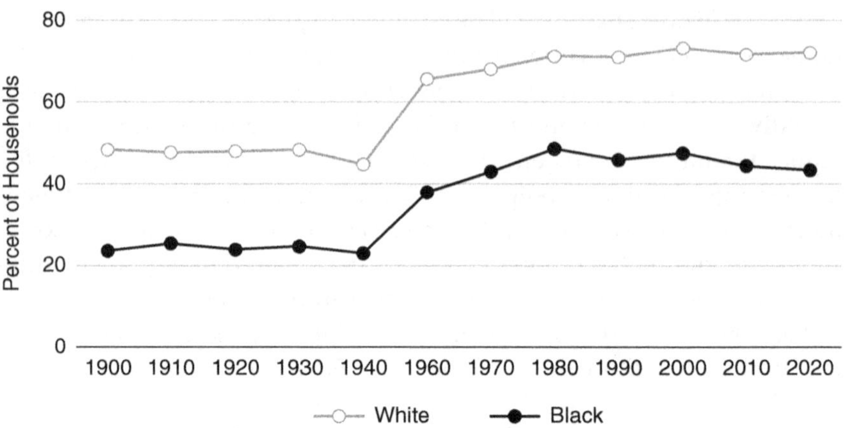

Figure 6.3 Homeownership rates by race
Note: the 1950 Census did not include questions about homeownership
Source: US Census Bureau retrieved from Ruggles et al. (n.d.)

Their higher homeownership rate aside, other reasons enabled White households to take greater advantage of the exclusion's generosity. As White employees earned higher wages and salaries, their incomes enabled them to purchase homes in more select neighborhoods that were primed to appreciate. These neighborhoods receive better public services and community assets like parks that raise property values further. Laws and norms that limited the search of prospective Black homebuyers, notably in the expanding suburbs, meant fewer competing buyers and lower home prices. Generous family and government help with down payments reduced the time needed to gather the means to buy a home. Becoming homeowners earlier in life offered greater opportunities to realize the capital gains and use the exclusion to "buy up." Of course, the well-paying defense jobs that were forcing so many homeowners to sell and relocate used segregated workforces. For all of these reasons, White households had the means to make better use of this exclusion in order to build generational wealth.

FOSTERING HEALTH SELECTIVELY

Our current system of employer-sponsored health insurance did not emerge until it was triggered by the same wartime rulings that sparked the use of employer-sponsored pension plans. Before 1930, most health plans were "sickness" plans that provided replacement income if the beneficiary was unable to work due to injury or sickness (Thomasson, 2003).

Viewed similarly to death benefits paid on life insurance, payments on these policies were made tax exempt by the Revenue Act of 1918.[14] Over time, advancing medical technologies brought improved patient care along with rising costs. Hospitalization and physician health plans emerged in response. Still, by 1940 less than 10 percent of the population were covered by some form of health insurance (Scofea, 1994). In most cases, these were individual insurance plans contracted with Blue Cross, Blue Shield and other carriers.[15]

Wartime conditions that froze wages and salaries, generated acute labor market shortages, and raised steeper income tax rates fueled the expansion of employer-sponsored health insurance plans across the economy. In an obscure and limited decision, the IRS exempted employer contributions to group health insurance on behalf of their employees. Looking to attract scarce workers, private employers began offering group health insurance to their employees. Commercial insurance carriers quickly saw the advantages of offering group insurance over individual insurance plans. Larger pools of insured lowered their administrative costs and limited the risks of adverse selection in which only those susceptible to illness would apply for insurance. Individuals who previously had been refused insurance coverage now could find it as part of an employee group. By the end of the decade, fully half of the population now had health insurance coverage (Scofea, 1994). This expansion encouraged innovation in the industry, including the introduction of Liberty Mutual Insurance's major medical plan. Unlike existing plans that placed caps on the provided coverage, this policy offered greater coverage for catastrophic circumstances, although it required cost-sharing like co-pays from the insured. It served as the forerunner for today's insurance policies.

In 1954, Congress undertook a massive review of the tax code that resulted in the Revenue Act of 1954. In contrast to its fifteen-page forerunner forty years earlier, this statute ran to 4,000 pages and produced 8,000 pages of testimony. At least in one area, this law brought needed clarity. The 1943 IRS ruling was narrowly drawn and subsequently undermined by later tax decisions. Confusion reigned. In section 106, Congress clearly codified that employer contributions to group as well as individual employee health plans were exempt from their employee's taxable income. The ensuing

[14] According to Employer Health or Accident Plans (1954), it is likely that Congress meant only to exempt payments from individual policies and not those generated by employer-sponsored policies.

[15] Blue Cross and Blue Shield were separate entities until 1978.

clarity along with extensive messaging conducted by the commercial insurance carriers kindled an immediate expansion of policies. In just four years after the law's passage, participation in group insurance plans jumped from 48 to 67 percent of Americans (Thomasson, 2003). Coverage rates by private health insurance would peak at nearly 80 percent in the early 1970s and then start a slow decline to around 62 percent before the advent of the Affordable Care Act (National Center for Health Statistics, 2019).

Surprisingly, employers face no federal requirements on offering health insurance to all employees, much less at the same level of coverage.[16] Federal law gives employers broad discretion on whether to provide different plans to diverse groups of employees. Companies can offer better health care packages to higher-paid employees, salaried workers, or those in professional occupations than they provide for hourly, part-time, or seasonal workers. According to one recent study, employees earning incomes more than four times the federal poverty level are more than twice as likely to have private health insurance than are workers earning incomes below the federal poverty threshold (Clemans-Cope et al., 2006). While making access to health care benefits based on race has been illegal since the 1960s, it still results. As White employees earn higher salaries, occupy more executive and professional positions, and experience shorter and fewer bouts of unemployment than Black employees, they are more likely to enjoy greater coverage and better health insurance benefits. As depicted in Figure 6.4, White employees have enjoyed higher rates of coverage from employer-sponsored health insurance. This disparity in coverage has remained remarkably stable over time, although it does not capture the expected differences in quality of plans available to White and Black employees.

ACKNOWLEDGING THE JIM CROW CONSEQUENCE

It is worth noting that nine out of the twelve tax expenditures have their origins during a period in which Congress counted no Black members among its ranks. Not until March 1929 would the House of Representatives seat its first Black colleague in nearly thirty years, and another fourteen years before there were just two members serving in the same Congress. The powerful Ways and Means Committee, the source of all federal tax legislation, did not include a Black member until 1975. Given the dearth of Black voices in Congress, one can surmise that White attitudes toward the needs of the Black community ranged from outright

[16] The Affordable Care Act does impose a penalty on larger businesses that fail to do so.

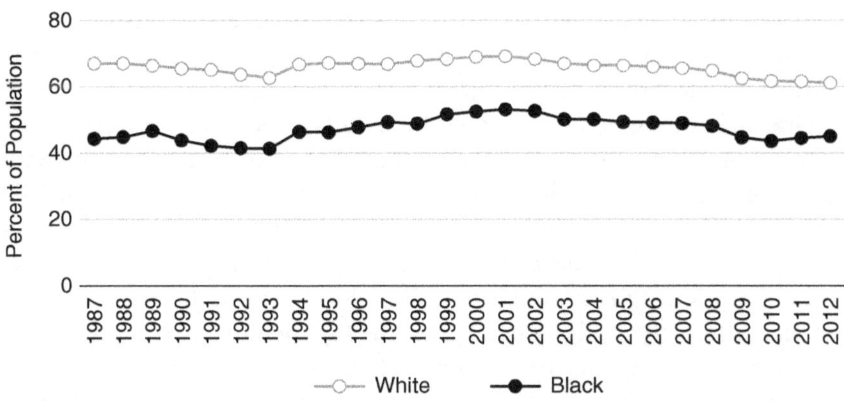

Figure 6.4 Private, employer-based health insurance coverage rates
Source: US Census Bureau, Health Insurance Historical Tables, Table HI

hostility to unthinking indifference. None of the tax expenditures appear to have overtly racial causes. Yet, tax policy is not color-blind given the very different circumstances that face Black households. In her excellent book, Dorothy Brown (2022) explains how technical fixes to the "marriage penalty" can impact typical White and Black households differently due to different marriage rates, salaries, and employment opportunities. Not having Black voices in the room when such decisions were made clearly have had consequences.

All of the dozen tax expenditures favor wealthy households; yet, in most cases, this does not appear to be the primary reason for their emergence in the tax code. The SALT and tax-exempt bond income deductions emerged mostly due to constitutional concerns regarding the limits of federal tax authority. Even the decision to treat capital gains as income only when they are realized was influenced by constitutional worries. Deductions for life insurance death benefits and charitable giving garnered support through arguments that each served the public good and reduced the need for public expenditures. The loophole that allowed noncash gifts to be deducted at their current value provides a notable exception to this point. At their inception, neither the mortgage interest nor the pension deduction attracted much interest as their financial benefits appeared far more modest. Deductions for employer-sponsored health insurance and pension contributions resulted more from wartime pressures and high tax rates than any desire to help wealthy households. Even the decision to exclude the imputed net rental income of homeowners is understandable given the expected political opposition to its administrative complexity and absent source of taxable income. That leaves the step-up in basis given to estates and the capital gains exclusion as two deductions that were established primarily to protect the income of the rich.

This attention given to personal income tax deductions diverts focus from a related issue, the tax itself. Although we take the federal income tax for granted, its establishment in 1913 launched a major shift in federal finance. It produced an elastic revenue source capable of financing an expansion of the federal government and imposing a more progressive tax burden, at least potentially. For a long period, this potential was tapped. After very modest beginnings, the top income tax rate was raised to above 70 percent and kept there for a half century. Assuredly, tax loopholes undermined the effectiveness of these high rates. Nonetheless, these marginal tax rates reflect a policy stance that is clearly not compatible with the narrow self-interests of the wealthy. Instead, they reflect a perception that the rich need to share more of their treasure to fund the legitimate needs of government. That this discussion within the White community occurred during a period in which Blacks were excluded from any meaningful political activity as well as from most educational, occupational, and business opportunities is not a coincidence. A receding Black threat allowed class schisms within the White community to emerge and develop.

While high marginal tax rates occupied the visible portion of the federal income tax, these tax expenditures did serve the interests of White supremacy in less noticeable ways. Mostly White households fortunate enough to own their own home, other property, or stocks and bonds were rewarded by the preferential tax treatment. Their desire to save amply for retirement wealth was generously assisted by tax deductions on pension plans crafted for their needs. All of this assistance enabled them to build generational wealth that would ensure their children could access the full range of opportunities. Even among those unfortunates who died prematurely, the ones who could afford life insurance or held appreciating assets were assured of transferring the bulk of their wealth to their heirs. As created, the system functioned to help those already affluent. It offered scant assistance to any households unable to achieve asset ownership on their own. And it ably resisted any elimination of these benefits. As one scholar argues, “Even where a mistake is reparable, it is hard to accomplish change after the mistake has been in place for decades because interests have been created and defensive institutions developed” (Brannon, 1986, p. 1766). That these tax expenditures served the interests of White supremacy certainly added to its effective resistance.

THE LAST HALF CENTURY

The struggle for civil rights finally gained the country's attention during the 1960s. Media images of nonviolent marches followed by police violence illuminated for all the ugly nature of American society. Urban protests erupted in numerous cities across the decade and signaled the immense anger in the Black community over a White-dominated society unwilling to make meaningful change in response to modest demands. To provide an explanation of these protests to a clueless, White America, President Johnson appointed the eleven-member Kerner Commission to study and report on their underlying causes. After a seven-month investigation, the Commission offered a clear diagnosis of the ills: "What white Americans have never fully understood – but what the Negro can never forget – is that white society is deeply implicated in the ghetto. White institutions created it, white institutions maintain it, and white society condones it" (National Advisory Commission, 1968, p. 1). No longer could White Americans pretend they did not know.

Along with a collective awareness, the period ushered in new possibilities. The Civil Rights Act of 1964 outlawed the system of legal segregation and discrimination that had maintained White domination in political, economic, and social spheres for seventy years. Previously Whites-only organizations like elite universities, professional organizations, and skilled trades slowly and reluctantly admitted Blacks to their ranks. This law created the need for new structures, policies, and social norms; what remained unanswered was whether these new arrangements would relentlessly eliminate the existing racial disparities or assure their perpetuation. A year later, the Voting Rights Act removed restrictions on Black voting, expanded the voter rolls, and instigated an increase in the number of Black officeholders, including in Congress. In 1975, the White monopoly over membership on the powerful Ways and Means Committee finally ended as two Black lawmakers, Rep. Harold Ford Sr. (D-TN) and Rep. Charles Rangel (D-NY), were selected as members. Given Secretary Surrey's high-profile warnings about the tax expenditures' "upside-down" subsidies, this moment offered a natural opportunity to target the needs of the Black community. It is instructive to examine what happened.

As Secretary Surrey warned, nearly half of the dozen tax expenditures have remained largely ignored by Congress over the past half century. These include the deductions for health insurance, imputed net rental income of homeowners, tax-exempt bond income, and life insurance buildup and death benefits. Each of these has remained virtually unchanged.[17] The estate step-up in basis rule should be included as well as it has remained unchanged despite attracting an enacted reform. In 1976, Congress finally moved to close the massive loophole by requiring that future estate assets would transfer with a *carryover basis* instead of the *step-up in basis*. This change would leave the heirs liable for any unrealized gains when they chose to sell the inherited assets. What was before a tax exclusion would now be a tax deferral. Nonetheless, this enacted change drew such a fierce response that Congress rescinded it before it ever was implemented. Although these tax expenditures effectively have remained untouched, that does not mean they have remained unaffected. Unrelated tax policy changes that raise or lower the income tax rates directly affect their value and appeal. Moreover, none of these have limits to their generosity. Wealthier households can make even greater use of these deductions. As they do, the demands on the US Treasury are obscure, but real and rising nonetheless.

Over the past half century, two other tax expenditures also attracted Congressional interest, but experienced only an expansion of their benefits. A third tax expenditure, the qualified business income deduction, was wholly created in 2017. Understanding how these deductions were expanded and who might benefit from them is instructive. As mentioned previously, Congress has expanded the home sales exclusion numerous times. Not only have they removed the roll-over purchase requirement, but they have continually raised the exclusion so that now married couples can protect up to $500,000 from income taxes. Only a few homeowners capable of purchasing a home in very selective neighborhoods are likely to experience this kind of appreciation. Similarly, Congress has expanded the pension deductions by adding the Roth Individual Retirement Account (IRA) as another savings option. Under the Roth guidelines, households can deposit after-tax dollars, leave them to earn income over time, and withdraw everything without any tax liability, ever. It is perfectly crafted for households affluent enough to have adequate savings and now looking for a way to save for retirement tax-free. These accounts offer nothing to households trying to build a rainy-day fund.

Lastly, the qualified business income deduction was created from scratch in 2017. It allows certain business owners the ability to exclude 20

[17] The Affordable Care Act did not alter the health insurance deduction but worked around it. It created financial penalties for larger firms that did not offer their employees the required level of insurance coverage.

percent of their business earnings from their personal tax liability. Similar to the other tax expenditures, this offers no help to those individuals interested in starting their own business, but serves only those who already have one. Not much help here for those looking for a hand up to start a business.

Two other tax expenditures, the exclusion on capital gains and deduction for charitable gifts, fall into the category of "suffered some setbacks, but ultimately experienced expansion over the period." Fifty years ago, the top capital gains tax rate stood at 35 percent while the top ordinary income tax rate was 70 percent. Since then, both rates have been adjusted numerous times, although the general trend has been downward for both. The capital gains rate was reduced at one point to 15 percent but has stabilized at 20 percent since 2013. It remains about half of the current top rate on ordinary income of 37 percent. These changes clearly favor those households affluent enough to invest in appreciating assets.

Similarly, Congress has loosened the limits on how much individuals can deduct by giving to charitable organizations and private foundations. Currently, individuals now receive deductions for cash gifts up to 60 percent of their AGI to charities and 30 percent to nonoperating foundations. Of course, only the wealthy are in a position to make such large gifts. Over the period, the deduction did experience a restriction, one that appears to be temporary. In 1992 Congressman Donald Pease (D-OH) advocated placing limits on the size of deductions that wealthy taxpayers could take on certain below-the-line deductions, including charitable gifts.[18]

Known as the Pease Limitation, it reduced the total deduction that taxpayers could take who earned above a threshold AGI. Known colloquially as a "financial haircut," it meant that the most affluent taxpayers could take only 20 percent of their expected deduction.[19] Removed once in 2010 for two years, the Pease Limitation was rescinded again by the 2017 Tax Cut and Jobs Act, at least until 2026.

Only the remaining two, the mortgage interest and the SALT deductions, suffered a net restriction of their benefits over the period. As both are below-the-line deductions, they experienced the "financial haircut" just discussed. Yet, they endured other limits as well.

[18] Worries about the federal budget deficits, then in the somewhat quaint range of $300 billion, rallied support for these limits.

[19] Curiously, this limitation had less impact on charitable giving than one might think. The Pease reduction is based on one's income, not one's charitable giving. Wealthy households that make larger charitable gifts will gain a larger deduction even as their income and Pease reduction remain the same.

Historically, the mortgage interest deduction was included with other household debt and had no limit. As Congress restricted the deduction to only mortgage debt, it placed a $1 million cap on the deduction and allowed another $100,000 on a related, home equity line. This was reduced further in 2017 to a $750,000 total. According to the 2019 SCF, very few households would have been harmed by the reduction. Similarly, the SALT deduction has experienced increased restrictions as Congress removed certain taxes like motor fuels tax (1978) and the sales taxes (1986) from the exempted list.[20] Yet, the most drastic cut in the deduction occurred in 2017. In a highly partisan battle that pitted higher-tax states against lower-tax states, the Congress capped the SALT deduction at $10,000. While this change captured most of the media attention, the increase in the standard deduction enacted that year likely had a far greater impact. This change caused far fewer taxpayers to itemize their deductions, making this and the mortgage interest deduction attractive only to the high-income taxpayers.

The changes made to these tax expenditures over the past half century exhibit a clear and consistent pattern. Most of the changes have led to expanded opportunities and benefits for those able to make use of them. In most cases, some form of property ownership is required to access these benefits. None of the changes over the past half century has addressed the needs of those households *seeking such property ownership.* Any acknowledgment of our nation's racial wealth divide and its roots in our past policies has had no impact on our tax expenditure policies. Instead, Congress has responded by doubling down on rewarding already affluent households – the overwhelming majority of whom are White – and neglecting those not yet able to overcome the barriers to property ownership.

CONCLUSION

The origins of these wealth-building tax expenditures are both fascinating and multifaceted. Some arose out of constitutional concerns as tax authorities and lawmakers struggled to create a new tax system amidst great uncertainty. Others resulted from overwhelmed lawmakers selecting ill-considered choices and ill-prepared Treasury officials making questionable calls. Other choices result from efforts to mitigate real or perceived tax administration challenges. Several deductions emerged during wartime, suggesting other priorities were given more attention. At least one

[20] In 2004, the sales tax exemption was partially restored as taxpayers had the option to deduct their state and local income tax payments or their state and local sales taxes.

materialized in response to the desires of a particularly affluent and powerful lobby. Whatever their particular origin story, they've all been influenced by key forces that have shaped tax policies over the past century. At times, the pressing need for increased revenues have caused rising tax rates and broader collection efforts. At other times, populist coalitions in Congress have pared back benefits. Through all of these changes, there has been one overriding constant. In assisting American households in their efforts to build wealth and attain financial security, they have targeted households that have already made it. They have focused their aid to households who already own assets, whether it is a home, pension, or business. They have showered their assistance to households wanting to transfer their wealth to future generations and neglected those responding to calls for help from current and preceding generations. Of course, these differences, due to our nation's history and current policies, also reflect the racial divide between Black and White.

Over the past half century, changes to these tax expenditures have almost exclusively targeted White, affluent households. While disturbing, this should not be surprising. The gains made by Black Americans over the past half century in educational attainment, professional employment, property ownership, business enterprise, political leadership, and cultural presence have been well documented here and elsewhere. In most cases, these gains are absolute in that they have been insufficient to close the racial gaps. Nonetheless, these gains have been sufficient to increase status threats among many White Americans. It is not so surprising that during this time of expanding opportunities for Black Americans, it has led to policies that reassert the dominion of White Americans.

In Chapter 7, we examine the emergence of the federal wealth transfer tax system. Both the estate tax and the subsequent federal gift tax emerged during this early period of the twentieth century. We examine the decisions that have led to a tax collection system that is full of leaks. It seems for every attempt lawmakers took to plug one leak, their decisions led to others springing forth. In recent decades, the persistent attempts to end the wealth transfer taxes serve the same interest of ensuring White dominion persists in the decades going forward.

7

Finding the Leaks

A GROUNDSWELL OF SUPPORT

Just two years after enacting the federal income tax, Congress took further aim at wealthy Americans as they considered an inheritance tax. Even as lawmakers increased the bite of the income tax, they viewed an inheritance tax as a more direct way of taxing the rich. During the previous half century, a laissez-faire attitude toward business along with the repression of union activity enabled growing disparities in incomes and wealth. Business-friendly Supreme Court rulings allowed the rise of monopolies and trusts as the "captains of industry" competed for control of vast commercial empires. Conspicuous consumption among the rich fueled further competition that led to lavish displays of wealth. They built mansions that reminded them of European castles from their tours abroad and hosted evermore outlandish parties, like one formal dinner served on horseback.

These displays of wealth and status gave witness to the vast disparities growing in American society. To redress this expanding gulf, prominent Americans declared their support for a tax on wealth. The rich and normally conservative steel magnate Andrew Carnegie lent his full support for a heavy inheritance tax:

> Of all forms of taxation, this seems the wisest. Men who continue hoarding great sums all their lives, the proper use of which for – public ends would work good to the community, should be made to feel that the community, in the form of the state, cannot thus be deprived of its proper share. *By taxing estates heavily at death* the state marks its condemnation of the selfish millionaire's unworthy life. (Carnegie, 1889, para. 12; emphasis mine)

Worried about the corrosive power of growing wealth, President Theodore Roosevelt announced his support for such a tax. Speaking before Congress in 1907, he argued:

> A heavy progressive tax upon a very large fortune is in no way such a tax upon thrift or industry as a like would be on a small fortune. No advantage comes either to the country as a whole or to the individuals inheriting the money by permitting the transmission in their entirety of the enormous fortunes which would be affected by such a tax; and as an incident to its function of revenue raising, *such a tax would help to preserve a measurable equality of opportunity* for the people of the generations growing to manhood. (Roosevelt, 1907, para. 31, emphasis added)

Supreme Court justice Louis Brandeis is believed to have the coined the pithy phrase: "We can have concentrated wealth in the hands of a few or we can have democracy. But we cannot have both" (Dilliard, 1941). Each of these leaders reasoned that an inheritance tax is essential to fund the public good, maintain some measure of a meritocratic society, and preserve democracy. In 1916, the country was facing the possibility of entering World War I, so the pressures for a new tax encouraged its enactment. Nonetheless, overcoming the powerful interests arrayed against such a tax and gaining Congressional ratification would require unusual circumstances.

Once again, Rep. Cordell Hull (D-TN) was asked to draft the new law. Yet, two committee chairmen, Sen. Furnifold Simmons (D-NC), who still chaired the Senate Finance Committee, and Rep. Claude Kitchin, (D-NC), who both chaired the House Ways and Means Committee and served as Majority Leader, would play prominent roles in the law's passage. Both committee chairmen hailed from North Carolina. Even more striking, they shared the experience of occupying the state's Second House District (NC-2). This particular district was known as the "Black Second." Over the last quarter of the nineteenth century, this House district sent more Black representatives to Congress than any other in the nation. This backstory needs recounting.

THE "BLACK SECOND"

Soon after North Carolina's readmission into the Union, the Democratic Party-controlled legislature redrew the legislative boundaries, including an oddly shaped district that snaked through the eastern part of the state. According to contemporaries, "The Second Congressional District is a masterpiece. It takes in Craven then wanders clear to the Virginia line, and turns a sharp corner around Nash and grasps Warren" (The Colored Nomination, 1878, p. 2). As the newly enfranchised freedmen voted overwhelmingly for the "party of Lincoln," Democratic legislators combined these Black-majority counties to limit Republican control of neighboring districts. This created a solidly Republican district that routinely elected

Black representatives to Congress as well as the North Carolina legislature. Over the last quarter of the nineteenth century, four different Black Republicans represented the district, giving voice to the concerns and aspirations of the freedpeople. White Democrats did win election occasionally, but only when the Republicans were divided and voting fraud was rampant.

One of these breakthrough White Democrats was Furnifold Simmons.[1] Born in 1853 on a large plantation near New Bern, North Carolina, Simmons came of age in a South undergoing sweeping change. Family wealth enabled him to study at both Wake Forest College and Trinity College, and after passing the bar, he practiced law back in New Bern. As a young leader in the Democratic Party, he decided to run for Congress in the Second District against the incumbent James O'Hara, a Black Republican. Factional disputes within the party caused a second Black Republican, Isaac Abbott, to run as well. Secretly, Simmons's father-in-law, Colonel L. W. Humphrey, was funneling money to all three campaigns to ensure a split vote (Zucchino, 2020). As a result, Simmons won despite facing a Black-majority electorate.

Always pragmatic, Simmons offered some support for his Black constituents while in office. He voted for a bill to repay Freedmen Bank depositors and argued against the high tariffs (Anderson, 1980). He ensured the construction of a post office in mostly Black James City and road projects that employed Black laborers. Running for reelection in 1888, Simmons faced a Republican Party more united in their support for Henry P. Cheatham. Also born on a plantation in 1857 – although to an enslaved mother – Cheatham gained an education in freedmen's schools and graduated from Shaw University with the help of a family friend. His decision to challenge Simmons pitted two individuals representing the competing Souths. Cheatham won and went on to serve two terms in the House of Representatives, while Simmons lost what he undoubtedly saw as his birthright.

Simmons sought a return to his seat two years later, but circumstances were shifting. Difficult economic times were causing many White farmers and sharecroppers to leave the Bourbon-dominated Democratic Party and join either the Farmer's Alliance or the Populists. Both parties were challenging entrenched economic interests as they supported public regulation of railroads and the sub-Treasury plan, which was designed to break the local merchant monopoly over agricultural credit. Due to this schism, many disaffected Whites joined an uneasy alliance with Republicans to defeat the

1 Another was W. W. Kitchin, Claude Kitchin's father.

Democratic Party. Sensing the threat to White unity, Simmons withdrew from the race. More importantly, he along with other Democratic Party leaders fully grasped the threat of a "Fusionist" coalition between Black and working-class White voters and began to plot a counterstrategy.

Twice during the 1890s, Simmons was called by the Democratic Party to serve as the state chairman. During these stints, he developed a reputation as a masterful organizer who oversaw the distribution of campaign literature, use of eloquent speakers, and assignment of poll-watchers to ensure meticulous voter canvassing (Watson, 1967). Moreover, he recognized that by developing racist tropes he could manipulate White fears and undermine the "Fusionist" coalition. After a disastrous 1896 electoral defeat, the party turned to him a second time. He orchestrated its campaign efforts during the infamous 1898 election, easily the most vicious and pivotal election in state history. Under his direction, a slate of speakers traveled the state raising the question "of whether in any part of North Carolina men of Anglo-Saxon blood should be subjected to the rule and mastery of the negro" (Rippy, 1936, p. 80). Years later, when reviewing the successful campaign, Simmons explained, "While we dealt with graft and advocated for the free coinage of silver, the keynote of the campaign was White Supremacy, and I believe I was chiefly responsible for the choice of the issue" (Rippy, 1936, p. 26).

One of the speakers traveling the state was a young lawyer from Scotland Neck, Claude Kitchin. Part of an influential political family, Claude began his political career that year organizing a local band of "Red Shirts." Distrusting the effectiveness of messaging alone, the campaign encouraged their deployment across the state. These "Red Shirts" were White vigilantes who paraded through Black neighborhoods brandishing guns and threatening violence to any Black citizens who dared to vote (Watson, 1978). Few did. An able orator, Claude Kitchin inflamed a crowd just days before the election, warning that any Black constable attempting to arrest a White man would be lynched (Zucchino, 2020).

One day after the election, a mob of 2,000 White insurrectionists overthrew the "Fusionist" local government in Wilmington, North Carolina, and stormed through Black neighborhoods burning businesses and homes and murdering upwards of 300 people (Tyson, 2006). Local leaders were banished under threat of further violence while others left fearing for their lives. Officials in Raleigh, including Simmons, clearly supported the insurrection as they saw the biracial government in Wilmington as a threat to White rule. To prevent any further challenges, Simmons shepherded a disenfranchisment amendment to the state constitution that effectively barred

Black voting in North Carolina for more than sixty years. Recognizing his fate, the lone remaining Black member of Congress, George Henry White, chose not to run for reelection in 1900. Instead, Claude Kitchin was easily elected to the Second Congressional District and held the seat for more than two decades.

Sixteen years later, these two White protagonists from the "Black Second" House district had each reached the peak of their political careers as they assumed their chairmanships of their respective tax-writing committees. In equal ascendance was the primacy of White supremacy in Washington, DC. This reality was cemented not simply by the evidence of a lily-White Congress or the segregation of the federal government workforce. A web of laws and norms at the federal, state, and local levels had extinguished the threat that Blacks might pose to White rule. The fear of a biracial coalition fused by shared economic interests had long passed away. It was under these circumstances that the debates on the federal estate and later gift taxes emerged. Few other issues could cut to the heart of the economic conflict festering within White America as much as the growing wealth divide.

ORIGINS OF THE FEDERAL ESTATE TAX

The Sixteenth Amendment cleared the income tax of any constitutional concerns, but not for a tax on wealth. Constitutional clouds remained despite the federal government's enacting wealth transfer taxes three times earlier, each time to deal with revenue needs wrought by war or its threat. Soon after the constitutional ink had dried, Congress faced a major crisis. French naval vessels were boarding American commercial ships to limit trade with its mortal enemy, Great Britain. Lacking a navy to protect American interests, Congress enacted a stamp tax as a requirement on documents that allowed the transfer of decedent wealth. The tax was repealed in 1802 once the diplomatic crisis ended and war had been avoided. Facing an existential threat in 1862, Congress enacted an inheritance tax on personal property above $1,000 to finance wartime expenditures. Once again, the tax was abolished after the need had ended. Lastly, in response to war with Spain, Congress established an estate tax on personal property that lasted little longer than the brief war itself. These examples demonstrated that taxes on wealth could raise needed public funds. This latest tax raised over $14 million (roughly $400 million today) despite its short life and modest design (Jacobson et al., 2007).

Despite these examples, taxes on wealth still generated questions of constitutional legitimacy. Recall that the Court's *Hylton v. United States (1796)* decision concluded that a tax on carriages could not be considered a direct tax, while any tax on real estate might still run afoul of this constitutional prohibition. Subsequent Court decisions offered more hope that an inheritance tax could pass constitutional muster. *Scholey v. Rew (1875)* argued the inheritance tax used during the Civil War represented an excise tax on the *transfer of wealth*; consequently, it was not a direct tax. In *Knowlton v. Moore (1900)*, the Court upheld the 1898 estate tax on personal property, with its graduated rate structure, as constitutional. Still left uncertain was whether an estate tax that included a much larger tax base, one that included real property, would meet constitutional approval.

The 1913 decision to exempt gifts and bequests from being considered taxable income is puzzling. Choosing differently could have saved future Congresses much time and effort spent developing an additional wealth transfer tax. Certainly, their decision was no oversight. The 1894 income tax included "money and the value of all personal property acquired by gift or inheritance" (Wilson-Gorman Tariff of 1894, sec. 28) as a source of taxable income. During Senate discussions of the income tax, Senator Norris (R-NE) offered an amendment that included an additional inheritance tax with graduated tax rates that exempted the first $50,000 and rose to 75 percent of any inheritance above $50 million (50 Congressional Record, 1913, 4422). Without much debate, this amendment was defeated 58–12 (50 Congressional Record, 1913, 4468). A second amendment designed as an estate tax with slightly lower tax rates also was defeated 39–29 without debate (Congressional Record, 1913, 4470). According to one contemporary, the decision to exempt inherited property was in recognition that most states already taxed inheritances as a revenue source (Blakey, 1914). Both amendments acknowledged this conflict by deducting any local tax paid from their federal tax bill. A later observer contended that the lawmakers viewed the two issues as sufficiently different as requiring separate tax systems, as suggested by the stand-alone 1898 estate tax (Klein, 1963). That the offered amendments both added a separate tax rather than amend the definition of income supports this view.

Less than two years after soundly rejecting any inheritance tax, Congress began earnest deliberations on its enactment in response to changing circumstances. The war in Europe had sharply curtailed international trade, causing the largest portion of federal revenues, custom duties, to decline by one-third. The sinking of the Lusitania with the loss of 128 American lives had shifted the American public away from neutrality and increased the prospect of war. In anticipation, the Wilson Administration was proposing $300 million annual increases in military spending. Just as it had done previously, Congress looked to an inheritance tax as a solution to its money woes. As the embryonic income tax was widely viewed as experimental and labeled "little more than ornamental" by the editors of the *Journal of Political Economy* (1915, p. 1001), many viewed estate wealth as a richer source of revenue.

Given its constitutional prerogative, work on the Revenue Act of 1916 commenced in the House Ways and Means Committee, under the supervision of Rep. Kitchin. Considering himself a Bryan Democrat, Rep. Kitchin represented a loose coalition of fifty southern and western Democrats (Brownlee, 1985). These lawmakers embraced a desire to shift the federal tax burden further onto more affluent shoulders along with a wariness for military preparedness and budget deficits. Once again, Rep. Hull was tasked with writing the draft law, which he completed by mid-May (Brownlee, 1985). In preparation, he had studied the inheritance and estate tax laws of European countries and settled on the latter, drawing heavily upon Great Britain's example (Hull, 1948). Taxing one estate versus multiple heirs imposed an easier administrative burden on the struggling Bureau of Internal Revenue (Joulfaian, 1998). Going after the estates of the deceased rather than the heirs would appeal to those lawmakers interested in taxing the "idle rich" while limiting the political fallout from the tax. In contrast to prior inheritance laws, Hull's estate tax included both personal and real property. He hoped to create a permanent estate tax that effectively taxed wealth despite the jurisdictional and administrative challenges (Brownlee, 1985).

One jurisdictional challenge facing Hull was that most states already taxed inheritances, creating a fear that the federal government would usurp this revenue source (Blakey, 1916). Several times in the debate, lawmakers disclosed that forty-two states had some form of an inheritance tax. Normally effective, this argument of states' rights was undercut as it was the Democrats who were pushing for the tax. Estate tax supporters argued the states were poorly positioned to enact an effective tax since the rich could simply move their residency. As evidence, supporters divulged that the state levies collected only $28 million in 1915, an amount far less than the $132 million raised by Great Britain's tax despite a much smaller wealth base (Blakey, 1916). To limit the states' rights argument, Hull proposed a high threshold of $50,000 (about $1 million today) before the federal tax would bite.

Working quickly and without the help of its Republican members, the Ways and Means Committee submitted their draft bill to the full House on July 1. Designed to raise needed revenue, it doubled the top tax rates on both the personal and corporate income taxes, added an excess profits tax on the munitions industry, increased certain "sin taxes" that targeted the urban middle class, and introduced an estate tax. Somewhat lost amidst these initiatives, Hull's new tax escaped much of the criticism leveled at the bill. Well aware of the powerful interests this tax proposal would arouse, Rep. Kitchin pushed it through to House approval with just a few days of debate. Senate rules gave the bill's opponents time to marshal their forces, causing Sen. Simmons to face greater headwinds in getting the bill approved. After three weeks of debate, the Senate approved a similar bill that quickly went to conference and final approval in both chambers. President Wilson signed the bill known as the Revenue Act of 1916. It has been called "the most dramatic departure toward progressive, re-distributional taxation" (Brownlee, 1985, p. 173) in the way that it shifted the federal tax structure from one based on consumption to one based on income and wealth.

Somewhat surprisingly, little of the Congressional debate focused on the estate tax provision. While Rep. Percy Quin (D-MS) defended it as enabling the government "to get it out of the class of idle rich who are riding around in $10,000 limousines, with poodle dogs on their laps" (53 Congressional Record, 1916, 10613), most supporters took a more measured approach. According to Rep. Dickinson (D-MO), "While the young men without wealth, the very flower of our country, bear the burden of battle and the exposure to disease, let wealth, secure at home, pay a reasonable percentage for the support for the Government and for this preparedness demanded by wealth and the country" (53 Congressional Record, 1916, 10602).

Indeed, the tax rates applied to the estates were quite modest, ranging from an initial rate of 1 percent rising to just 10 percent on net estates above $5 million (about $100 million today). Still, Rep. Collier (D-MS) insisted that this tax on estates offers the "only way that some of the largest estates worth millions, which heretofore escaped Federal taxation and, in many instances, have paid no taxes at all either to State or Federal authority, will be reached" (53 Congressional Record, 1916, 10583). While offering a means of taxing this wealth, its modest tax bite and the absence of a companion gift tax limited its actual threat.

While Congress left the gift tax absence unresolved, it did address the low tax rates the following year. With the country's entry into World War I, the need for additional federal funds became even more pressing. In response, Congress raised the top estate tax rate from 10 to 25 percent and doubled the bottom rate to 2 percent. To lessen opposition to the higher rates, Congress doubled the threshold to $10 million (about $200 million today) before the highest rate would apply. Although Congress lowered the bottom rate back to 1 percent the following year, the higher rates remained in place. Yet, these higher rates would remain cosmetic until Congress added the companion gift tax.

CHALLENGES TO THE ESTATE TAX

The estate tax suffered major challenges to its existence and effectiveness, both legal and political. Rather quickly, the New York Trust Bank on behalf of a decedent client sued to test the law's constitutional basis. The plaintiffs argued the estate tax imposed the burden *prior* to any transfer of wealth, unlike an inheritance tax that assesses the beneficiary *after* the transfer. Since the transfer had not yet occurred, the plaintiffs disputed that the tax could be viewed as an excise or indirect tax. Moreover, they contended that an estate tax limited a key property right – the right to transfer the asset – while the inheritance tax dealt with the privilege of receiving a gift. In upholding the estate tax, Justice Oliver Wendell Holmes found the distinction immaterial as he argued, "if a tax on property distributed by the laws of a State, determined by the fact that distribution has been accomplished, is valid, a tax determined by the fact that distribution is about to begin is no greater interference and is equally good" (*New York Trust v. Eisner*, 1921, para. 5).While this decision appears to have become settled law, there are some who find this argument unpersuasive and continue to question the constitutionality of the estate tax (Lowenstein & Kisska-Schulze, 2018).

Other Court decisions undermined the effectiveness of the law. Under the Revenue Act of 1916, the gross estate is defined as "value at time of death of all property, real or personal, tangible or intangible, wherever situated" (Title II, §202). It also includes any gifts transferred within two years of death or any claims to jointly held property. The law then details the possible deductions to the gross estate, including funeral and executor's expenses, support payments to dependents during settlement, outstanding debt, or uninsured losses, as well as any estate tax payments made to other jurisdictions. Clearly, Congress intended to define the taxable estate broadly and comprehensively. Regrettably, the Supreme Court demonstrated other ideas in a series of decisions. In *Crooks v. Harrelson (1930)*, the Court ruled that land belonging to the decedent in states where land passed directly to heirs would not be considered part of the estate. The Court dismantled the two-year prior gift rule in *Heiner v. Donnan (1932)* as it could not discern which gifts were made in contemplation of death. Even worse, the Court, in a series of rulings including *May v. Heiner (1930)*, argued that transfers of wealth through trusts that did not transfer its possession, enjoyment, and title at the time of death could not be taxed under the estate tax (Lowndes, 1960). These rulings offered tax lawyers numerous opportunities to devise legal maneuvers like large insurance policies, life estates, and generation-skipping trusts to avoid the estate tax.

In some cases, Congress roused itself and produced a response as these leaks were recognized. The *May v. Heiner* (1930) decision so severely limited which property transfers were subject to the estate tax that an outraged Congress passed a joint resolution the following day that partially closed the newly created loophole (Lowndes, 1960). In other cases, Congressional action created leaks. In 1918, Congress added charitable giving as one new exemption to reduce the net estate. On a smaller scale, they transformed the deduction for any state inheritance taxes into a federal tax credit, effectively enabling more wealth to transfer. Initially, this credit was limited to 25 percent of the federal tax owed but subsequently was raised to 80 percent. Not until 1924 did the Congress finally enact a federal gift tax and thereby plug the largest leak in the wealth transfer bucket.

The second major challenge, this time a political one, occurred several years later. Relief and joy at gaining victory in Europe gave way to the challenges of enduring the Spanish flu pandemic and an economy struggling to find peacetime prosperity. Hampered by wartime controls, organized labor insisted on recapturing wages lost to inflation during the war years. Reluctance among employers to meet these demands led to a period of strikes, lockouts, and violent confrontations. Black servicemen returned from Europe after fighting to "keep the world safe for democracy" with a raised awareness of the racial oppression operating back home. Rising aspirations for change were met with equally committed responses of force and violence in support of the status quo. As racial tensions escalated, cities like East St. Louis (1917) and then a host of cities during the Red Summer of 1919, ranging from Omaha and Chicago in the west to Syracuse and Charleston in the east erupted in racial violence. On the promise of returning prosperity and "normalcy," the Republican Party swept back into power in the 1920 election, capturing the White House as well as both houses of Congress. Restoring prosperity would include revisiting the income and estate taxes, while normalcy would be on display as the KKK marched in full regalia down Constitution Avenue between the White House and the Capitol.

President-elect Warren Harding quickly named Andrew Mellon, one of country's wealthiest men, as Treasury Secretary; Mellon would remain in this role for over a decade through the Coolidge and Hoover Administrations. At the time, some quipped that all three Republican presidents worked under the Secretary. Born into the wealthy Mellon family,

Andrew expanded the family's banking and industrial empire. As Treasury Secretary, he made tax reform one of his top priorities, including the repeal of the estate tax (Blakey, 1924). Given the precedence that all previous wealth taxes had served as temporary sources to fund wartime expenses, there was a strong argument that this tax should follow the same fate. By 1924, the federal government had repaid most of its war debts and was running budget surpluses, making this argument persuasive (Blakey, 1924). Despite Republican control of the federal government, a coalition of fiscal conservatives, progressive Republicans, and Democrats resisted efforts to repeal the tax. Notwithstanding his antipathy and nearly eleven years as Treasury Secretary, Mellon was never successful in eliminating the estate tax. When the Depression hit, it was ready to serve as a source of needed revenue to help a floundering economy.

SHOWING AMBIVALENCE TO THE GIFT TAX

Even more surprising, the same disparate coalition of lawmakers who defended the estate tax were able to enact a federal gift tax over the objections of Secretary Mellon and now President Coolidge. To forestall any interest in raising taxes, the Coolidge Administration presented an appealing array of tax cuts known as the Mellon Plan. This included slashing the top income tax rate in half while making substantial cuts in excise taxes on telephones, telegrams, and theater admissions. These cuts were carefully crafted to appeal to both the rich and working class. The Mellon Plan's supporters believed the allure of lower taxes would blunt support for a gift tax, particularly among those lawmakers running for reelection. However, the Mellon Plan met its match in facing the Bonus Plan for World War I veterans.

Having missed a booming economy while at war, World War I veterans returned home to an economy mired in recession. Facing high unemployment, veteran organizations, like the powerful American Legion, lobbied for an "adjusted service compensation" that became known colloquially as a "bonus" (Alstott & Novick, 2005). Initially, the bonus called for $1.25 per day of service abroad up to a maximum of $625. In addition, veterans could apply their benefit toward vocational training or loan assistance in buying a home or farm (Alstott & Novick, 2005). Arguing the nation could not afford both tax cuts and bonus payments, Secretary Mellon miscalculated politically as he pitted the Mellon Plan directly against the Bonus Plan. Recognizing his mistakes, his opponents swooped in. As Rep. Quin framed the issue:

> The people who have the wealth, the ones who stayed at home, the ones who profiteered during the war, lying down in good warm beds, eating three square meals a day, asking the divine blessing every morning at table, now oppose giving these boys the bonus, while these boys, who were on the high seas with submarines and German assassins trying to sink them every day, who, while they were across, yonder in France, in Belgium, and even on the soil of Germany itself, were standing waist deep in mud, with bullets whistling all around their heads, gas floating around them, now simply ask through their organizations that the people of the United States give them one little lousy dollar a day, none of them to get in excess of $500. Yet these great fortune holders of the country object to that, and upon what grounds? They say that it will disturb business. (64 Congressional Record, 1924, 3110)

The appeal of lower taxes could not overcome this argument.

Much to the dismay of Secretary Mellon and other fiscal conservatives, Congress chose both tempting options, what some called the "pie a la mode" option. They did so by offering key concessions to gain the support of lawmakers concerned about federal deficits. First, the bill shifted the veteran bonus from cash to a $650 bonus (roughly $9,800 today) payable as a Certificate of Service maturing in twenty years. While veterans could use this certificate to leverage bank loans for cash, it curtailed the immediate need for federal revenues.[2] Second, the tax bill included some of Mellon's proposed tax cuts, although scaled back.[3] To raise needed revenues, the bill raised the top estate tax rate to 40 percent and created a federal gift tax. Under this law, donors could avoid the tax if they kept their separate gifts below $500 and their total lifetime gifts below $50,000. Like the estate tax, the high thresholds exempted most gifts. Still, very large gifts would be subject to this tax.

Unlike the estate tax, the federal gift tax was not long-lived. Forced to sign the Revenue Act of 1924 that passed both the House and Senate by veto-proof margins, President Coolidge vowed he would "bend all of his energies" to produce a tax bill more to his liking (Blakey, 1926). Buoyed by the 1924 election results and the increased Republican majorities in both houses, the Administration planned a concerted strategy to ensure a different outcome. Wanting to meet an early spring deadline, the Congress took unprecedented action by starting hearings on the bill the previous fall

[2] One questions whether Black veterans could gain such credit given the level of racism at the time.

[3] Some may recall hearing in recent years about the Revenue Act of 1924. One of the provisions of the bill was the option of Congressional leaders to request any individual's federal income tax filings. Recent efforts to gain former President Trump's tax statements have relied upon this law.

(Blakey, 1926). That way, the Revenue Act of 1926 was the first bill filed on the first day of the spring session. At the hearings, Secretary Mellon reasserted his dislike for both the estate and gift taxes but gave primary focus to the latter. He claimed that reducing estate tax rates to moderate levels made the gift tax unnecessary. Moreover, levying a gift tax conflicted with the aim of breaking up large fortunes (Blakey, 1926). Given the overwhelming Republican majorities, Congress repealed the two-year-old gift tax without much public debate. Although the legislation reduced the estate tax rates by about half, it did leave the tax in place, although just barely. The provision allowing tax payments to the states to replace up to 80 percent of the federal estate bill assured the states would gain the primary share of any revenues (Luckey, 2003). This change along with the elimination of the federal gift tax left the estate tax on life support, undermining its value as a source of federal revenues or restraint on the growing concentration of wealth.

THE ASCENDANT PERIOD

Just six years later, the country found itself mired in the Great Depression. The shuttering of factories and businesses, skyrocketing unemployment, foreclosures of homes and farms, and migrating families dominated the landscape. Once again, the federal government faced collapsing tax revenues, rising demands for help, and spiraling budget deficits. The Treasury forecasts predicted federal revenues would fall by nearly half from their 1930 levels (Blakey & Blakey, 1932). Despite the pervasive distress throughout the country, Congress mostly worried about finding new revenues to limit budget deficits that would further dampen "business confidence." At one point during the debate, House Speaker Garner (D-TX) challenged any member who did not believe the federal budget should be balanced to stand up. No one did (Cooper, 2010).

While the Democrats had secured a modest majority in the House, the Republicans retained slim control in the Senate, albeit with the help of an insurgent bloc of progressive Republicans (Blakey & Blakey, 1932). Once again, the two parties were locked in vitriolic debate over tax policy – whether to tax consumption in the form of a national sales tax or to tax income and wealth. As negotiations stalled with the pivotal 1932 election looming, Rep. Ramseyer (R-IA) offered what became known as the Ramseyer Amendment. His plan reintroduced the federal gift tax and expanded the estate tax. Long an advocate of both, he argued that the growing wealth offered the federal government "a large and inexhaustible reservoir"[4] of tax revenue, one that could lessen other "burdensome taxes now weighing so heavily on the backs of the people."[5] Without much debate, the Congress adopted the Ramseyer Amendment over an alternative proposal that aimed to raise the estate tax even higher (Cooper, 2010).

The enacted legislation expanded the federal estate tax in several ways. It returned the exemption on taxable estates back to $50,000, thereby increasing its collection.[6] It doubled the top rate on estates exceeding $10 million from 20 to 45 percent. Over the next three years, Congress extended the reach of this tax as it lowered the exemption to $30,000 and raised the top rate to 70 percent.[7] To impede easy tax avoidance, the law resurrected the federal gift tax. This tax carried an annual gift exclusion of $5,000 per recipient and offered a similar $50,000 lifetime exemption. Support for these changes clearly resulted from the recognition that the wealthy were exempt from much of a tax burden. As Rep. Swing (R-CA) contended, "After allowing the big boys to play with their money during their lifetime and after allowing them the pleasure and pride of piling up dollar on dollar, while living, a generous estate tax should be levied on their death" (75 Congressional Record, 1932, 5906). Yet, Congress designed these taxes with objectives other than simply soaking the rich.

Rep. Ramseyer, along with other members of Congress, was acutely aware of the estate tax's long gestation. Delays caused by the need to probate estates meant any increase in revenues were several years away. But Congress needed more money, and sooner rather than later. Rep. Hill (D-WA) bluntly stated the dilemma: "It takes a period of 18 months under existing law before you can get settlements of these estates, and we need money now" (75 Congressional Record, 1932, 6352). To meet this need, Congress designed the gift tax with special features to advance this flow. First, they separated the gift and estate tax exemptions, giving the wealthy an additional exemption if they transferred wealth while living. Second, Congress set the gift tax at 75 percent of their estate tax rates to offer further encouragement. Lastly, they designed the gift tax levy as tax inclusive, making this option even more attractive. According to Rep. Canfield (D-IN), Congress designed this tax "with the expressed hope that it would persuade

4 Statement of Rep. Ramseyer, House Hearings, 1921, as cited in Cooper (2010, p. 891).

5 Statement of Rep. Ramseyer, House Hearings, 1921, as cited in Cooper (2010, p. 892).

6 The exemption was raised to $100,000 in 1926.

7 In addition, the law froze the state estate tax credit to its 1926 levels. This would allow the federal government to collect more of the rising revenues expected from the tax. This would remain until the tax credit was reverted to a tax deduction in 2001.

owners of large estates to make gifts to their heirs as soon as possible" (75 Congressional Record, 1932, 5903). Their efforts bore relatively quick dividends. Within five years, tax collections increased nearly ten times and the two taxes collectively contributed nearly 10 percent of federal revenue, their highest share ever over their entire history (Joulfaian, 1998).

Over the next decade, Congress expanded both taxes as Depression-era and then wartime expenses mounted. Congress raised the top rate on the estate tax several times until it reached 77 percent. To preempt opposition to the high rates, Congress initially raised the required threshold to $50 million before returning it to $10 million. At the other end, Congress settled on an estate exemption of $60,000 before triggering the tax while raising the minimum rate from 1 to 3 percent. Gift tax rates adjusted accordingly at their 75 percent levels, while the separate gift tax exemption was lowered to $30,000. Although not without substantial leaks, this highly progressive tax structure gave the country a legitimate wealth transfer tax system for the first time. Amazingly, it remained largely untouched until the mid-1970s. Perhaps, speaking for many of his colleagues, Rep. Davis (D-TN) stated, "I do not want to 'soak' anybody, but it would be better to soak the rich than to starve the poor" (75 Congressional Record, 1932, 6258).

The available evidence supports the view that the federal estate and gift taxes functioned reasonably well over this period. Figure 7.1 depicts the growth of real household wealth, the percentage of adult decedents required to file and their real gross estate. All of the variables are indexed to 1933 to illustrate what happened during this ascendant period. Over the forty-year period, real household wealth nearly quadrupled, with most of that growth occurring in the post-World War II boom. As a result of this good fortune, more estates became subject to the tax, causing both the rate of filers and their gross estates to grow even faster. The progressive nature of this tax appears to respond effectively to the rising household wealth. One legitimate concern at the time was the rising rate of decedents required to file. A period of high inflation pushed a greater number of smaller estates over the fixed exemption level, causing a surge in the tax's administrative costs. Even in the peak year, not quite 8 percent of decedents were required to file. Moreover, simply adding an inflation adjustment to the threshold could easily remedy this problem.

It is likely that another problem triggered the changes that were about to come. Figure 7.2 retains the three variables in Figure 7.1 but adds the real value of the estate and gift tax collections over the period. As is evident, the growth in tax collections dwarfs those shown in Figure 7.1. The tax collections increase 40 to 50 times in real terms from their 1933 levels. This surge

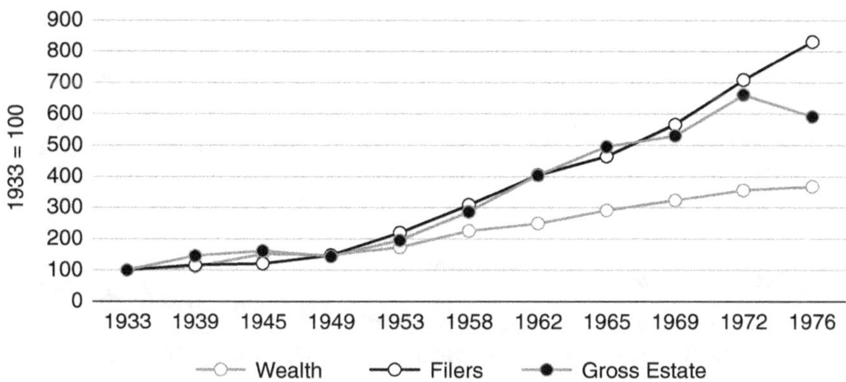

Figure 7.1 Impact of wealth transfer taxes, 1933–76, Take I
Source: Author's calculations; Bureau of Internal Revenue (1935); Internal Revenue Service (n.d.) Taxable Estate Returns; Joulfaian (1998); US Census (1936); Wolff (2018), p. 558

in taxes stems from two main sources. Clearly, the changes made by lawmakers in the 1930s had an impact as the tax revenues expanded over the decade or so. However, the main growth occurred during the postwar boom. As households were experiencing prosperity and the accompanying rising asset values, more of that wealth was being captured by the estate and gift taxes. Of course, most of that captured wealth was being collected from White families, thereby raising the threat posed by these taxes.

During the postwar period, Congress amended several marital deductions that each added leaks to the tax collection effort. In the first instance, Congress remedied an issue of tax fairness caused by differences in state laws. In *common law* states, joint property acquired during marriage is assigned to the spouse who acquired it. This acquisition rule would affect the estate of the deceased spouse. In *community property* states, any acquired property is assigned equally to both spouses. The death of either spouse would leave half of their joint property in the estate. Given progressive tax rates, married households in *community property* states would pay lower estate taxes after both spouses are deceased. Congress resolved this disparity in 1948 by creating a 50 percent marital deduction whereby half of the deceased's gross estate is shielded from any tax. In practical terms, this change enabled married households to keep more of their wealth longer. In 1981, Congress doubled down and expanded the deduction to 100 percent. Effectively, this change treats both spouses as one tax unit, except for two notable exceptions. The deceased spouse's assets are stepped up in basis before being transferred to the surviving spouse, suggesting they are still

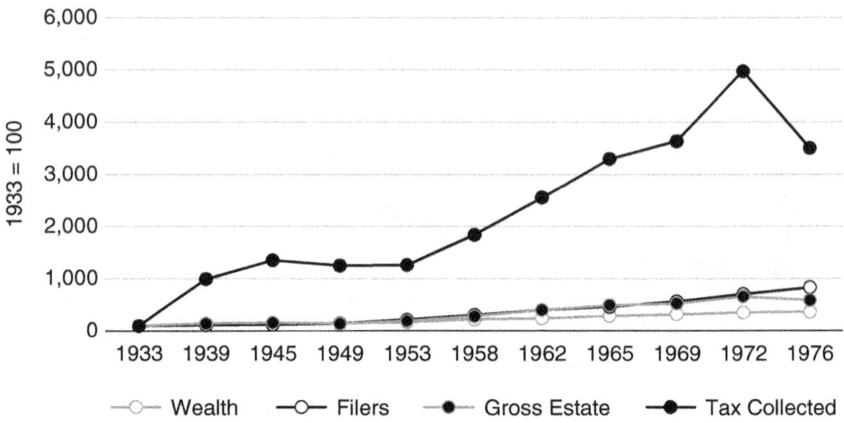

Figure 7.2 Impact of wealth transfer taxes, 1933–76, Take II
Source: Author's calculations; Bureau of Internal Revenue (1935); Internal Revenue Service (n.d.) Taxable Estate Returns; Joulfaian (1998); US Census (1936); Wolff (2018), p. 558

two distinct individuals (Joulfaian, 2007). Death of the first spouse not only brings relief from any estate tax, but also removes any income tax liability on the sale of appreciating assets.

Congress made one other important change in 1948. They enacted what is known as the *split-gift rule.* With the consent of both spouses, any gift from one can be split by both spouses, thereby allowing the household to be viewed as two individual givers. This effectively allows married households to double their gifts before they become liable to file or pay any gift taxes. Again, this exception allows families to transfer more wealth to their heirs. These exceptions reveal the arcane and contradictory nature of many tax rules. What they demonstrate is how the specific tax treatment depends on which interpretation works best for affluent households. Again, this inconsistent treatment works to the benefit of White households due to their greater net worth.

THE UNRAVELING

Other than these technical changes in the treatment of married households, Congress largely left the federal estate and gift taxes untouched through the postwar period. This neglect persisted despite their awareness of large leaks in the wealth transfer system caused by generation-skipping trusts and the preferential treatment given to inter vivos gifts. Technically separate but still related were the loopholes created by the step-up in basis given to appreciating assets at death and noncash charitable gifts. By the 1970s, many lawmakers were eager to tackle these issues after leaving them ignored for a generation (Senzaki, 1976). In retrospect, this effort stands as the last time that Congress marshalled a collective will to strengthen the wealth transfer tax system and redress remaining leaks. However, the resultant Tax Reform Act of 1976 must be judged as a regrettable failure. Nearly all of its major accomplishments were quickly rescinded, while its efforts were compromised by the need to make concessions (Senzaki, 1976). It marks the beginning of a slow dissolution of the wealth transfer tax system.

One important accomplishment is that the law did unify the estate and gift taxes. Although the two taxes functioned as complements, their separate design offered wealthy households several ways to avoid paying taxes. First, the annual and lifetime gift exemptions of $3,000 and $30,000, respectively, gave the rich varied ways to reduce their estates. As long as they did not exceed the $3,000 annual limit per recipient, the wealthy could reduce their estate as much as they desired. Gifts above that level would need to accumulate above the $30,000 lifetime cap before they would be trigger a gift tax liability. Second, the wealthy could lower their tax bill by splitting their wealth between inter vivos gifts and estate bequests and qualify for lower tax rates on both. Third, the preferential tax rates given to inter vivos gifts allowed the wealthy to save even further by transferring their wealth now rather than later. Lastly, the gift tax was assessed on a tax-exclusive basis which lowered further the taxes due. In each of these ways, tax policy encouraged households to make inter vivos gifts in order to avoid paying taxes. These gifts likely assisted in the growth of dynastic wealth in families across generations as the earlier gifts gave younger generations more time to leverage that wealth.

The tax bill created a unified tax framework in which tax rates and exemption levels would apply similarly to both gifts and bequests. To harmonize the tax rates, Congress compromised between the two; for example, the top estate tax rate was reduced from 77 to 70, while the gift tax was raised from its 57.5 percent rate. Regarding the exemption, Congress took a different approach. It combined the two exemptions into one and enacted regular increases starting at $120,000 in 1977 and rising to $175,000 by 1981. This effectively doubled the available exemption over five years and ignited continual increases thereafter. This initial increase was largely driven by influential farmers worried that rising land prices might jeopardize the transfer of their farm to the next generation. Although this problem was hardly an extensive one, their outsized impact on the deliberations is undeniable (Surrey, 1976b). This pressure to offer preferential tax treatment to family farms (and closely held businesses) overcame warnings raised during the hearings about the rising concentration of wealth (Surrey, 1976b). In response to the higher exemption, Congress did raise the minimum tax rate from 3 to 18 percent. While all of these changes effectively unified the two taxes, they did leave one difference unchanged – the dissimilar ways the two taxes are calculated.

Raising the exemption levels required Congress to find ways to offset the expected revenue losses. This prompted a review of a long-standing problem, the (income) tax forgiveness extended to unrealized capital gains in the deceased's estate. Back in 1969, a Treasury Department study recommended redesignating death as a "realization event" and then levying a capital gains assessment against the deceased's last income tax filing (Zaritsky, 1977). This would eliminate the estate step-up in basis exclusion and generate significant revenue. Powerful lobbies like the American Bankers Association fiercely resisted this remedy and nearly stalled the whole reform effort. This forced Congress to choose a compromise that few desired – treating the assets on a carryover basis. This would make the heirs liable for a substantial tax bill whenever they chose to sell the asset. While this solution would have reduced the tax leakage somewhat, it created such a political backlash that it was quickly rescinded.

The need for more revenue also encouraged Congress to close the tax loophole made available through the use of GSTs. In tackling this problem, the House Ways and Means Committee emphasized the need for tax uniformity and fairness. According to the Committee Report:

> The purpose of the Federal estate and gift taxes is not only to raise revenue, but also to do so in a manner which has *as nearly as possible a uniform effect, generation by generation*. These policies of revenue raising and equal treatment are best served where the transfer taxes (estate and gift) are imposed, on the average, at reasonably uniform intervals. Likewise, these policies are frustrated where the imposition of transfer taxes is deferred for very long intervals, as possible, under present law, through the use of generation-skipping trusts ... Your committee recognized that there are many legitimate nontax purposes for establishing trusts. However, it also believes that the tax laws should be neutral and that there should be no tax advantage available in setting up trusts.[8] (emphasis mine)

Hewing to the concept of tax uniformity, lawmakers drafted a bill that tried to treat GST assets as if the wealth is simply transferred from one generation to the next. However, arcane tax laws and complex estate planning strategies stymied this effort. The result was a tax law that failed the test of

[8] House Committee Report HR 14844, as cited in Surrey (1976b).

tax simplicity and easy understanding. According to one expert, the new law "failed to provide a tax system that is readily understandable in routine transfer situations" (Radford, 1977, p. 575). In the interest of tax equity, Congress created a tax that generated so much confusion and consternation that it was rescinded and replaced a decade later (Zaritsky, 1977).

Despite its demise, this initial GST tax did have two lasting consequences. Most importantly, the law grandfathered all prior GSTs, thereby shielding vast sums of wealth from the federal tax system (Surrey, 1976b). In setting up the new tax, Congress created another generous exemption as an offer of compromise. Under the law, donors could transfer $250,000 tax free into their GST, a figure that could be doubled by the split transfer option available to married households. This figure would become the standard for future increases in exemption levels.

As disappointing as this effort proved to be, it represented the last major action to tighten the federal wealth transfer tax system. Since then, opponents of the "death tax" have relentlessly undermined its effectiveness in collecting federal revenues and restraining the growing concentration of dynastic wealth. This effort started quickly. In 1981, Congress bestowed several gifts to the wealthy. They doubled down on raising the lifetime exemption of gifts and estates, increasing both to $600,000 in five years. Over a mere decade, Congress had increased these exemptions by ten- and twenty-fold. Exhibiting some restraint, the law only increased the annual gift exemption three-fold, from $3,000 to $10,000 per recipient. Past limits on marital transfers were eliminated, making them fully tax exempt. Moreover, the law reduced the top tax bracket from 70 to 55 percent. Each of these changes offered direct assistance to families wanting to keep and transfer dynastic wealth. Lastly, the legislation boosted the special exclusion given to family farms and closely held businesses from $500,000 to $750,000.[9] Most of these family farms can trace their lineage back to the homesteading laws discussed in earlier chapters.

Just five years later, Congress engaged in a tax reform effort that many tax policy experts look upon with nostalgia. The Tax Reform Act of 1986 reflected a Congress able to ignore powerful special interests as it eliminated tax loopholes and slashed income tax rates. As discussed in Chapter 6, several of the wealth-based tax expenditures were pruned during this effort. Amidst this extensive tax review, the estate and gift taxes

[9] Rather than value these assets at their fair market value, they could be assessed based on their capitalized income or on similarly engaged enterprises. The difference between these two values could be excluded from the estate up to the limit designated.

were largely ignored. One exception was the unworkable GST tax. Its replacement swapped a simple, flat rate equal to the top estate tax rate for the graduated tax rates in the earlier tax. The new version is designed to tax wealth each time it crosses a generation, including direct transfers to distant generations (grandchildren and great-grandchildren) that wholly skip a generation. As a peace offering to the wealthy and their estate attorneys, the law increased the initial exemption from $250,000 to $1,000,000. Of course, the split rule meant that both adults in the married household could exercise this exemption, thereby doubling it.

Over the last thirty-five years, Congress has relentlessly expanded the tax leakages and reduced the effectiveness of all three taxes. In several steps, the top tax bracket, now unified across all three taxes, has been slashed from 55 to 40 percent. By 2002, the estate and gift tax exemptions were raised to $1 million to unify them with the GST exclusion; additionally, all are now subject to an automatic inflation adjustment. Several times subsequently, Congress has raised the exemption substantially to its current level of $13.61 million in 2024.[10] Of course, the split-gift rule means that married couples can double this exclusion. For one year, the estate and GST taxes were eliminated, although the gift tax was retained. The primary result of these changes is that many fewer households, other than the extremely rich, really need to engage in estate planning.

The impact of these changes can be seen in Figure 7.3. Similar to the previous figure, I illustrate the recent trends in real household wealth, the percentage of adult decedents required to file, real gross estate, and real tax collections. Each of these values is indexed at their level in 1976, the year we see the modern shift toward dismantling the wealth tax system begin. As the figure illustrates, real household wealth has quadrupled over the past forty years. In contrast, the number of filers has fallen almost to zero while the value of gross estates considered along with tax collections are below their 1976 levels. The disparate trends are particularly apparent after 2001 as the exemption was increased without restraint. These changes have effectively dismantled the federal wealth taxes in all but name only.

One graphic in particular illustrates how the nation's wealth transfer tax system has been undermined in recent decades. Over the years, the estate tax has provided the overwhelming share of collected revenue while the gift tax has functioned simply to limit tax avoidance. This means we need

[10] This increase over the prior year's exemption of $690,000 is greater than the total exemption offered over the first eighty-five years of the estate tax.

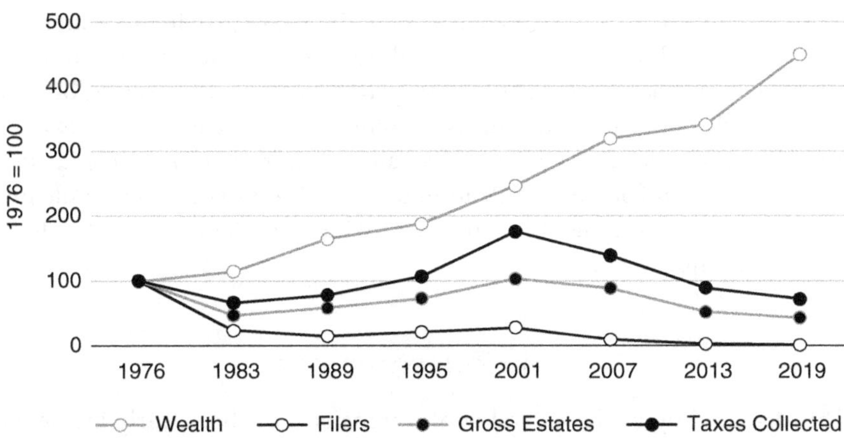

Figure 7.3 Impact of wealth transfer taxes since 1976
Source: Author's calculations; Internal Revenue Service (n.d.) Taxable Estate Returns; Wolff (2018), p. 558

Figure 7.4 Estate tax exemptions
Source: Author's calculations; US Department of Treasury

only examine the history of the estate tax exemption to understand what has happened.[11] Figure 7.4 depicts this history as it tracks the exemption over the period in real dollars. Over the first sixty years, the estate tax exemption remained relatively stable as it fluctuated around what would

[11] Since 1977, the estate and gift tax exemptions have been unified.

be equivalent to $1 million today. As such, it always provided a generous threshold that allowed many households to transfer moderate amounts of wealth without bother. Over the past quarter century, the exemption has been raised numerous times to its current astronomical heights. Today, no one but the very rich need to worry about estate planning. Indeed, just two-tenths of one percent of all adult decedent's estates needed to file for the tax in 2019. And the tax currently provides less than 1 percent of federal tax revenue.

THE CONSEQUENCES

This dismantling of the federal wealth transfer taxes has clearly impacted the intergenerational transfers of household wealth. On the one hand, there is no evidence that these changes have broadened the transfer of wealth. Returning to the SCF data, the share of households reporting the receipt of some substantial gift or bequest has hovered around 21 percent over a thirty-year period. Similarly, the number of households who *expect* to receive a gift or inheritance has fluctuated around 14 percent. In contrast, the average amounts reported on both figures have increased significantly, indicating the wealth transfers are deepening. Typically, White households account for over 90 percent of the transfers even as their share of the population falls below 70 percent. Figure 7.5 compares how much past family gifts and bequests have benefited White and Black households and depicts

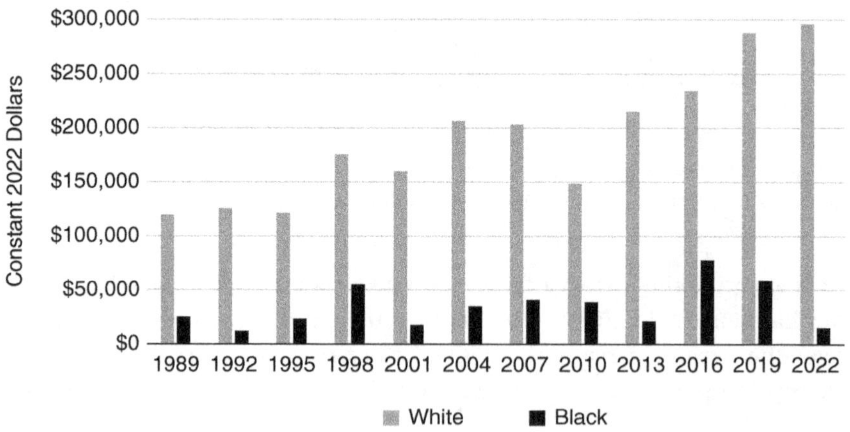

Figure 7.5 Average inherited wealth
Source: Author's calculations; Federal Reserve Board, Survey of Consumer Finances

the changes over time.[12] In both cases, the annual values are subject to a cyclical pattern. However, White inherited wealth is clearly increasing over time while the pattern among Black households is static. Moreover, the absolute advantage experienced by White households is growing dramatically. What was less than a $100,000 gap in 1989 grew to almost $300,000 in 2022. The efforts to dismantle the federal wealth transfer taxes are clearly working to expand White wealth and cement further the persistence of White supremacy.

CONCLUSION

The origins of our federal estate and gift taxes, like the wealth-related tax expenditures discussed previously, reside during a period in which White treatment of Black civil rights was at its nadir. Overt displays of White supremacy were constructed throughout the country, not simply in the South. The KKK experienced a wave of ascendancy as membership swelled and social acceptance expanded. Violence against Blacks, whether in the form of lynching or mob carnage in Black neighborhoods, was all too common. Neither stirred local law enforcement into action. Racially tailored voting restrictions and gerrymandering ensured a lily-White Congress. Worse, the main stewards of the federal estate tax, Sen. Furnifold Simmons and Rep. Claude Kitchin orchestrated and benefited from a violence-laden political campaign that ended Black voting in North Carolina for sixty years.[13] Given their experiences with the "Black Second," it is unlikely that either along with their political allies would have championed the estate tax as long as Black political power was freely exercised. The need for White racial unity would have trumped any desire to realign the federal tax burden.

The enactment and expansion of the federal estate and gift taxes stemmed as much from the need for federal revenues as from any concern about the expanding wealth divide. Fear of war birthed the federal estate tax in 1916, while financial desperation led to the federal gift tax's resurrection. Even the introduction of the GST tax in 1976 owes its enactment to revenue concerns as much as to limiting intergenerational

[12] Many of these transfers were received years before the survey date. To account for their value over time, I assume that the recipients deposited them the following January 1 in an S&P index fund and left them until July 1 of the survey year. I then took the values from each survey year and calculated their values in 2022 dollars.

[13] Two other primary sponsors of the estate tax, Cordell Hull and President Woodrow Wilson, also held deep-seated anti-Black views.

transfers of wealth. Assuredly, their progressive tax rates that targeted the rich engendered significant political support. Yet, the persistent loopholes argue that Congress was never able to mobilize sufficient backing to create a truly effective tax system. Consequently, a potentially rich source of federal funds was never adequately tapped. Unlike the personal income tax, these wealth transfer taxes have never been given their due as a significant source of federal revenue.

The most striking aspect of our nation's history with the modern wealth transfer tax system is what has happened since 1976. Whatever consensus existed regarding the need to limit dynastic family wealth disintegrated over recent decades. One Congress after another has unraveled this system, even to the point of repeal for one year. At one level, there is nothing overtly racialized by these actions. However, the persistent undermining of these taxes solely benefits wealthy households and their heirs. The overwhelming majority of these beneficiaries are White, many of whom benefit indirectly and directly from past and current federal assistance, respectively. All of these policies have fueled a massive increase in inheritances among White households over the past generation, thereby adding another wedge to the widening racial wealth gap.

As we have seen throughout this book, federal wealth policies have played an important role in the expansion of White household wealth that has allowed White Americans to dominate American society. Whether constitutional protections offered to enslavers, free land offered to White homesteaders, loan guarantees offered to White homebuyers, or generous benefits provided to White veterans, past federal policies targeted their assistance to White households, frequently overtly, in their efforts to achieve financial security. In countless cases, this federal generosity enabled White households the means to endow their children with a head start. These past policies meant that many White households over the past half century owned homes and other assets, making them eligible to receive the ever-increasing tax breaks. As this wealth swelled in White America, there was increasing pressure to dismantle the estate and gift taxes to allow easier and more complete transmission of this wealth across generations. Taken collectively, these three streams of federal wealth policy have created and currently foster the widening racial wealth gap. It is a system that cannot help but cement economic stratification and expand racial disparities.

One cannot ignore that the 1970s serve as a watershed for our contemporary federal wealth policies. The Kerner Commission had recently offered its frank appraisal of the structural racism deeply rooted in American society. The Commission's findings argued for federal policies that targeted Black households in their efforts to build wealth and work toward financial independence. Yet, the modest opportunities afforded to Black Americans due to the dismantling of Jim Crow barriers threatened the racial hierarchy and upset many White Americans. Rather than refocus the federal wealth policies to narrow the racial wealth gap, we saw in Chapter 6 how the tax expenditures were revamped to expand their assistance to those already affluent. In this chapter, the wealth transfer taxes have been dismantled to ensure that the accumulated family wealth can be passed on to descendants, in some cases in perpetuity.

At the same time that federal wealth policies were turning to satisfy the demands of White supremacy, an important federal effort was emerging to expand opportunity to those households left behind. Recognizing the importance of the higher education ladder to better paying jobs, advocates were pressuring the federal government to expand access to a college education. With the aspiration of making college accessible to all who are academically ready, Congress funded the Basic Educational Opportunity Grants (BEOGs) in the 1970s. These grants offered one modest step to redress existing disparities, including those detailed in the Kerner Commission report. Chapter 8 will investigate the circumstances and consequences of this program.

8

Assessing the Higher Education Ladder

ACCESS TO HIGHER EDUCATION

In December 1899, representatives from twelve elite northeastern universities gathered at Columbia University to address the growing "educational anarchy" in higher education (Stewart & Johanek, 1996, p. 277). Growing numbers of high school graduates were overloading college admissions as schools sought to enroll the most qualified students. Back then, colleges either administered their own admission exam or individually certified high schools based on their curriculum and standards. The former method was labor intensive while the latter gave secondary schools undue influence on their admissions. The meeting created the College Entrance Examination Board (CEEB), a nonprofit consortium of the initial twelve colleges that today includes over 6,000 universities and secondary schools. Its original goal was to develop and administer a common college entrance exam to assess student readiness for college-level work and report the results to member schools. These early exams, known informally as the "College Boards," gauged student knowledge in nine subject areas including English, history, Greek, Latin, and physics. This battery of tests could take up to five days as students wrote their responses to essay questions in "blue books" (Jacobsen, n.d.). Students paid $5 for the privilege of taking these exams. While burdensome to the student applicant, this testing relieved the colleges of spending their own resources on in-house entrance exams. Moreover, this test assured the matriculation of students who knew the traditional canon.

Interestingly, these exams attracted notable criticism. Malcolm Barnes, clearly an indefatigable educator from the Thacher School in Ojai, California, took the exam ten different times "in cognito qua candidate" and then asked to see his graded answers. Writing in the *Harvard Alumni*

Bulletin, Barnes (1922) raised warnings about the incompetent grading, the impact of "teaching for the test" in the classroom, and the folly of relying solely upon the test for admissions criteria. Much of this sounds quite familiar.

Looking for a more streamlined test, the CEEB considered whether the emerging "intelligence" and standardized aptitude tests might be adapted to assessing student readiness. They turned to psychologist Carl Brigham to oversee the project. Recently, Brigham had written a book entitled *A Study of American Intelligence* (1923) that analyzed data from the Army mental tests given to World War I servicemen. He concluded these aptitude tests demonstrated convincing evidence of a racial hierarchy. According to one of his conclusions:

> It is also possible to make a picture of the elements now entering into the American intelligence. At one extreme, we have the distribution of the Nordic race group. At the other extreme, we have the American negro. Between the Nordic and the negro, but closer to the negro than to the Nordic, we find the Alpine and the Mediterranean types. (p. 197)

With this worldview, Brigham and the CEEB developed an aptitude test that purportedly assessed general intelligence and readiness for learning rather than student understanding of select subject areas. Multiple choice replaced essay questions to enable objective assessment and avoid arbitrary grading. The earliest versions took students only ninety minutes to complete, making this exam both impartial and efficient. Once the technology was ready, the exam could be machine graded, adding further economies. Over time, it reached its mass audience as millions of students annually experienced it as a painful rite of passage – the dreaded SATs.

As the SAT was designed to predict accurately which students would thrive in college, it is understandable how the worldview of its creators would produce an exam with massive racial and cultural biases. Inevitably, questions would reflect the cultural experiences of their makers, who were overwhelmingly White and middle class. One of the analogy questions used for years included the term "regatta," an activity with clear racial and class bias (Carlton, 2022). Like any standardized test, potential questions were tested on sample populations (Lomax et al., 1995). Given the prevailing thinking, those questions that scored low among the favored Nordic group would be viewed as inaccurate predictors and rejected as "defective." Throughout much of the country, the tests were administered along strictly segregated lines. No doubt, White and Black students alike recognized the underlying message that segregated testing sent.

Designed as an educational gatekeeper, the SAT exam performed its function well, as it funneled the young heirs of White families into the nation's elite colleges and universities.

In 1959, a young Lois Dickson Rice started working at the CEEB, now known as the College Board. At that time, about 94 percent of the enrolled college students were White,[1] while it would be another six years before the College Board had fully complied with the *Brown v. Board of Education* (1954) decision to offer integrated testing (Wheeler, 2013). Despite working in an organization and larger society that discouraged access to college, Ms. Rice resolved to remove the obstacles. She knew firsthand the importance of getting an education. Recent emigres from Jamaica, her father worked as a janitor at a local music store while her mother worked as a maid. Nonetheless, Ms. Rice and her four brothers all graduated from college. Over her long career at the College Board, Ms. Rice rose through the ranks as she became an executive vice president and director of the Washington, DC office. She developed an expertise in higher education financing and used her position at the College Board to influence educational policies. Reflecting on her achievements, former Education Secretary Arne Duncan said, "For so many of us, she was a hero, a role model and an example of what true service is all about. She helped create a pathway to college for literally millions of low-income and first-generation college goers, changing the trajectories of their families forever" (Roberts, 2017, para. 13).

From personal experience, Ms. Rice knew that other talented young adults came from households with few resources. In 1971, the average annual cost of a four-year public university was $1,410, while the average four-year private college was $2,930. Even these price tags were largely out of the reach of most Black households. Figure 8.1 considers Black households earning at the twentieth and fortieth income percentiles and the share of their income needed to pay for one member to attend college. For those households fortunate to live near a public university, a college education might be possible. Having only to pay tuition and fees would require 15 and 8 percent of the household income, depending on whether they had earnings at the twentieth or fortieth percentile. Still, commuting would likely require a car and the attendant transportation costs. The remaining options of paying for room and board at a public university or going to a private college were increasingly out of their reach. Centuries of restricted opportunities and their impact on prevailing incomes meant that a private

[1] US Census Bureau (1962).

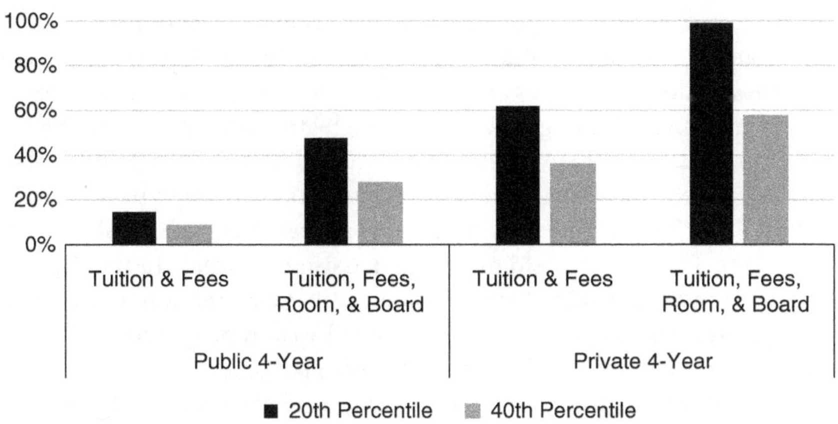

Figure 8.1 College burden on Black households, 1971
Source: College Board, Trends in College Pricing 2023; Census Bureau, Table F-1 Income Limits for Each Fifth and Top 5 Percent of Households

college education was beyond the means of most Black families unless they garnered ample financial assistance.

Acutely aware of the financial barriers facing many capable students from historically marginalized communities, Ms. Rice labored to develop new funding sources to assist their efforts. Working with other educational leaders, she lobbied Congress tirelessly to enact the Basic Educational Opportunity Grant (BEOG) in order to expand access to college. Eventually, she gained tacit Presidential support as President Nixon argued that "equal educational opportunity, which has long been a goal, must now become a reality for every young person in the United States, whatever his economic circumstances" (Nixon, 1970, para. 24). Still, the heavy lifting of gaining legislative approval lay ahead. Finally, Congress took her advice and included the BEOG as part of the 1972 Education Amendment to the Higher Education Act of 1965. Rather than providing a loan that students would be required to repay, the BEOG offered a substantial need-based federal grant to academically able students. In stark contrast to the prevailing policy, these grants were allocated directly to the student recipients based on their income and not given to the colleges to distribute as they saw fit.

Initially, these new education grants were dwarfed by two other federal programs that also offered educational assistance. To help returning Vietnam veterans, the federal government had reprised the GI Bill to expand access to a college education. Additionally, Social Security offered benefits to those aged 18–22 wanting a college education but whose parents had died or were disabled. In 1976, these two programs, neither of which were need-based, provided over $6.5 billion in educational assistance, far more than the $1.5 billion doled out by the BEOGs. Ms. Rice continued to lobby Congress unremittently to ensure the BEOGs would gain full funding and not get overshadowed by the larger programs. By the end of the decade, the VA benefits were in decline as the eligible number of Vietnam vets dwindled (Rivlin, 1978) and Congress pared back benefits to those older than eighteen as part of the restructuring of Social Security (Lee, 2013). This left the field of financial assistance largely to the BEOGs. That the most important form of federal financial aid was need-based represented a notable achievement in federal wealth programs and serves as witness to Ms. Rice's tireless and persuasive advocacy.

Cognizant of its growing role, Congress decided to remove the grant's cumbersome name by renaming it. Calling it the Rice Grant would have remedied the marketing problem and given due credit to Ms. Rice's efforts. However, Congress decided to name the grant after one of its own members, Sen. Claiborne Pell (D-RI). As chairman of the Senate Education Subcommittee, he had served as a close ally and effective shepherd of the program through its initial and subsequent authorizations. Hence, we know it today as the Pell Grant. What is less well known is Ms. Rice's recognition as the "mother of the Pell Grants." Having reached its fiftieth anniversary, estimates indicate that more than eighty million students have been assisted as they aspired to gain a college education and climb the higher education ladder to financial security (Rice, 2021).

THE COLLEGE PREMIUM

As discussed in Chapter 3, the original GI Bill transformed higher education from a sanctuary of the privileged elite to a realistic achievement for millions of returning veterans. Since then, earning a college diploma has assumed increasing importance for those aspiring to gain financial security through building personal wealth. Emerging technologies and global shifts have reshaped the US economy, causing many well-paying jobs, ones that did not require a college diploma, to shift abroad or disappear entirely. Increasingly, employers began requiring a college degree to gain consideration for more selective jobs. As illustrated in Figure 8.2, college graduates earn a substantial premium over those with only a high school diploma. In recent years, this premium has increased to nearly 80 percent higher. Over a working career, this dividend can total hundreds of thousands of dollars of additional income. While those who complete two years of college can capture a portion of this premium, the figure demonstrates

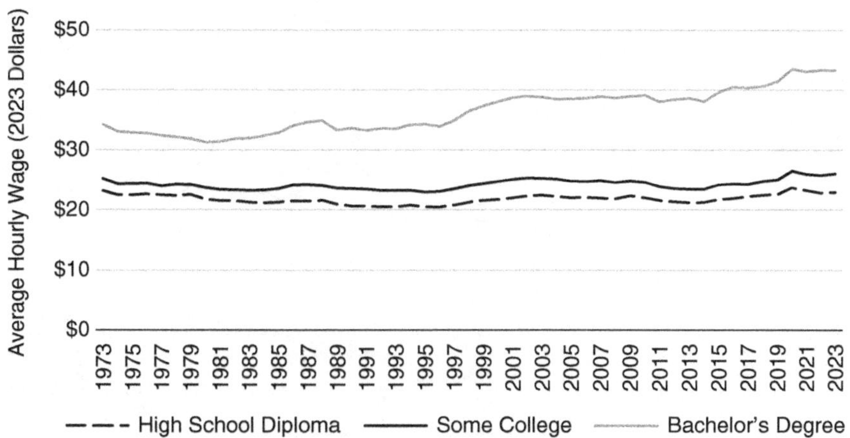

Figure 8.2 College wage premium
Source: Census Bureau, Current Population Survey retrieved from Economic Policy Institute (n.d.) State of American Working Data Library

that completing a bachelor's degree is essential to securing the full measure of these benefits. Further, it appears the college premium continues to grow, thereby adding greater value to acquiring a college education.

A college diploma offers more than merely a ticket to a higher-paying job; it typically brings increased job security and income stability. College graduates experience fewer and shorter bouts of unemployment. Avoiding job loss limits periods of dissaving and the need to liquidate previously accumulated wealth. As a college diploma is required for most professional and managerial positions, it typically brings jobs with better benefits in addition to higher pay. Access to employer-sponsored health insurance limits out-of-pocket medical expenses and encourages greater use of preventative care. Most professional jobs come with employer-sponsored retirement benefits that enhance the accumulation of retirement wealth. In these ways, a college diploma affords its holder much greater access to the Household Saving pathway discussed in Chapter 2.

Of course, Black employees experience the college premium somewhat differently. Black college graduates experience a much smaller boost from earning a college degree, despite starting from a substantially lower high school wage.[2] Black college graduates experience greater difficulty in obtaining employment as they report sending out more resumes to land a job interview (Bertrand & Mullainathan, 2004). They earn lower

[2] Economic Policy Institute (n.d.) analysis of Census Current Population Survey.

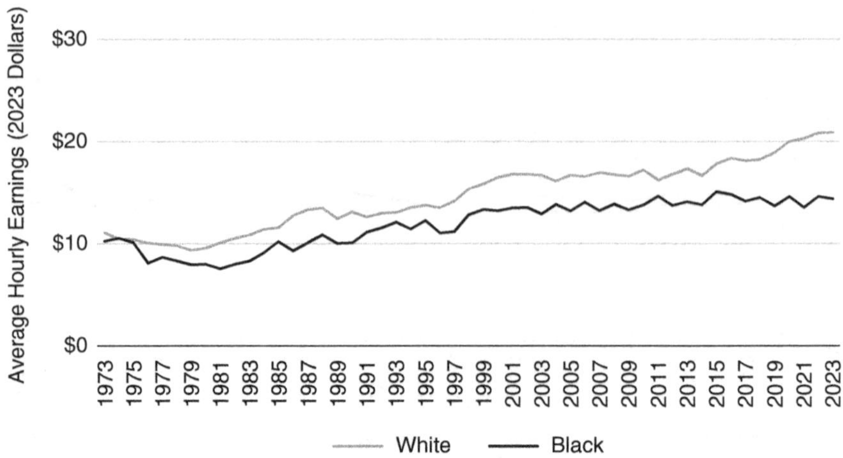

Figure 8.3 Racial gap in the college wage premium
Source: Census Bureau, Current Population Survey retrieved from Economic Policy Institute (n.d.) State of American Working Data Library

starting salaries than their White colleagues holding similar degrees (Hamilton et al., 2011). Moreover, Black college graduates are more likely to work in jobs that do not require a degree (Jones & Schmitt, 2014). Black workers suffer more frequent and longer bouts of unemployment, no matter their educational attainment (Williams & Wilson, 2019). For these reasons and more, the financial payoff to Black college graduates is markedly less than for White graduates. Figure 8.3 shows the boost in average hourly earnings that a college degree generates for Black and White workers. While the college wage premium was virtually identical for both groups in 1973, they've each experienced a different trend since then. The White wage premium has almost doubled to $20 per hour, while the Black college premium has grown only 40 percent to $14 per hour. This difference of $6 per hour means an extra $12,000 per year on top of the other salary and benefit advantages. Despite the lower benefits to Black graduates, there are few alternatives to a college degree if one wants to achieve economic security.

While the financial rewards to a college education have grown over time, the cost of attendance has risen even faster. Over the past fifty years, few prices have climbed as fast as the tuition, room, and board (TRB) charges at private colleges. The cost of attending a public university has escalated almost as much. As shown in Figure 8.4, both have increased exponentially over the period, doubling time after time after time. On average, the cost of college has increased fifteen to seventeen times since 1971. These increases

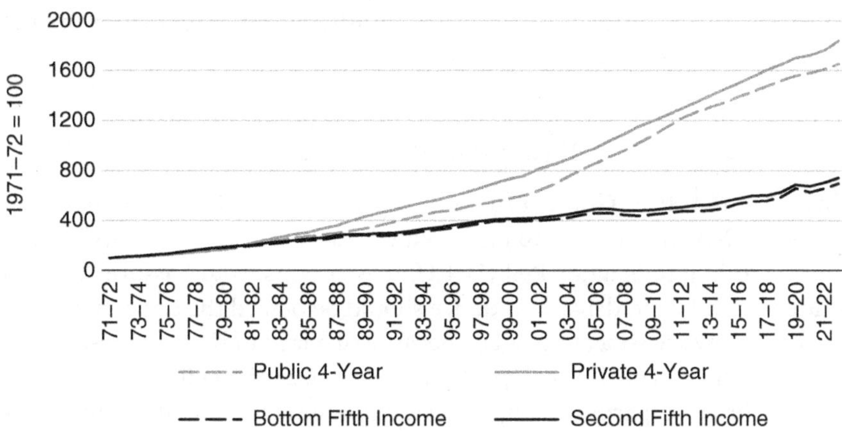

Figure 8.4 Rising burden of a college education
Source: College Board, Trends in College Pricing 2023; Census Bureau, Table F-1 Income Limits for Each Fifth and Top 5 Percent of Households

far outstrip the increase in income among households at the twentieth and fortieth income percentiles.[3] Skyrocketing TRB costs have left these households far behind.

These disparate trends reveal the conundrum of the higher education ladder. Today, a college diploma is more essential than ever in providing households the means to attain financial security. Yet, the costs of earning a college degree have escalated even faster, putting it beyond the reach of increasing numbers of households. Once again, it appears that it takes wealth to build wealth. Absent some other form of financial assistance, the lack of family resources creates financial obstacles that preclude many aspiring young students from garnering the benefits of a college education. These obstacles block a singularly crucial path toward upward mobility for many young Americans. Given the historical policies and practices discussed in Chapter 3, these barriers thwart far more aspiring Black students than White. Far more White students come from households that earn higher incomes as well as hold generational wealth. The enactment of Pell Grants offered the country an opportunity to redress this conundrum and expand access to higher education and its rewards. It offered the promise of wealth-building help to the aspiring rather than

[3] Most of these increases are the result of inflation over the years. Adjusting these figures for inflation offers the following insights. In real terms, college TRB costs have more than doubled over the period while the income levels of both the twentieth and fortieth income percentiles have barely kept pace with inflation.

to those already affluent. In this way, it differs profoundly from the tax expenditures discussed in Chapters 4 and 6.

THE PROMISE OF PELL

Enacting the Pell Grant Program represented a down payment on President Nixon's promise to make "equal educational opportunity" a reality. According to Senator Pell (D-RI), these grants would assure "that no student with talent, drive, and desire should be denied the opportunity for a post-secondary education solely because of a lack of financial resources" (As cited in Curs et al., 2007, p. 284). At its outset, the Pell Program experienced broad bipartisan support (Heller, 2013). Democratic lawmakers welcomed its potential to expand access to higher education and mitigate structural disparities while Republican policymakers, including the Nixon Administration, valued its example as a voucher program (Gladieux, 1995). As a direct grant to the applicant, the Pell Grant followed the student's college choice, thereby applying market pressures. Likely, legislators from both sides of the aisle viewed it as a sound investment in the country's future as more of the country's best and brightest gained the means to exploit their talents more fully.

Starting with an initial class in 1973–74, the program was phased in over the following three years. In its first full year of operation, the program assisted almost two million students. Rather than use a blunt income threshold to limit eligibility, the program required applicants to complete a worksheet. This questionnaire requested information on family income, number of dependents, certain household assets, and any unusual circumstances that might impact their effective family contribution (EFC). Grant awards varied inversely with the household's financial means as measured by the EFC.[4] In the inaugural 1976–77 academic year, the maximum grant allowed was $1,400, which covered over two-thirds of the cost of a typical public university and one-third of a typical private college. By design, Pell Grants were not expected to cover the full cost of college; the legislation limited assistance to 50 percent of the entire costs.[5] Students were expected to draw upon other federal aid sources like federal work study, federal loan programs, institutional aid, and family contributions to pay the balance. Fears of "spoiling" wealth-poor students certainly haunted this aspect of the program.

[4] Applicants with a lower EFC had a greater probability of receiving an award since funds were generally limited below the actual need.

[5] This limit was raised to 60 percent in 1986 and then eliminated completely in 1992.

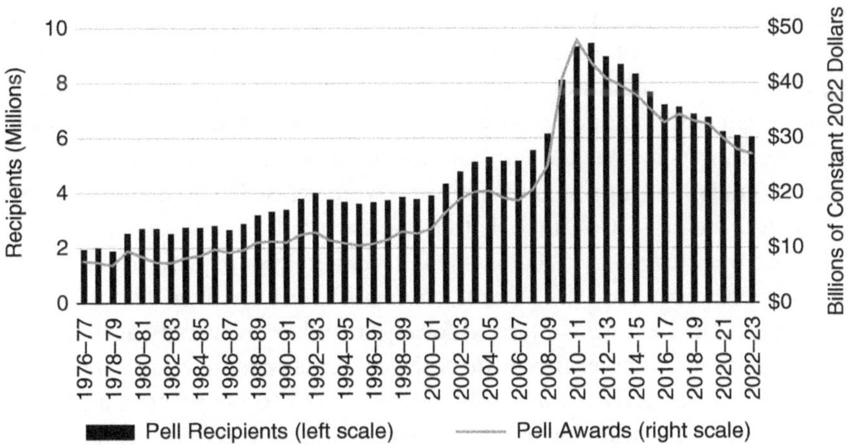

Figure 8.5 Pell Grant Program trends
Source: Federal Student Aid Data Center, Table 8; Federal Pell Grants in Current and in 2022 Dollars, 1973–74 to 2022–23

For much of its existence, the Pell Program has grown as it helped increasing numbers of students enroll in college. As Figure 8.5 depicts, the program reached four million students by the early 1990s and spiked to nine million during the Great Recession and its aftermath. Since then, improving employment prospects among other factors have caused the numbers to subside to six million recipients in 2022–23. Of course, an important outcome is how many of these students actually graduate. Early studies concluded that Pell Grants had minimal impact on graduation rates. However, these studies were hampered by the fact that students who are *eligible for Pell* have much lower graduation rates. More recent studies that control for this effect have found that Pell assistance increases persistence and graduation rates among students from low-wealth households.[6] These gains in both access and graduation rates represent notable successes of the Pell Program. Figure 8.5 also illustrates the program's costs, which unsurprisingly rise and fall with the number of recipients.

THE UNKEPT PROMISE OF PELL

While Pell Grants have enabled millions of young Americans to earn a college diploma and seek otherwise unavailable occupational opportunities,

[6] The interested reader should review Alon (2005), Flowers (2011), and Umbricht (2016).

the program has not matched its promise to provide "equal educational opportunity" to all deserving students. Several causes are to blame. Required paperwork that is more onerous than filing federal tax forms deters many applicants from even applying (Deming & Dynarski, 2009). An uncertain aid process with late decisions on actual awards discourages financially strapped households (Dynarski & Scott-Clayton, 2006). However, the largest obstacle is that the awards have not kept pace with the cost of attending college, as illustrated in Figure 8.6. Initially, the authorized maximum Pell Grants were sufficient to cover 80 percent of the full cost of attending a typical four-year public university and 40 percent of a typical four-year private college. While specific grants were limited to 50 percent of actual costs – later raised to 60 percent and then eliminated – the initial awards had the potential to provide greater access to college. Subsequent increases over the years never matched the spiraling costs of college. By the 1990s, the authorized maximum award could cover only 60 percent of the cost of a public university and 20 percent of a private college. Since then, Pell awards have continued to erode in value until the maximum award now covers only 30 percent of the typical public university. No longer can one plausibly insist that the Pell Grants ensure "equal educational opportunity."

Actually, the maximum Pell awards have been lower than the values illustrated in Figure 8.6. Despite repeated attempts by Congressional allies to make the program an entitlement, most consider Pell Grants as only

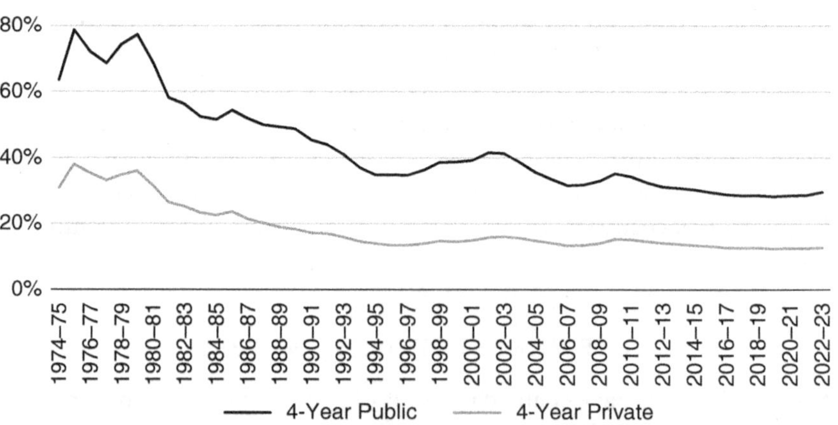

Figure 8.6 Share of college costs covered by maximum Pell Grant
Source: College Board, Trends in College Pricing 2023; Federal Student Aid Data Center, Table 8; Federal Pell Grants in Current and in 2022 Dollars, 1973–74 to 2022–23

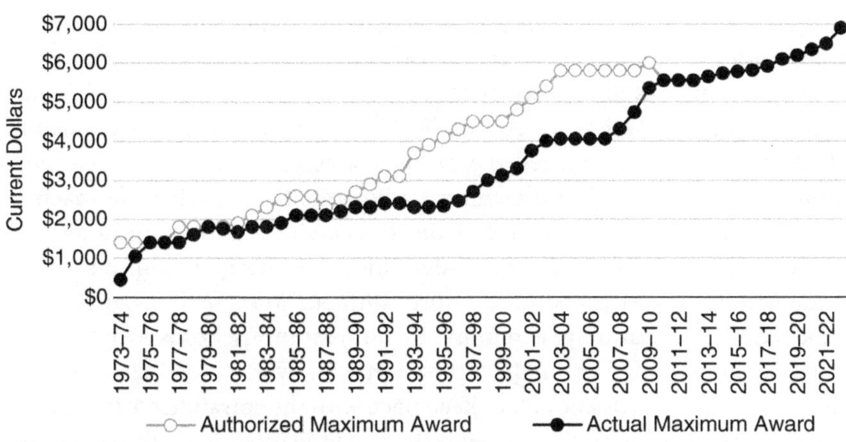

Figure 8.7 Funding impact on maximum awards
Source: Dortch (2023)

a "quasi-entitlement."[7] Congress regularly authorized maximum awards, but funding shortfalls often led to reduced awards, generally on a prorated basis (Boren, 1989). Although seemingly equitable, this decision caused those with the greatest need to suffer the largest reductions. As shown in Figure 8.7, the actual maximum awards often fell short of the authorized maximum.[8] At times, these discrepancies have been substantial. One study from the 1990s found that for every $1,000 (1998 dollars) increase in financial aid, the probability of attendance increased by 4 percent (Dynarski, 2003). Due to these smaller awards, students from modest backgrounds faced significantly larger financial challenges in completing or even contemplating their education. According to a Congressional Budget Office study in the early 1980s (*Testimony on Student Aid Programs*, 1984), changing the Pell Grant Program into an entitlement would have cost the Treasury $6 billion annually. Rather than make this highly beneficial investment, federal aid priorities were shifting in new directions.

GOING IN A NEW DIRECTION

The Pell Program's initial successes actually triggered the earliest shift in federal student aid. The early Pell Grants caused parents and lawmakers

[7] This means eligible students will likely receive a grant, although its amount is dependent on actual funding.

[8] In recent years, Congress has stopped the practice of specifying an authorized maximum award.

to question why such financial assistance was unavailable to students from middle- and upper-income households (Umbricht, 2016). This pressure from influential sources encouraged Congress to enact the Middle-Income Student Assistance Act of 1978 (Gladieux, 1995). To expand Pell eligibility, the law liberalized the needs analysis formula to include more affluent households. These technical adjustments expanded the reach of Pell Grants, but at the expense of those receiving the maximum award.[9] Some of these changes were rescinded under the Reagan Administration; nonetheless, they foreshadowed future conflicts. Many Pell Program allies believed that expanding eligibility to affluent households would build political support. Unfortunately, this support never materialized to boost the maximum awards enough to keep pace with the spiraling costs. Instead, broadening the program's assistance diverted the focus from those the program was created to help.

Two other decisions continued this trend. Financial aid forms that determined economic need considered household income and net worth. Over time, both retirement savings and home equity were excluded from consideration. The justification that households should not be forced to jeopardize their home or their retirement savings certainly makes sense. Yet, both decisions clearly favor more affluent households and enable them to gain more financial assistance (Edlin, 1993; Levine & Ritter, 2022). Although significant, these decisions were overshadowed by what followed.

Speaking before the 1996 graduates of Princeton University, President Clinton announced a new direction in federal student aid for higher education. He outlined a new federal tax credit, based on Georgia's statewide Hope Scholarships, that offered up to $1,500 to eligible households for two years of college. He boldly promised this proposal would make the "13th and 14th years of education as universal to all Americans as the first 12 are today" (Clinton, 1996, para. 34). The president continually pushed for his tax proposal as he traveled across the country seeking reelection. Just fifteen months later, he got his wish as he signed into law the Taxpayer Relief Act of 1997. The law included his signature proposal as well as the Lifelong Learning Tax Credit, which offered any eligible student a tax credit of up to $1,000 for any post-secondary education without limit to the number of years. Together, these two tax credits offered financial assistance to millions of American households as they invested in post-secondary education.

The use of tax credits signaled a major change in the federal government's role in higher education. Rather than guaranteeing student loans

[9] For a detailed explanation of these changes, see Mortenson (1988).

or using outright grants, the federal government was utilizing tax policy in support of higher education. Doing so established these tax credits as entitlements, a status long sought but never achieved by the Pell Program. Recognizing the value of tax credits over deductions to less affluent households, the Administration made sure to design the assistance in this way. Moreover, both tax credits included income phaseouts that limited participation by high-income households.[10] As designed, these tax credits served two other political purposes. Their targeting of benefits to middle- and upper-middle-income households earned them strong political support among those paying the rising college tuition bills. Additionally, the tax credits enabled President Clinton and Congress to unveil new avenues of federal assistance while engaged in significant tax reduction. While these tax credits never quite cost the Treasury as much as the Pell Grants, they did divert scarce funds from those students in greatest need of help.

Even within the Clinton Administration, there was disagreement over this new direction. Treasury Secretary Robert Rubin, a long-time Wall Street financier, insisted the tax credits would do little to expand educational opportunity (Sanchez & Chandler, 1997; Hartford Courant, 1997). Designed as nonrefundable, neither tax credit would assist households who paid little or no federal income tax. This feature effectively excluded one-third of American households (Long & McPherson, 2007). Additionally, households would need to wait a year before receiving the credit, further limiting their value to those unable to afford the delay. Lastly, they applied only to net expenses, making them even less valuable to Pell Grant recipients. Eliminating potential recipients at both the bottom and top of the income continuum, these tax credits targeted their help to middle- and upper-middle-class students with laser focus. One study confirmed Rubin's suspicions and concluded these tax credits had little impact on enrollments (Long & McPherson, 2007).

The federal government soon followed these tax credits with other education-related tax expenditures with the professed goal to lower college costs and expand access. Qualified tuition plans (also known as 529s) and Coverdell IRAs are designed to encourage saving for future college expenses by extending preferential tax treatment. Any earnings generated by these accounts are exempt from federal taxation. Any scholarship income or employer-sponsored educational reimbursements are deemed tax-exempt income. In addition to the tax credits already discussed, several provisions

10 Individuals and married households with an AGI above $50,000 and $100,000, respectively, were excluded from the tax credits.

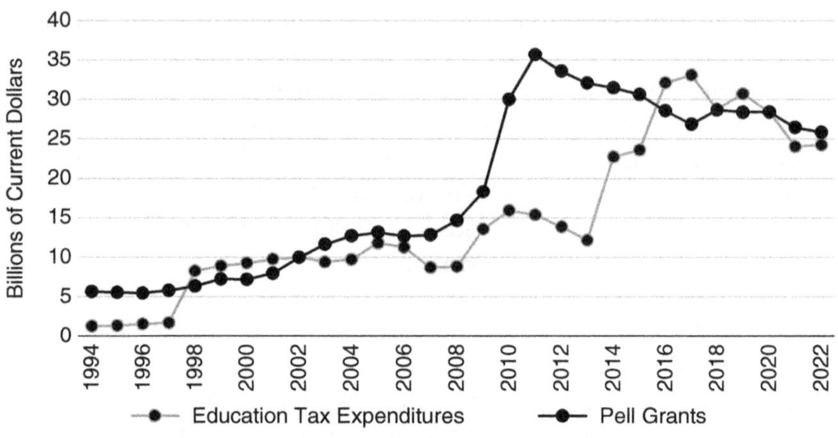

Figure 8.8 Comparing educational assistance

reduce the tax liability of households paying college-related expenses. These include the parental personal exemption for adult children enrolled in college and a tax deduction for college expenses. Although disparate in their focus, each of these provisions uses the tax code to convey their benefits to eligible households. As such, they shift their focus and assistance away from Pell-eligible households to those more affluent. Inevitably, this change carries racial consequences as it swings more aid toward White households.

President Clinton's call for a new direction in higher education assistance did cause a major shift in federal help. Prior to his announcement, federal use of the tax code to help households pay for college was negligible.[11] Since then, their importance has grown as illustrated in Figure 8.8, which compares their cost to the Treasury to those of Pell awards. Two major initiatives drive the rise of the education-targeted tax expenditures. The enactment of the Hope and Life Learning Tax Credits under President Clinton led to the first major increase. The second major jump occurred during the Obama Administration as Congress expanded the Hope Tax Credit to four years and a maximum value of $2,500 annually.[12] Over the past decade, the rising cost of these tax expenditures frequently superseded that of the Pell awards. Their magnitude illustrates the shift in federal help as it increasingly funneled assistance to middle- and upper-income households at the expense of those most challenged by the high costs of college.

[11] The exclusion on scholarship income and the parental personal exemption for enrolled children both predate his speech at Princeton by decades.

[12] Congress did change the credit from nonrefundable to partially refundable thereby extending some help to Pell-eligible households.

ENROLLMENT MANAGEMENT COMES TO THE PUBLICS

Historically, the states offered access to a college degree through their taxpayer-supported public universities. With generous taxpayer support, the public universities could offer a wide variety of academic programs at low tuition. By locating campuses around the state, they served aspiring students from low-income households even better, as they could save by living at home. They offered modest institutional grants to those students still needing financial aid even after using their Pell Grants. This "low tuition – low aid" strategy helped many students from financially strapped households gain access to college and earn their degrees.

As President Clinton addressed the Princeton graduates, two trends were shifting the finances of higher education. Political support for the "low tuition – low aid" model was waning as state lawmakers refused to appropriate funds to meet the rising enrollments and operating costs. During recessions, state legislatures reduced their contributions to the public universities as they faced declining tax revenues. Verbal commitments to restore these cuts once prosperity returned were often forgotten. In 1993, state funds met 34 percent of the revenues for the four-year public universities in the US. By 2014, the comparable figure had fallen nearly by half to 18 percent (Zhao, 2018). Facing budget shortfalls, university administrators had few options other than raise TRB rates. According to the College Board, the average published TRB rates of four-year universities have nearly tripled since 1990 and doubled since 2000, even after adjusting for inflation (Ma et al., 2020). While some argue that the rapid increase in the price of the publics is simply the result of state disinvestment in higher education, the story is likely more complicated.[13]

For obvious reasons, public university administrators prefer to experience robust student enrollments. Yet, rapid increases in tuition over many years make this much more challenging. In response, school administrators have deployed various enrollment management strategies. Curiously, one such strategy is to raise tuition substantially, since higher tuition is linked with increased status for the school. The obvious downside is that higher tuition deters many potential students, particularly those from low-income households. Supporters of this approach contend that a portion of the additional revenues can fund need-based grants and thereby lower the financial barriers imposed by the rising tuition. The evidence indicates that

[13] Delisle (2017) argues there is little evidence in the literature that the two are strongly linked.

need-based aid has increased over the past twenty-five years, but not as much as the growth in merit-based aid.

Enrollment management consultants advised a shift in institutional aid priorities away from helping needy students afford the cost of college. Instead, they counseled that institutional aid should be deployed to boost enrollments and maximize net tuition revenues. Although universities publish their TRB rates, very few students pay full freight. Typically, students are offered an institutional grant or discount off the full price. Net tuition revenue measures the actual TRB revenues once these grants are deducted. Following the strategy of "financial aid leveraging," institutional aid should be distributed in amounts just enough to lure prospective students, but not one dollar more. Under this strategy, the college maximizes its limited financial aid funds by attracting the largest number of matriculants. Students with high financial need lose out as they require more institutional aid to gain their attendance.

Of course, universities do not simply want any student; they are interested in attracting certain students. By attracting students with high SAT scores, college administrators keep their restive faculty happy and, more importantly, improve their position in the coveted college rankings. As SAT scores are highly correlated with household income, these students typically can pay a larger share of their tuition. Generating increased net tuition revenue permits the university to heighten their appeal by renovating residence halls, offering extensive cocurricular programs, and providing such amenities as bowling alleys and climbing walls. This spending not only attracts more students but enables the institution to climb higher in the rankings. Driving this system is the lure of increased prestige and status that results from an improved ranking. Universities unwilling to join the game find increasing numbers of their talented matriculants getting poached by better offers elsewhere. Either they join the competition or suffer the consequences, creating what one observer has labeled the "merit-aid arms race" (Burd, 2020).

This allure of gaining an "improved student profile" has encouraged an explosive increase in merit-based aid and influenced changes in the awarding of need-based aid. Rather than give enough aid to eliminate as much need as possible, the new strategy calls for giving just enough to attract the student. Students are then required to cover the difference, whether it means placing heavy burdens on their family, taking out loans, working long hours, or going part-time to school. Each of these options generates added stress and undermines student persistence to graduation. While universities are offering larger amounts of need-based aid than ever before, this aid is meeting a smaller share of the total need and leaving students more vulnerable.

This shift in institutional aid has occurred with breathtaking speed, as documented in Woo and Choy (2011). During the 1995–96 academic year, more college students received need-based than merit-based aid. At public universities, students receiving need-based aid exceeded those getting merit-based aid (13 vs. 8 percent), while the numbers at private colleges were 43 versus 24 percent, respectively. Just twelve years later, the emphasis was reversed. More students at public universities received merit aid (18 vs. 16 percent) as did at private colleges (44 vs. 42 percent). Shifting priorities also affected the relative size of grants. At public universities, average grants for merit-based aid were larger and rose faster (from $3,600 to $4,200) than did the need-based grants (from $2,600 to $2,700). As merit-based aid is offered without respect to financial need, it benefits students from affluent households. Assuredly, these shifts have racialized consequences. In 1995–96, fewer White students than Black students received institutional aid (15 vs. 18 percent), although their average grant was higher ($3,200 vs. $2,700). Twelve years later, White students received more grants (21 vs. 17 percent) and collected larger average grants ($5,600 vs. $4,400). In just twelve years, institutional aid had shifted its focus and redeployed its benefits.

The rush to offer students merit-based aid has only increased since. A recent study examined the financial aid spending of 339 four-year public universities from 2001 to 2017. The author found that merit-based institutional aid had skyrocketed from $1 billion annually in 2000–2001 to nearly $3 billion annually in 2016–17 (Burd, 2020). While the report acknowledges that need-based aid also soared during the period, it cautions that this surge did not increase access among students from low-income households. The evidence indicates that the four-year publics are drawing fewer students from the bottom 40 percent of household incomes while luring more students from the top 20 percent (Burd, 2017). These trends simply demonstrate how enrollment management has transformed the financial aid practices in higher education.

THE BROKEN LADDER

Lois Dickson Rice fully appreciated the benefits a college degree might bring to students from families like her own. From personal experience, she knew how a college diploma could open doors to professional employment that offered job security, ample pay, and generous benefits. Even with these opportunities, working toward financial security is challenging.

Table 8.1 *Comparing young (under 36) householder prospects*

	Professional Employment (%)	Median Salary	Retirement Plan (%)	Homeownership Rate (%)
Black				
Without Bachelor's	15	$23,780	21	12
With Bachelor's	73	$58,369	51	41
White				
Without Bachelor's	24	$52,965	47	43
With Bachelor's	74	$83,230	70	50

Source: Author's calculations; Federal Reserve Board 2022 Survey of Consumer Finances.

Completing a college degree takes persistence and hard work. Saving a portion of one's salary requires discipline and self-control. Yet, she recognized how a bachelor's degree offered those who exhibited these personal characteristics expanded opportunities and greater rewards. After accumulating some savings, one could invest that money in a home or business opportunity and access the asset accumulation pathway. She fully grasped the singular role that a college education played in giving millions of young adults the opportunity to realize economic security.

The promise of a college education, if anything, is more important today than in Ms. Rice's day. Simply compare the prospects of young householders – both Black and White – in 2022. Table 8.1 offers some striking insights. First, earning a college diploma offers young households a dramatically different economic trajectory. Young householders with a college degree are far more likely to land professional employment, earn substantially higher salaries, hold a retirement account, and attain homeownership. The differences are striking. Second, the gains from a college degree are arguably greater for Black households than White. A college degree enables young Black households to close the gap on professional employment and make striking gains in the other three areas. This demonstrates how a college degree continues to provide a meaningful ladder to those striving for financial security. Yet, the evidence in Table 8.1 offers one less rosy insight. Regarding typical salaries as well as access to retirement plans and homeownership, Black college graduates more closely resemble young Whites without a college degree than their educated peers. Earning a college diploma dramatically improves the economic prospects of young Black householders, but it only modestly reduces the salary and asset-ownership disparities. Simply equalizing educational opportunities, although very important, will not by itself reduce the racial wealth gap.

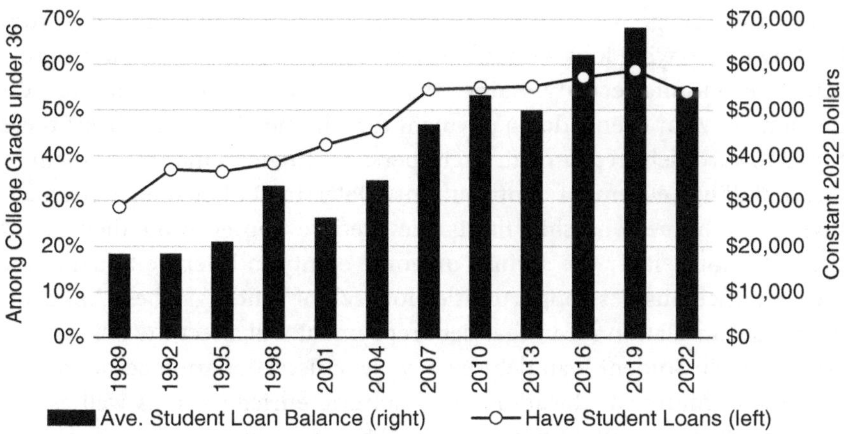

Figure 8.9 Growing student debt burden

While a college diploma continues to offer considerable benefits, fewer students graduate with only a diploma in hand; most now leave with substantial amounts of student loan debt. Over the past quarter century, state lawmakers have balked at keeping the cost of their public university low and accessible to all. The adoption of enrollment management strategies has encouraged sharp increases in college tuition and judicious use of financial aid to maximize enrollment. Financial aid priorities have shifted from need-based to merit-based aid. These changes have shifted the burden of gaining a college education increasingly onto the students and their families. While Pell Grants at one time plugged much of this gap, they no longer do so. Without family wealth to fall back on, students are forced to use student loans to finance their college education or go without.

Like the rising cost of college, the growth of student loan debt has been striking. Figure 8.9 depicts the rate of student loan debt among recent college graduates as well as the average debt burden. In 1989, 29 percent of young households (under 36) with a college graduate had outstanding student loans. Just thirty-three years later, the comparable figure had nearly doubled to 54 percent. It is now the norm for college graduates to leave with both a diploma and a substantial IOU. Worse, the size of that debt has tripled in real dollars from $18,254 to almost $55,000 in 2022, although this figure is a modest reduction of what it was several years earlier. The magnitude of this debt undermines the promise of a college diploma as it places a substantial obstacle in the path to economic security. Moreover, these debt figures ignore an extremely vulnerable group – households that incurred considerable debt but were unable to complete their degree, at least to this point.

Leaving college with a sizable debt need not preclude graduates from landing well-paying jobs with full benefits, but it will inhibit their progress toward economic security. Rather than use their current income to save for rainy days or even a down payment for a home, they must divert these funds toward debt repayment. Tight personal finances may force them to forgo making retirement contributions. Deferring either their retirement savings or homeownership limits the lifetime appreciation they might gain. Without either the savings or home equity to leverage a loan, they may sacrifice business opportunities for lack of funding. These limits on wealth accumulation mean that debt repayment will affect the next generation as well. Student loan debtors have less discretionary income to support their children's educational and cultural enrichment, as well as less to offer when they attain majority age. The rising burden of student loan debt imposes limitations and risks not experienced by prior generations of college graduates.

This debt burden threat is even worse. Most student loans require monthly payments sufficient to repay the debt over a ten-year period, much like a mortgage. Those borrowers who experience low-paying or unstable employment may miss payments, causing their loans to be delinquent or even in default. In response, the federal government designed programs that adjusted repayment levels to reflect the borrower's actual earnings. Called income-dependent repayment (IDR), this alternative has reduced loan delinquencies but has contributed to another problem. Either nonpayment or reduced payment can allow the loan balance to rise as any unpaid interest continues to mount. Many borrowers are making monthly payments but nonetheless watching nervously as their debt obligation increases. According to one study, 64 percent of those loans originating in 2018 had higher balances a year later, while those originating between 2013 and 2015 had a similar rate of 60 percent (Steinbaum, 2020). Worse still, many older borrowers with more mature loans are watching their loan balances continue to rise, raising the specter of a new form of debt peonage. Rather than use their college degree to leverage a path toward economic security, these borrowers are finding their future tethered to their unyielding student loan debt.

To be sure, the burden of college debt is not equally shared. Figure 8.10 compares the incidence and extent of debt held by young, college-educated households, Black and White. What is most striking about the evidence is how much the debt measures have grown. Over the past generation, the share of Black college graduates with student loan debt has nearly doubled from around 40 percent to nearly 80 percent. The rates

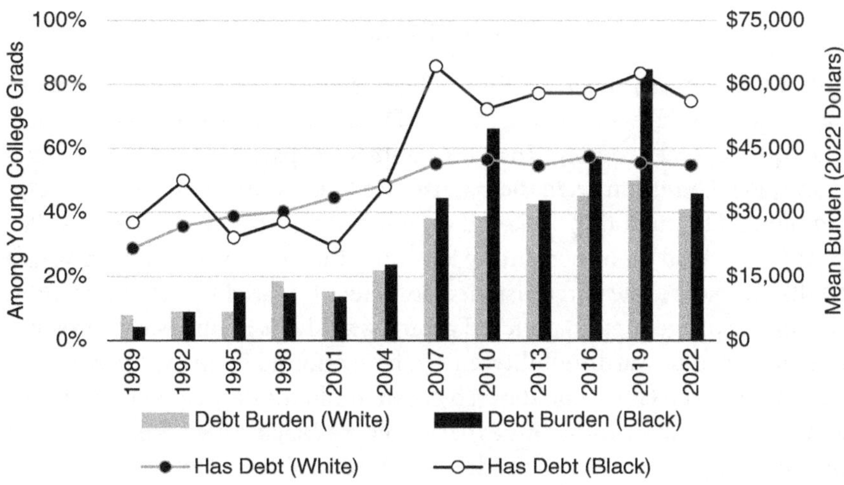

Figure 8.10 The debt burden by race

among Whites have remained about twenty points lower. Over the years, college graduates have had to assume far greater loans, with the increase in debt burden growing faster among Black college graduates.[14] One might wonder whether Black graduates simply borrow too heavily. Despite being raised in households with fewer resources, they leave college with modestly higher debt, by about $4,000 (NCES, 2020). Upon graduation, they enter an unwelcoming labor market where they earn 23 percent lower salaries (Economic Policy Institute, n.d.) and experience less employment security than their White peers. Immediately, they must juggle higher monthly debt payments on significantly lower budgets. Finding this challenge unrealistic, many choose an IDR plan rather than let their loan fall delinquent. Consequently, many Black borrowers observe anxiously as their outstanding balances have grown rather than diminished as expected (National Center for Education Statistics, 2023). This rising debt burden obstructs their efforts to build wealth, causes their credit score to plummet, and generates acute financial stress. Rather than a ladder to upward mobility and economic security, they are finding their college diploma comes with a deadweight.

[14] Whereas the average burden in Figure 8.8 was calculated among student debt holders only, the averages here are calculated across all young college graduates, whether Black or White. Interestingly, among these young householders, White college graduates tend to have higher average loan balances. In many cases, this is the result of higher rates of attending graduate programs that will likely boost their earning capacity even higher.

CONCLUSION

Fifty years ago, Lois Dickson Rice's creative vision and persistent determination in tandem with Senator Pell's (D-RI) legislative prowess launched a unique federal program. In stark contrast to past wealth-building programs, Pell Grants targeted their assistance to those most in need of a helping hand. Although they lacked the generosity of the GI Bill benefits, Pell Grants provided an important opportunity for millions of talented young adults to escape the circumstances of their birthright.[15] Then, as now, earning a college diploma offered aspiring students an unrivaled prospect to experience upward mobility and gain economic security. Of course, a fully funded Pell Grant could not, by itself, undo the decades of educational and economic discrimination experienced by Black Americans. Although the Pell Program serves as a model for future wealth programs, it functions as well as a cautionary tale.

In its early years, Pell Grants gave gifted students from impoverished families a realistic opportunity to select among the elite colleges and universities. The 50 percent cap on assistance excluded some potential students, but others were able to leverage their grant with other forms of aid to cover most of their college expenses. Pell's narrow focus on economic need meant that millions of Black students, along with many more White students, gained access to a college education otherwise unavailable. Recent studies support the contention that Pell Grants not only increase access to college but also encourage increased persistence and graduation rates.[16] Further evidence suggests that Pell Grants encourage more Black students to graduate with STEM degrees, thereby filling an important social need and ensuring more lucrative careers (Flowers, 2011). One can only wonder at the benefits we might reap today if Congress had granted Pell Grants entitlement status, full funding, and maximum awards that rose as college costs soared.

As beneficial as an unflawed Pell Program might be, we should not overestimate its potential impact. Singular programs by themselves cannot remedy the centuries of systemic disparities and institutional racism that is embedded in our societal fabric. Even if Pell Grants fully covered the costs of college, they could not single-handedly ensure "equal educational

[15] The GI Bill education benefits paid the full costs of attending college plus a modest stipend for living expenses.

[16] The interested reader should review Alon (2005), Chen & DesJardins (2010) and Umbricht (2016).

opportunity," nor substantially reduce the racial wealth gap. A major cost of attending college is the "lost earnings" from not working full-time. Many households simply cannot afford to have their adult children not working to sustain the family's income. Inferior educational quality at under-resourced schools causes many smart high school graduates to lack academic preparation for college without some additional academic help. Many prospective first-generation students are unable to navigate the college admissions process or persist to graduation without targeted advising. Each of these examples suggest systemic barriers that impede equal educational opportunity. Even if these barriers were eliminated, Black college graduates still encounter substantial discrimination in the labor, credit, and housing markets. While an effective program that assures equal educational opportunities in higher education is necessary to achieve an inclusive economy, it is not sufficient by itself.

A remarkable lesson of the Pell Program's history is the multifaceted pushback it generated by threatening economic stratification. The early generosity of the Pell Grants spawned envy among households whose income made them ineligible. Resultant pressure led to relaxed eligibility guidelines that diverted assistance to more affluent and White households. As Pell Grants permitted increased numbers of students from marginalized communities to attend state universities, lawmakers displayed decreased interest in funding these institutions. In response to the funding reductions, college administrators had few options other than raise tuition and fees, which undermined the Pell awards. Worse, they listened to their enrollment management consultants and shifted their institutional aid from need-based to merit-based. Responding to parental worries about the rising cost of college, Congress enacted tax credits to encourage saving for college and reimburse the costs of college. Curiously, Congress designed these credits as nonrefundable, thereby assuring their benefits would not reach households with the greatest needs, a feature that Ms. Rice, now a scholar at the Brookings Institution, saw perfectly well (Hauptman & Rice, 1997). All the while, Pell Grants have languished to their lowest levels relative to the cost of college. At one time, Pell Grants threatened to undermine higher education's role in maintaining economic stratification; more recently, this threat has been effectively repulsed.

No doubt, racial animus motivated some of this pushback. Increased matriculation of students from Black and other marginalized communities certainly influenced lagging support to restoring the real value of Pell awards as well as maintaining low-tuition public universities. Just as likely, race played a role in the shifting emphasis within institutional financial aid as school administrators sought the ideal student profile. Similarly, the decision by Congress to enact nonrefundable education tax credits strongly suggests another example where race considerations influenced the outcome.

Even if one questions whether these decisions were racially motivated, one cannot dispute the racialized consequences they produce. The return to a system of economic stratification in higher education clearly benefits White, affluent households. In anticipation of college's rising cost, affluent households can use generous tax deductions to save for their children's education tax-free without limit.[17] Raised in households and educated in schools each endowed with greater resources enables White students to score higher on standardized tests that frequently drive merit-based aid offers. That their family has some financial means makes them even more attractive recipients of aid from college administrators looking to fund their academic program. Exclusion of both home equity and retirement savings allows some middle-class households to qualify for Pell Grants and other forms of need-based aid. All of this help permits White college graduates to leave college with less debt even though they tend to enroll at higher-cost schools.

Their advantages do not stop there. Landing jobs that offer higher salaries, better benefits, and greater job security grants White college graduates an easier path to repaying their college loans without worry of late fees or accumulating interest. Less likely to be a first-generation graduate, they will field fewer requests for help from family members. Instead, they can marshal their resources to build their own savings. At some point, many can expect to receive a substantial family gift which they can use to complete their debt reduction or add to their savings. In eliminating their debt burden more quickly, White college graduates can focus on funding homeownership, business ventures, or other investments. Their student debt will pose much smaller obstacles in their pursuit of economic security. As they do, they are able to pass along their advantages to their children in ways that those entrapped by student debt peonage cannot.

We should take the lessons from the Pell Program experience as we consider the ways that we might truly reduce the racial wealth gap and erode the base of White supremacy. That is the task of the remaining chapter.

[17] Some states allow contributions to be tax-deductible.

9

Ending Malign Neglect

TIME FOR "BENIGN NEGLECT"

A mere two years after the Kerner Commission report was issued, *The New York Times* reported a released memo from Daniel Patrick Moynihan, counselor to the President, arguing that the Nixon Administration should pursue a policy of "benign neglect" toward African Americans. According to the memo, Black Americans had made "extraordinary progress" over the previous decade that could be expected to continue given the programs in place. He argued that continued attention to the issue of race only serves to cause "more people to get polarized, the more the crazy racists on the left and maybe crazy racists on the right shout and yell and make things seem worse than they are" (Kihss, 1970, p. 69). Certainly, one can dispute Moynihan's political judgment, but what seems less debatable is the likelihood that much of White America by the early 1970s was ready for a period of "benign neglect."

Three years later, *Commentary* magazine published an article entitled "Black Progress and Liberal Rhetoric" that gained wide attention. Drawing upon extensive data, the authors Ben Wattenberg and Richard Scammon concluded the progress attained by Black Americans as nothing short of "remarkable" and "striking" (Wattenberg & Scammon, 1973). Indeed, they insisted that a majority of Black households had achieved their definition of "middle class." To buttress their conclusions, they cited the rapid increase in Black high school graduation rates and white-collar employment, the doubling of real family incomes, and a decline in the Black unemployment rate. They attributed this progress to the strong economy during the 1960s, various Great Society programs and an end of the "logjam," their opaque reference to the dismantling of Jim Crow structures. Although they acknowledged that many disparities remained, they predicted "the continued march toward statistical parity with whites" (sec. 6, para. 4) would resume with the return of strong economic growth. One takeaway from their analysis was that the remaining racial disparities would shrink with time.

From some quarters, the *Commentary* article generated swift responses. Dr. John Morsell of the NAACP accused Wattenberg and Scammon of cherry-picking their statistics in support of their conclusions. Yes, from 1961 to 1971 median Black incomes had increased from 53 to 63 percent of White incomes, suggesting rapid improvement. Yet, Morsell (1973) noted that in 1945, median Black incomes had stood at 57 percent of White incomes, indicating much less progress over a far longer period. In a speech before the Chicago Economic Development Corporation, Dr. Karl Gregory (1973) noted that despite the improvement in Black incomes, the inflation-adjusted, absolute income gap had increased from $2,700 in 1947 to $3,700 in 1970. As proof of the remarkable Black progress, the *Commentary* article noted that young Black married households living outside the South had achieved income parity with their White counterparts. Dr. H. J. Bryce (1974) observed that Black married women were far more likely to work for pay than White married women, making this apparent parity the result of unequal labor effort. After reviewing extensive evidence that generated more ambiguous conclusions, Dr. Spratlen (1974) argued that the *Commentary* article would simply reinforce the policy of "benign neglect."

Despite these persuasive rebuttals, all made by prominent Black economists, few White economists rose to challenge the conclusions made by Wattenberg and Scammon. It is likely that the views expressed in the *Commentary* article resonated within the White economic orthodoxy. Quite incredibly, mainstream economics had largely ignored the role of racism and Jim Crow segregation through much of the twentieth century. Sure, Gunnar Myrdal (1944) had completed his monumental and influential work entitled *An American dilemma: The Negro problem and modern democracy*; its absence of economic theory and emphasis on norms and mores caused most in the discipline to view it as sociology, not economics.[1] Its conclusions that Black poverty was the direct result of White discrimination and not innate differences in ability did not sit well with most economists. Nor would have his call for substantial public policies in housing, civil rights, and education to resolve what he viewed as a massive moral

1 See Fleury (2012). According to Dewey (1958), "In the two-volume *An American Dilemma*, Myrdal the sociologist firmly held in check the analytical bent of Myrdal the economist" (p. 494).

paradox at the heart of American society. While Myrdal's work was influential among sociologists and psychologists studying race, it generated little interest among the overwhelmingly White economists who viewed racism as irrational and outside the field (Fleury, 2012). Labor relations specialists like Herbert Northrup, Richard Lester, and Donald Dewey examined the impact of race on employment outcomes, but their work was largely ignored by the broader profession (Fleury, 2012). One contemporary identified Dewey at Duke University as "virtually the only white economist in any Southern university to devote a substantial amount of research to the economic aspects of race" (Nicholls, 1960, p. 197). Similarly ignored by their White colleagues was the work of Black economists like Sadie T. M. Alexander, Abram Harris, and Oliver Cox, who examined the role and consequences of racism (Malveaux, 1991; Banks, 2022).

In 1957, a young economics professor at the University of Chicago published his PhD dissertation under the title of *The Economics of Discrimination*. By focusing on racial discrimination, Gary Becker tackled one of the milder forms of racial oppression then in operation (Alexis, 1998). Rather than examine the causes of this discrimination, Becker simply examined its economic consequences. Further narrowing his focus, he examined discrimination as it operated in market settings and ignored nonmarket forms like voting restrictions and school segregation. According to Becker, racially prejudiced White employers could decide not to employ Black employees for any host of reasons. If practiced widely, the lost opportunities for employment would reduce the earnings of Black employees relative to comparable White employees. Becker's model of taste-based discrimination explains both the segregated workplaces of the period as well as the obvious wage discrimination. Curiously, Becker's framing of discrimination in this way concluded that racially prejudiced employers would lose as well. Their refusal to hire equally competent Black workers at a lower wage would cost them lost profit. Moreover, Becker predicted the disappearance of this discrimination as nonprejudiced employers outcompeted their rivals by employing undervalued but fully capable Black employees. Drawing upon trade theory, he argued that discrimination had the same effect as a tariff; presumably, remove the obstacle and market equilibrium will return (Darity, 1975). Implementing pro-competitive policies could eliminate the uneconomical discrimination with time.

As others have noted, Becker's theory of taste-based discrimination has an extremely narrow focus, causing it to ignore broader elements of systemic racism. His theory emphasizes the issue of proximity in which Whites prefer physical distance from Blacks. Clearly, discrimination is not simply a physical phenomenon, but about creating status and hierarchy for those in the dominant group (Marshall, 1974). Becker's theory neglects to explain the underlying causes of this discrimination and assumes that institutions are fixed and inert. Despite these substantial shortcomings, most economists embraced his theory. Undoubtedly, its insistence on irrational behavior as the source of discriminatory behavior appealed to the profession. Even more attractive was its prediction that market corrections would eventually eliminate the behavior without worry of persistent recidivism. Like the conclusions of the *Commentary* article, racism and the attendant disparities would simply vanish with time.

A small group of economists rejected this view of racial discrimination along with its conclusion that racial disparities would naturally disappear. After examining household wealth data, Terrell (1971) concluded that Black households, despite their higher saving rates, had little hope of erasing the vast wealth gap even if they narrowed the racial income gap. Alexis (1971) perceptively argued how past centuries of enslavement and denied opportunity continued to stunt Black educational attainment, occupational choice, earnings, and income in ways that preclude any hope of erasing the wealth gap. America (1971) extended this argument as he explained how centuries of racial oppression did not just create losses for Black Americans but produced wealth transfers to Whites. Whether through profitable slave breeding or wage suppression, White owners pocketed the profit that seeded their current wealth. He insisted that any Whites who might view these past practices as immoral ought to acknowledge the contemporary moral obligation to repay this debt in the form of reparations. In two articles that remarkably anticipate the themes raised in this book, Robert Browne (1974) argues that reparations offer the only realistic way that Black Americans can overcome the racial wealth gap and become full participants in the American economy. He contends that a reparations policy represents a debt repayment which he links to Dr. King's iconic metaphor of a" promissory note that is now coming due." Further, he notes that the bill could be paid by ending the raids on the Treasury by White America (Browne, 1970). Lastly, two economists estimated the transfer of wealth from the enslaved to the enslaver during a portion of the time that slavery was legal. Depending on the discount rates used, they argued that the bill for this debt ranges from \$306 billion to \$30.5 trillion in 1973 dollars (Simon & Neal, 1974).[2]

[2] As noted elsewhere, other scholars have estimated the losses borne by Black Americans as a result of enslavement, the reneged promise to freedmen, and Jim Crow.

Finally, a group of seven economists published a remarkable document entitled "An Economic Bill of Rights" that documented the strengths and glaring challenges that dogged the American economy (Alexis et al, 1972). They argue persuasively that only when the economy functions effectively on behalf of all Americans can it achieve its true economic promise. As part of their recommendations to produce such an economy, they advocate an effective full-employment mandate, a tax system that effectively redistributes both income and wealth, the replacement of indirect tax expenditures with direct expenditure programs, greater federal support for public education to ensure more equal resources, public-funded health insurance, and a negative income tax system using up-front tax credits to provide basic income support. In addition to these nonracially targeted policies, they conclude that simply using "a color-blind approach will be totally inadequate" (p. 39) to remedy the prevailing racial wealth gap. They recommend reparations "to a group whose current, economic handicap is directly traceable to its historic victimization and from the group which has benefited the most from that victimization" (p. 39).

A HALF CENTURY OF MALIGN NEGLECT

It is unclear what the supporters of the "benign neglect" policies were hoping would actually occur. Undoubtedly, they wished the overt conflicts over race and racism would die down. Likely, many desired that Black Americans would continue to experience greater education, higher earnings, and increased economic security. What is less likely is whether the advocates were hoping that the racial disparities in educational attainment, income, and wealth would narrow. There is much evidence in our nation's history to suggest that White Americans would view such a narrowing of opportunities and outcomes as a threat to their status. What we do know from the last half century is that these racial disparities have not dissipated. Yes, Black Americans have experienced gains in educational attainment, income, and – more ambiguously – wealth. But the gaps between Black and White achievement in these key areas have persisted or even grown. Consequently, there is no reason to expect that the issues of race and racism should subside given these large and persistent disparities in opportunities and outcomes.

One cannot describe the past half century as a period of benign neglect. One major policy to redress the centuries of racial oppression is affirmative action. Inaugurated by President Kennedy's Executive Order 10925, its objective was to ensure equal opportunity in employment hiring and promotion, with an emphasis on groups like Blacks and women that had been historically marginalized. After some modest efforts that mostly "encouraged" employers to hire more women and minority employees, the program's successes generated a strident response among Whites who labeled the program "reverse discrimination" and accused it of undermining meritocracy. From the Reagan Administration onward, the program lost its modest political support while multiple Supreme Court rulings, including the 2023 rulings against Harvard University and UNC-Chapel Hill (*Students for Fair Admissions v. Harvard,* 2023), have effectively ended this mild experiment. Like the Pell Grants, its early successes triggered concerted White responses that effectively undermined the program's effectiveness.

Worse, the last half century has witnessed a persistent expansion of tax exclusions and deductions targeting their generous assistance to already-wealthy households. As Secretary Surrey warned, the expansion of these policies would covertly help those with the least need. In most cases, these tax expenditures offer their generosity without limit on their benevolence. At the same time, Congress has repeatedly undermined the effectiveness of the federal estate and gift taxes so that more family wealth is passed to future generations. Newly created loopholes are permitting the very rich to transfer their wealth in trusts that might escape future taxes forever. The overwhelming number of these beneficiaries are White, most of whom have benefited from their privileged position during centuries of enslavement and de jure discrimination. These policies of the past half century can only be judged as showing malign neglect when one considers the racial wealth gap.

MOVING AWAY FROM MALIGN NEGLECT

Upon realizing we are digging ourselves deeper into a hole, the usual initial advice is to stop digging. Our current tax policies target their assistance to the affluent, widen the racial wealth gap, and reinforce the basis of White supremacy. The first order of business is to revamp these policies. According to government estimates, these twelve tax expenditures are expected to cost the Treasury over \$1.2 trillion in 2023 and grow to over \$1.33 trillion by 2025.[3] As discussed, the overwhelming share of this aid goes to White households and those already wealthy. Reducing and redirecting this source of wealth accumulation is required.

[3] Author's calculations using Joint Committee on Taxation (2022) and US Department of Treasury (2023).

Offering a careful review of all twelve tax expenditures to consider their elimination or substantial revision is beyond the scope of this book. Indeed, Myers and Ha (2018) offer a thoughtful analysis of the complexities one should consider before implementing policies to reduce racial inequality. Nonetheless, we can make certain observations at this point. Ending the step-up in basis on estate assets and ensuring any unrealized capital gains are subject to federal taxation is a suitable first step. Eliminating or severely curtailing the exclusion of capital gains – whether on one's primary residence or otherwise – offers further low-hanging fruit. Enacted with little debate in 2017, the exclusion of qualified business income rewards certain business owners without offering any help to aspiring entrepreneurs. Its elimination makes sense. Similarly, ending the income exclusions of employer-sponsored health insurance and the imputed net rental value of one's principal residence both make good sense. However, each carries specific administrative challenges and powerful political advocates that must be overcome. Rather than continue the mortgage interest deduction that helps current homeowners, this tax deduction should be revamped as a first-time homebuyer tax credit that would aid households attain homeownership. Some curtailment of the tax preferences offered to retirement plans, charitable giving, and tax-exempt bonds should be made, although with due consideration of their impact on the affected areas. In some cases, legitimate policy objectives may justify replacement with a fully refundable tax credit that can provide encouragement and assistance in a more inclusive way. Serious work here has the potential to free up hundreds of billions of dollars annually that could be repurposed for other ends.

Next, we must restructure our wealth transfer tax system. As already detailed, our system of estate, gift, and GST taxes is largely voluntary and wholly ineffective. Rather than attempt to remedy its flaws, it makes more sense to take a different direction. We should replace our current system with an inheritance tax that works seamlessly with our federal income tax system. Shifting to an inheritance tax offers greater transparency, simplicity, efficiency, and fairness. Moving in this direction would shift the tax burden from the deceased or donor to the recipient. It would correct the unfortunate choice taken by Rep. Hull (D-TN) a century ago.

According to one recent tax proposal, implementing an inheritance tax would work in the following way (Batchelder, 2020). Any gifts, inheritances, or income from trusts would be subject to income and payroll taxes paid by the recipient. Amounts below a threshold, say $15,000 for a given year, would be exempted to limit the compliance costs generated by many small gifts. Amounts above that threshold would be subject to a lifetime exemption, say $500,000 per recipient. Any further sources of inherited income above that threshold would be subject to the taxpayer's income tax rate plus the full payroll tax rate, currently 15.3 percent.[4] In the case of large gifts, the income would be averaged over five years to limit the distortions that one-time gifts might have on the recipient's tax bracket. The beauty of moving in this direction is its simplicity and fairness. Any gifts or inherited funds are simply treated like employment earnings. Of course, one might argue that the $500,000 lifetime exemption is overly generous as it currently represents about one-half of the average wealth of a household. Once set, the exemption levels should adjust annually to offset inflation.

To prevent the transfer of unrealized capital gains that escape any taxation, the proposal adopts the concept of *constructive realization*. Under this idea, either the gifting of assets to an heir or death triggers a tax realization event. In either case, any unrealized gains in the transferred assets are the responsibility of the donor or estate as part of their income tax liability. These assets then carry a new tax basis as a result. If further gains are generated by these assets prior to their receipt by the recipient, then these unrealized gains become part of the recipient's income tax liability when they receive the gift. In this way, the proposed inheritance tax functions to create a seamless vehicle to ensure that any capital gains do not elude taxation.

A concrete example provides added clarity. Suppose a wealthy donor contributes appreciated assets to a GRAT with the expectation that 60 percent would go to an heir and 40 percent would remain with the donor. As the assets are contributed to the GRAT, the donor would be liable for 60 percent of any unrealized gains and the tax basis of the assets would be adjusted accordingly. When the heir eventually receives the GRAT assets, they would be responsible for any remaining unrealized gains, including those that accrued during the intervening years. By applying this concept of constructive realization, the inheritance tax can ensure that capital assets are taxed despite the efforts of well-advised donors and heirs. In the case of dynasty trusts that spin off income for recipient generations, the inheritance tax will capture any income that exceeds the prevailing exemption.

The inheritance tax is much better suited to overcoming many of the tax avoidance strategies previously discussed. While the GST tax is determined at the time the trust is created, the inheritance tax operates later when the income or gift is received. The former encourages tax evasion strategies that undervalue the trust assets. The inheritance tax simply waits until the

[4] The payroll tax cap on normal income – $160,200 in 2023 – is waived for this source of income.

actual transfers are known and assesses the tax then. Some complicated trusts may require a tax-withholding provision that collects a tax up front and then offers tax credits as the heirs receive their benefits. Nonetheless, the inheritance tax's simplicity and transparency eliminate most of the opaque gaming that currently exists.

Using their simulation tax model, the Urban-Brookings Tax Policy Center estimates how much tax revenue this inheritance tax proposal might raise. Using the $15,000 annual and $500,000 lifetime thresholds, they estimate that the tax would raise almost $1.4 trillion over a ten-year period (Batchelder, 2020). Given the modeling challenges posed by incomplete data, this estimate is considered a lower-bound figure. In comparison, the current estate and gift taxes are predicted to raise less than $300 billion over a ten-year period. By eliminating many of the major leaks in our current wealth transfer tax system, the inheritance tax can raise over one trillion dollars over the course of a decade. Of course, this amount can be expanded by simply lowering the lifetime threshold below the designated value of $500,000.

ENHANCING WEALTH-BUILDING CAPACITY

The Wealth Privilege model discussed in Chapter 2 explains how wealth-poor households face multiple financial headwinds as they strive for economic security. They experience earnings that are neither adequate nor reliable to permit steady and substantial saving. They can afford depreciating assets like furniture, appliances, and vehicles, but few assets that appreciate significantly over time. Those able to achieve modest prosperity often attract less fortunate family members seeking financial help. These households need help overcoming the minimal wealth thresholds required to access the virtuous cycles that wealth generation yields. Our nation's wealth policies should assist low-wealth households surmount the wealth barriers rather than support those who have already attained this access. These policies that work to reduce wealth disparities should also reduce the racial wealth gap (Darity & Myers, 1998).

Implementing Baby Bonds

While many young adults in White households can expect some assistance from generational wealth, the Baby Bonds program is an attempt to provide universal access to capital to all young adults (Markoff et al., 2022). As initially designed, all American children are enrolled into the program, assigned a specific account, and receive an initial deposit from the federal government (Hamilton & Darity, 2010). Each year, the government would make additional deposits inversely related to the household's economic circumstances to ensure program progressivity. Managed by the Treasury Department, these accounts would earn interest. The funds could not be touched until the account holder reaches the age of eighteen. Under some proposals, limits are placed on how the funds might be spent – whether on education, homeownership, or retirement. While states and some cities are considering their own program, the focus here is on providing a federal program that provides universal access to capital (Brown et al., 2023).

Sen. Cory Booker (D-NJ) became an early advocate of the concept and has regularly co-sponsored legislation to gain its enactment. Under a recent version, entitled the American Opportunity Accounts Act and filed in 2023 with co-sponsor Rep. Ayanna Pressley (D-MA), the proposal envisions an initial deposit of $1,000 in each child's account. The federal government would make annual deposits of $2,000 or less depending on the household income. For example, households whose income is below the poverty line would receive the full $2,000 while those whose income is twice the poverty line would receive only $1,000 each year.[5] Future payments would adjust with inflation. The deposited funds would earn interest as they are invested in government bonds. At eighteen, account holders can withdraw funds to pay for education, purchase a home, start a business, or begin a retirement savings plan. In this way, the Baby Bond would enable each young adult the opportunity to access the Asset Appreciation pathway as they start their working careers.

According to the bill's sponsors, this proposal could generate as much as $46,215 for a young adult to invest in their future (Booker, 2023). Further estimates indicate that the average Black young adult would find nearly $30,000 in their account while the average White adult would gain just under $12,000. In this way, the proposal would offset modestly the current wealth advantages experienced by young Whites. One cost estimate of an earlier version of this proposal placed it at $82 billion, an amount that is less than the added revenue that the inheritance tax proposal would generate. Tying the Baby Bonds to a newly enacted inheritance tax makes good political as well as economic sense. The tax on large gifts and bequests would finance actual opportunities for the next generation as well as providing the Baby Bonds with an enduring revenue source.

[5] See S.441-American Opportunity Account Act (2023–2024).

Doubling the Pell Grant Awards

One glaring weakness of the Baby Bonds proposal is its long gestation period. Under current versions, it will take eighteen years for account holders and their balances to mature fully. Until then, there is a need for bridge programs to help older children whose age makes them unable to benefit significantly from the Baby Bonds. Pell Grants offer one such bridge to post-secondary education, whether technical or higher education. However, the erosion of Pell awards requires new funding to restore its original vision of providing equal opportunity to higher education. One such proposal is the Pell Grant Preservation and Expansion Act of 2021. It proposes to double the Pell awards over five years, extend eligibility to Deferred Action for Childhood Arrivals (DACA) students, ease qualifying requirements to students from households eligible for Medicaid and Supplemental Nutrition Assistance Program (SNAP) benefits, and offer these recipients an extra $1,500 annually on top of the maximum award (Pell Grant Preservation and Expansion Act, 2021). Although the bill did not pass, it does offer a model of how policymakers might restore the promise of Pell.

According to the Department of Education, the maximum Pell Grant in the 2023–24 academic year will be $7,395, while the anticipated award costs are expected to total to $29.8 billion.[6] Doubling the award and adding the extra $1,500 could mean $16,300 a year to students whose families have modest resources. Grants of that size could cover about two-thirds of the cost of attending a typical four-year public university. While this still leaves a considerable gap, many could leverage this with other federal aid as well as institutional aid to make college a realistic choice. Easing the qualifying process would also make the Pell Grant more attractive to those students and their families who find the paperwork overwhelming.

This proposal comes with a twist. Under the normal Pell Grant formulation, an increase in the awards automatically expands eligibility (Blagg, 2022). For example, a doubling of awards will double the income thresholds that determine grant eligibility. That means that much of the additional program costs assist more affluent households rather than target the neediest of recipients. In this proposal, I suggest that the doubling of awards initially only go to those students eligible under the current guidelines. This means that the benefit reduction rate must also double. That is, for every $1,000 of additional family contribution, the Pell award will

[6] See US Department of Education (n.d.) Student Financial Assistance FY 2024 Budget Request.

decline by $2,000, not the current $1,000 (Klebs, 2020). By making this adjustment, not only does the extra assistance continue to focus on the highest-need recipients, but also it precludes the real possibility that students from very affluent households will become eligible. Designing the expansion in this way also will serve to limit the overall program costs. One would expect this proposal to cause the overall program costs to slightly more than double their current total of $30 billion. Any costs above this level would result only if a considerable number of high-need individuals found the awards attractive enough to matriculate.

Requiring Guaranteed Retirement Accounts

The shift away from defined benefit to defined contribution retirement plans has left far too many American households without adequate savings. As of 2016, Jeszeck (2019) found that nearly a third of households with someone fifty-five years or older had neither a defined benefit pension nor any retirement savings. Households between the ages of forty and fifty-five have on average less than $15,000 in retirement savings, far less than they will need during retirement (Ghilarducci & James, 2016). Clearly, households recognize the need to save for retirement but are unable to do so for a variety of personal and institutional reasons. As one would expect, there is a clear racial divide to the retirement savings issue as well.

Guaranteed Retirement Accounts (GRAs) would require all employers to offer their employees a fully portable retirement savings account. Each employee would be required to contribute 1.5 percent of their earnings, while employers would offer a matching contribution of 1.5 percent as a minimum. Both parties could contribute more. To help low-wage employees make this contribution, the federal government would provide a fully refundable tax credit of $600 to each contributing employee. This money would offset fully the contributions made by workers earning $40,000 or less. All contributions would vest immediately, allowing employees to take the accounts with them as they change employers. Each account holder could select among different pension funds and profit from the higher returns and lower risks provided by pooled savings. To ensure these funds benefit fully from long-term investments, they cannot be withdrawn for emergency or otherwise until the account holder becomes eligible for Social Security, currently at age sixty-two.

Once the employee reaches retirement age, they can decide with limits how to allocate their account balance between a lump sum payment and a lifetime annuity. In the case of the latter, the Treasury Department would determine the lifetime annuity based on the individual's age, family structure, and accumulated savings. This annuity would then complement their Social Security benefit. Guaranteeing the annuity shifts the life expectancy risks from the individual retiree to the federal government; retirees would no longer worry about outliving their accumulated savings. Those able to participate from early adulthood would benefit from regular saving and matching employer contributions that would appreciate significantly over the years. Along with their Social Security benefits, most households would find their retirement incomes adequate to meeting their living expenses.

In 2017, the Tax Policy Center of the Urban Institute generated an estimated cost of this proposal. According to their analysis, this program would cost less than $40 billion annually (Toder & Khitatrakun, 2017). In contrast, the lost revenue to the Treasury from the current tax treatment of pension assets totaled $329 billion in 2022. While the latter aid helps primarily affluent households, the GRA proposal would target the assistance more toward less affluent households.

To be sure, the GRA proposal does not address the systemic advantages experienced by White households. Their higher earnings would allow them to save more each year and benefit from larger employer contributions. Less frequent and shorter bouts of unemployment would add further to this advantage. Higher levels of wealth among White households would make the prohibition against early withdrawals a less severe sacrifice. And longer life expectancy among Whites would likely mean they would benefit disproportionately from the annuitized payments. Nonetheless, implementing the GRA proposal would do much to reduce the current racial retirement gap. According to the 2022 SCF, two-thirds of White households aged between forty and sixty-five have retirement funds, and these hold 82 percent of the pension assets. Only 44 percent of similarly aged Black households hold pension assets, and they hold less than 4 percent of the pension assets.[7] Among those who hold retirement funds in this age group, White balances are typically more than double Black holdings. Implementing the GRA proposal will undoubtedly reduce the racial retirement gap, although only partially.

THE REMAINING NEED FOR REPARATIONS

Recent research requiring extraordinary archival work now traces the racial wealth gap over the entire post-Emancipation era (Derenoncourt et al., 2022). Drawing upon multiple sources, the authors estimate a White

[7] To provide benchmarks, White and Black households comprise less than 64 and 13 percent, respectively, of this age group.

to Black wealth gap of 23 to 1 in 1870 that rapidly declines to 11 to 1 by 1900 before narrowing much more slowly through the first half of the twentieth century. From that point, they document a period of stagnation followed by a trend reversal as the gap has widened over recent decades to 6 to 1. Likening the trend to a hockey stick, they explain the initial progress and recent regress in the following way. After 1870, a modest convergence of White and Black incomes enabled Black household saving to slowly erode the initial gap. As Black freedpeople were starting from low levels of wealth, their efforts substantially reduced the wealth gap but yielded diminishing returns over time. White backlash to this modest Black progress in the early twentieth century ended the income convergence, preventing any further narrowing of wealth. Worse, as household wealth over the past half century has increased faster than income, the role of savings takes a back seat to asset appreciation as a source of wealth accumulation. The authors conclude that even under the most favorable circumstances – (1) that income convergence quickly reaches parity and (2) Black households experience similar saving and capital gains as Whites despite their reduced income and wealth – "it will be centuries before per capita Black and white wealth equalize" (Derenoncourt et al., 2022, p. 23).

The more likely result, as explained throughout this book, is that the racial wealth gap will continue to widen. While the evidence demonstrates that Black households save more than White households when income is considered, their lower household income limits the extent that Black households can "outsave" Whites to wealth parity. Far more important is the increasing role that wealth and capital assets play. As the WP model clearly shows, White households with their expanded wealth can invest in higher-risk but higher-return assets that fuel their wealth accumulation. Various tax expenditures are designed to shelter these capital gains not only from the federal income tax, but the estate tax as well. There is no realistic way that Black households, starting from their lower wealth holdings, can realistically hope to equalize these capital gains, much less exceed them. Further, the recent dismantling of the federal estate and gift taxes means that more of the past advantages enjoyed by White households will be transferred to their heirs. The momentum for wealth expansion is undeniable and growing in force. Not even an immediate and full enactment of the policies just discussed will yield a substantial reversion of this trend. The centuries of singular privilege fully supported by a mix of federal policies have created a dynamic that calls for one remedy – a substantial transfer of wealth from the beneficiaries of these policies to the primary victims.

Such a transfer, usually referred to as reparations, can trace its modern roots back to 1969 when civil rights activist James Forman challenged White churches and synagogues to pay $500 million to African Americans for their complicity in benefiting from a system of enslaved labor. Since that time, there has been an ongoing discussion, mostly among Black economists, about the key details of such a policy. Robert Browne (1972) argued that reparations should punish Whites for the sins of enslavement, compensate current descendants for the unpaid labor of their ancestors, and restore the rightful shares of income and wealth to the Black community. Richard America (1998) offered key principles that should guide the design and implementation of a reparations program. These include the recognition that Whites continue to benefit from past (unjust) policies, levels of compensation should reflect these past amounts of White enrichment, and compensation should be paid in ways that increase wealth across the Black community. Any compensation should largely come from affluent Whites and primarily benefit low-wealth Black households. Various studies have estimated the consequences of state-sanctioned enslavement, Jim Crow discrimination, and reneging on the promise of "forty acres and a mule" on White and Black wealth today.[8] To limit any moral hazard problem, Darity and Frank (2003) recommend restricting compensation to African Americans who can show documentation regarding enslaved ancestors as well as having self-identified as Black over the preceding ten years. Lastly, Swinton (1990) argues that as the state-sanctioned policies harmed Blacks while privileging Whites, the reparations payment should provide racial equity by equalizing capital wealth in both communities.

Currently, the most detailed reparations policy is explained in a recent book by Darity and Mullen (2020). They recommend that payments should target US citizens who can document at least one enslaved ancestor as well as their self-identification as Black for a dozen years prior to program implementation. They estimate this would include about forty million Americans. Regarding the payment, they argue that transfers sufficient to equalize the current racial wealth gap should be considered the bottom-line figure. Based on 2016 data, they estimate the reparations bill would require a payment of $267,000 per recipient that would total $10.7 trillion. They recommend the payments include a mix of direct transfers to individual recipients, newly created trust funds that would provide wealth-building

[8] See America (1990) for an excellent compendium of these studies along with a rich and insightful discussion of the issues. Craemer et al. (2020) provides a more recent estimate as well.

grants for homeownership, higher education, and business startups as well adding to the endowments of historically black colleges and universities (HBCUs). While some estimates of Black harm and White enrichment from state-sanctioned policies are less than this amount, none can account for the violence and trauma experienced by Black Americans throughout our nation's history. Even after the wealth is transferred, Black Americans still will face persistent discrimination in education, labor markets, credit markets, and housing.

Although the $10.7 trillion figure seems overwhelming, it resides in the realm of possibilities as current GDP, a measure of annual income generated, runs more than double this figure. Darity and Mullen recommend the transfers occur in staggered amounts over a ten-year period. Regarding financing, they cite the experience of the Great Recession, in which the Federal Reserve transferred $1 trillion to financial institutions largely overnight along with subsequent monthly purchases of around $50 billion as part of "quantitative easing." Consequently, they recommend that the Federal Reserve cover some or all this transfer. Worries about resultant inflation could be mitigated by transferring more nonliquid assets that would assist wealth building rather than spur consumption. In addition, substantial curtailment of the current wealth-building tax expenditures could reliably raise $6 to $8 trillion over a decade. Using this source would meet the earlier requirement that affluent Whites bear the burden of reparation payments.

CONCLUSION

Reflecting on our nation's racial history generates some important lessons. Throughout much of that history, White treatment of Black Americans has been horrific. The system of chattel slavery that enriched White Americans as the enslaved toiled under harsh conditions while enslaved females were used to breed children later sold for profit was a uniquely immoral system. After Emancipation, the elimination of the freed peoples' political and civil rights despite constitutional guarantees represents another badge of dishonor. The subsequent political violence perpetrated by Whites on Black Americans – whether through individual lynchings or mob violence against whole communities while law enforcement stood mute – reeks of both corrupt and depraved behavior. Even the longstanding Jim Crow laws and norms that denied educational and occupational opportunities to Black Americans and communicated a persistent reality of inferior status through separate and substandard public accommodations reflect a willingness to accept a debauched bargain. Of course, White Americans today are not responsible for these past behaviors, except as beneficiaries.

The durability, transferability, and fecundity of household wealth confirms how these long-past policies that advantaged White households still leave their mark today. Different forms of wealth have long been prized for their capacity to hold their value through good times and bad. For just as long, parents have used any accumulated wealth to offer their children whatever opportunities and advantages that were available. Despite the federal estate and later gift taxes functioning through most of the twentieth century, families had numerous opportunities to transfer wealth to their offspring, whether in the form of physical, financial, cultural, or human capital. In whatever form, this family help enabled the recipients to access the pathways of wealth accumulation and take advantage of the privileges of wealth. With this stake, these recipients could effectively accumulate wealth during their lifetimes, enabling them to leverage this wealth for their children's futures. Whether we examine the racial wealth gap in 1962 or today, we can see concrete evidence of this legacy.

Reflecting on our nation's racial history evokes another insight – that White racism against Black Americans will not evaporate if Whites hold superior wealth. As even Becker's theory of discrimination suggests, White wealth offers its holders the luxury of practicing discrimination even if it produces self-inflicted economic harm. More importantly, the racial wealth divide ensures the replacement of the de jure segregation under Jim Crow with a de facto system today. Household wealth effectively determines where people live, what schools their kids attend, which jobs and occupations are available, and whether upward mobility is an option or not. Moreover, the racial wealth divide is the vehicle that allows White Americans to retain their superior position within the racial hierarchy that defines American society. The concentration of wealth within the White community is a source of the economic, political, and social power available to Whites to impose their will and maintain the racial hierarchy.

At the same time, there have been periods in our racial history, however brief, ambivalent, and episodic, in which White Americans have considered the possibility of truly offering the promise of America to Black Americans. The post-Emancipation period of Reconstruction and the brief Civil Rights era of the 1960s offer two examples where there existed strong impulses to remedy the racial hierarchy. Both efforts underestimated the difficulty of the challenge as well as the power of the countervailing impulse to reassert the racial hierarchy under new circumstances. An effective reparations policy seeking to eliminate the racial wealth gap and implemented over a ten-year period could meet both challenges. We should take inspiration from the courage and foresight of these two periods and enact an effective reparations policy with haste.

Appendix

The interested reader can learn more about how the estimates reported in Chapter 4 were determined.

The estimated revenue losses for each of the tax expenditures were taken from the Joint Committee on Taxation (JCT) or from Treasury Department publications. Both estimate the revenue losses suffered by the Treasury assuming current economic conditions and prevailing tax law. Each estimates these losses assuming the other tax deductions are unchanged. For example, the value of the home sales exclusion measures the savings to home sellers who pay no taxes on the gain versus the capital gains rate they would pay if the exclusion only was eliminated. Both conduct forward estimates of these losses, with the JCT making estimates over five years while the Treasury reports ten years. I use two different annual estimates and average them to determine the annual cost of each tax deduction. I use the JCT estimates except for estimates of the imputed net rental value of one's principal residence.

To determine the racial shares received from each tax expenditure, I use the detailed information on household balance sheets to determine these estimates. I describe later how I make each of the calculations.

PENSION ASSETS EXCLUSION

The Survey of Consumer Finances (SCF) surveys respondents and calculates their pension assets including employer-sponsored defined contribution plans, individual retirement accounts (IRAs) and Keogh Plans, as well as current or future defined benefit pensions. I calculate the relative shares held collectively by White and Black households. I then apply a tax bracket adjustment to reflect the value of these tax savings to households in higher tax brackets. See later details on this adjustment.

LIFE INSURANCE EXCLUSION

The SCF queries respondents regarding the cash value of any whole life insurance policies they may hold to estimate the value of inside buildup. I calculate the relative shares held collectively by White and Black households and then apply a tax bracket adjustment to reflect the value of these savings to households in higher tax brackets. See later details on this adjustment.

HOME MORTGAGE INTEREST DEDUCTION

The SCF asks respondents for any mortgage payments they make on their principal residences. Of course, these payments do include both principal and interest payments. I use the relative share of these payments made collectively by White and Black households as the basis of the estimated shares. I top edit any monthly payments to reflect the mortgage interest cap, whether $1 million or $750,000. As a below-the-line deduction, I make adjustments according to the respondent's reporting on whether or not they itemized on their taxes. I apply a tax bracket adjustment to reflect the value of these savings to households in higher tax brackets. See later details on this adjustment.

CHARITABLE CONTRIBUTIONS DEDUCTION

The SCF queries respondents for the level of charitable giving over the previous year. These responses form the basis of estimating the share of benefits from this deduction. To reflect the deduction caps of 30 percent of household adjusted gross income (AGI) for noncash gifts and 60 percent for cash gifts, I use the lower cap of 30 percent to place an upper bound on the deduction value. Although this deduction is subject to the Pease Limitation (see final section in this appendix), I use the lower cap as an alternative method to capture the limits on benefits to highly generous givers. As a below-the-line deduction, I make adjustments on whether the respondent reported on whether they itemized on their taxes or not.

I apply a tax bracket adjustment to reflect the value of these savings to households in higher tax brackets. See later details on this adjustment.

CAPITAL GAINS EXCLUSION

The SCF queries the respondents about income realized from any capital gains over the previous year. After editing any capital losses, I then calculate the share of reported capital gains by White and Black households. I then apply a capital gains tax bracket adjustment that considers the likely value of the exclusion based on the existing personal income and capital gains tax rates. See later sections for details.

STATE AND LOCAL TAX (SALT) DEDUCTION

Prior to the Tax Cuts and Jobs Act of 2017 (TCJA 2017), the JCT reported benefits from a Home Property Deduction and a SALT deduction. Since 2018, they have combined the two into one deduction.

HOME PROPERTY TAX DEDUCTION

The SCF asks respondents for the value of their share in any residential properties. I use this value since taxpayers can deduct their property taxes on multiple residences. As the SCF does not report any geographical information regarding the respondents, one cannot estimate the actual property tax liabilities that result from differences in local tax rates. I assume a standard rate. As a below-the-line deduction, I make adjustments on whether the respondent reported on whether they itemized on their taxes or not. I apply a tax bracket adjustment to reflect the value of these savings to households in higher tax brackets. See later details on this adjustment.

OTHER STATE AND LOCAL TAX DEDUCTION

This deduction includes state and local income tax, sales tax, and personal property tax payments. To capture the share of benefits, I use household income as the best proxy for each of these. Of course, there is no accounting for the different tax rates used across the states and localities. As a below-the-line deduction, I make adjustments on whether the respondent reported on whether they itemized on their taxes or not. I apply a tax bracket adjustment to reflect the value of these savings to households in higher tax brackets. See later details on this adjustment.

Since the decision to lump this with the Home Property Tax Deduction, I use the latter method to estimate the combined tax benefits. Residential property owners across the country pay local property taxes, while not all states impose a personal income tax. Consistent with the tax law, this deduction is capped at $10,000 since 2018.

IMPUTED RENT EXCLUSION

Similar to the Home Property Tax Deduction, I use the reported value of all residential properties owned. Presumably, the current property value offers an accurate estimate of its potential rental income. I apply a tax bracket adjustment to reflect the value of these savings to households in higher tax brackets. See later details on this adjustment.

HEALTH INSURANCE EXCLUSION

Unfortunately, the SCF has never asked very detailed questions regarding the quality or extent of health insurance coverage other than whether some or all members of the household are covered. As such, the benefits of this tax expenditure reflect solely the proportion of White and Black households fully covered by some form of health insurance. By necessity, any differences in the quality of insurance coverage are ignored. I apply a tax bracket adjustment to reflect the value of these savings to households in higher tax brackets. See later details on this adjustment.

HOME SALES EXCLUSION

The SCF asks respondents about the purchase price, current market value, and the value of any improvements made to their principal residence to determine the unrealized capital gains. I use this value to determine the potential value of the exclusion when they do indeed sell their home. As this exclusion has an upper limit, I cap any gains by the prevailing limit based on whether they are a single or married household. I apply a unique tax bracket adjustment that estimates the value of the exclusion relative to the capital gains rate the household would have otherwise paid. See details in the next sections.

TAX-EXEMPT BOND DEDUCTION

The SCF asks respondents for the value of all tax-exempt bonds they own. I use this to estimate the relative share of this tax deduction. I apply a tax bracket adjustment to reflect the value of these savings to households in higher tax brackets. See later details on this adjustment.

ESTATE STEP-UP IN BASIS EXCLUSION

The SCF queries respondents on any unrealized capital gains on their real assets, business assets, and financial securities. I subtract from this value any unrealized gains in their principal residence to reflect the home sales exclusion. Of course, this measures the potential benefits as opposed to the actual benefits. Assuming unbiased mortality rates, this estimate should offer a reasonable view of the value of this tax expenditure across different groups. I apply a unique tax bracket adjustment that estimates the value of the exclusion relative to the capital gains rate the household would have otherwise paid. See details in the following sections.

QUALIFIED BUSINESS INCOME EXCLUSION

Created by the TCJA of 2017, this newest tax expenditure is subject to elimination after 2025 unless Congressional action intervenes. To estimate its share of benefits, I use the business (and farm) income variable to estimate its benefits as it captures much of the "pass-through" income earned from small business. The deduction is limited to 20 percent of this income and carries a very complicated cap. To capture this, I limit the deduction to 90 percent of the lower income threshold available to married households or all other households. I apply a tax bracket adjustment to reflect the value of these savings to households in higher tax brackets. See details in the following sections on this adjustment.

TAX BRACKET ESTIMATES

To estimate the personal income tax bracket, I simply use household income, marriage status, and the standard deductions taken from each year. To generate an estimate of AGI, I subtract the standard deduction from household income. I use this figure to estimate both the personal income tax rate as well as the long-term capital gains rate. I use the former to calculate the personal income tax bracket.

When calculating the benefits of the capital gains exclusion, I use the difference between the applicable personal income tax rate and the capital gains rate.

When calculating the benefits of the Home Sales Exclusion and the Estate Step-Up in Basis Exclusion, I use the difference with the applicable capital gains rate.

PEASE LIMITATION

Named after Rep. Donald Pease (D-OH), the limitation reduced the value of tax deductions available to higher-income households. Beyond some income threshold, households would suffer a 3 percent reduction in their allowable deduction for every dollar of additional income. This reduction could not exceed a maximum loss of 80 percent of expected deduction. This "financial haircut" was applied to selected deductions including the home mortgage interest, charitable giving, and the SALT deductions. Since the first two already have deduction caps, I apply the Pease Limitation to the SALT deduction only. The limitation was enacted in 1991, rescinded in 2009, reinstated in 2013, and rescinded again in 2017.

References

Ajilore, O. (2020). On the Persistence of the Black-White Unemployment Gap. Center for the American Progress. February 20, 2020. www.americanprogress.org/article/persistence-black-white-unemployment-gap/.

Akbar, P. A., Li, S., Shertzer, A., & Walsh, R. P. (2019). *Racial segregation in housing markets and the erosion of black wealth* (No. w25805). National Bureau of Economic Research.

Alexis, M. (1962). Some negro-white differences in consumption. *The American Journal of Economics and Sociology*, *21*(1), 11–28. www.jstor.org/stable/3484315.

Alexis, M. (1971). Wealth accumulation of black and white families: The empirical evidence: Discussion. *The Journal of Finance*, *26*(2), 458–465.

Alexis, M. (1998). The economics of racism. *The Review of Black Political Economy*, *26*(3), 51–75.

Alexis, M., Anderson, B., Bell, D., Browne, R., Dixon, V., Gregory, K., & O'Dell, J. (1972). An economic bill of rights. *The Review of Black Political Economy*, *3*(1), 1–41.

Aliprantis, D., Carroll, D., & Young, E. (2019). "The Dynamics of the Racial Wealth Gap." Federal Reserve Bank of Cleveland, Working Paper no. 19-18. https://doi.org/10.26509/frbc-wp-201918.

Alon, S. (2005). Model mis-specification in assessing the impact of financial aid on academic outcomes. *Research in Higher Education*, *46*, 109–125.

Alstott, A. L., & Novick, B. (2005). War, taxes, and income redistribution in the twenties: The 1924 veterans' bonus and the defeat of the Mellon plan. *Tax Law Review*, *59*, 373.

America, R. F. (1971). A new rationale for income redistribution. *The Review of Black Political Economy*, *2*(2), 3–21.

America, R. F. (Ed.). (1990). *The wealth of races: The present value of benefits from past injustices* (No. 132). Greenwood Publishing Group.

America, R. F. (1998). Reparations and public policy. *The Review of Black Political Economy*, *26*(3), 77–83.

Anderson, E. (1980). *Race and politics in North Carolina, 1872–1901: The black second.* Louisiana State University Press.

Anstey, R. (1975). The volume of the North-American slave-carrying trade from Africa, 1761–1810. *Outre-Mers. Revue d'histoire*, *62*(226), 47–66.

AP-NORC Center for Public Affairs Research (2022, March). "Evaluating Progress for Racial Equality" [https://apnorc.org/projects/evaluating-progress-for-racial-equality/].

Austin, A. (2016). *The color of entrepreneurship: Why the racial gap among firms costs the U.S. millions*. Center for Global Policy Solution.

Babcock, F. M. (1924). *The appraisal of real estate* (Vol. 3). Macmillan.

Banks, N. (2022). Retrospectives: Sadie TM Alexander: Black women and a "taste of freedom in the economic world." *Journal of Economic Perspectives, 36*(4), 205–220.

Baradaran, M. (2017). *The color of money: Black banks and the racial wealth gap*. Harvard University Press.

Barnes, M. (1922). College entrance examinations. In College Entrance and Examination Board *22nd Annual Report*. HathiTrust Digital Library. Retrieved June 30, 2023, from https://babel.hathitrust.org/cgi/pt?id=pst.000060014443&view=1up&seq=17&skin=2021.

Batchelder, L. L. (2020). Leveling the playing field between inherited income and income from work through an inheritance tax. In J. Shambaugh and R. Nunn (Eds.), *Tackling the tax code: Efficient and equitable ways to raise revenue* (pp. 48–88). The Hamilton Project at Brookings.

Bates, T. (1997). Unequal access: Financial institution lending to black-and white-owned small business start-ups. *Journal of Urban Affairs, 19*(4), 487–495.

Bayer, P., Casey, M., Ferreira, F., & McMillan, R. (2017). Racial and ethnic price differentials in the housing market. *Journal of Urban Economics, 102*, 91–105.

Becker, G. (1957). *The economics of discrimination*. University of Chicago Press.

Berkhofer, R. F. (1972). Jefferson, the ordinance of 1784, and the origins of the American territorial system. *The William and Mary Quarterly: A Magazine of Early American History*, 231–262.

Bertrand, M., & Mullainathan, S. (2004). Are Emily and Greg more employable than Lakisha and Jamal? A field experiment on labor market discrimination. *American Economic Review, 94*(4), 991–1013.

Blagg, K. (2022). *How would doubling the Pell Grant expand aid eligibility?* Urban Institute.

Blakey, R. G. (1914). The new income tax. *The American Economic Review, 4*(1), 25–46.

Blakey, R. G. (1915). Amending the federal income tax. *The ANNALS of the American Academy of Political and Social Science, 59*(1), 32–43.

Blakey, R. G. (1916). The new revenue act. *The American Economic Review, 6*(4), 837–850.

Blakey, R. G. (1924). The revenue act of 1924. *The American Economic Review, 14*(3), 475–504. Retrieved May 11, 2021, from www.jstor.org/stable/742.

Blakey, R. G. (1926). The revenue act of 1926. *The American Economic Review, 16*(3), 401–425. Retrieved May 11, 2021, from www.jstor.org/stable/691.

Blakey, R. G., & Blakey, G. (1932). The revenue act of 1932. *The American Economic Review, 22*(4), 620–640. Published by: American Economic Association Stable. www.jstor.org/stable/1805167.

Blanchflower, D. G., Levine, P. B., & Zimmerman, D. J. (2003). Discrimination in the small-business credit market. *Review of Economics and Statistics, 85*(4), 930–943.

Bonilla-Silva, E., Goar, C., & Embrick, D. G. (2006). When whites flock together: The social psychology of white habitus. *Critical Sociology, 32*(2–3), 229–253.

Booker, Sen. C. (2023, February 15). "Booker, Pressley Re-introduce Bicameral 'Baby Bonds' Legislation to Tackle Wealth Inequality." [Press Release].

Boren, S. (1989). The Pell Grant Program: Background and Issues. CRS Report for Congress.

Borjas, G. J., & Bronars, S. G. (1989). Consumer discrimination and self-employment. *Journal of Political Economy, 97*(3), 581–605.

Borowczyk-Martins, D., Bradley, J., & Tarasonis, L. (2017). Racial discrimination in the US labor market: Employment and wage differentials by skill. *Labour Economics, 49*, 106–127.

Boshara, R., Emmons, W. R., & Noeth, B. (2015). The demographics of wealth: How age, education and race separate thrivers from strugglers in today's economy. Federal Reserve Bank of St. Louis.

Brannon, G. M. (1986). Tax loopholes as original sin: Lessons from tax history. *Villanova Law Review, 31*, 1763.

Brenner, J. C. (1992, July 26). Life on Mars: The Mars family has all of the classic elements. Independent.

Brigham, C. C. (1923). *A study of American intelligence*. Princeton: Princeton University Press.

Brown v. Board of Education of Topeka, 347 U.S. 483 (1954).

Brown, A. (2018). Appraisal narratives: Reading race on the midcentury block. *American Quarterly, 70*(2), 211–234.

Brown, D. A. (2022). *The whiteness of wealth: How the tax system impoverishes Black Americans – and how we can fix it*. Crown.

Brown, M., Biu, O., Harvey, C., & Shanks, T. (2023). The state of baby bonds. *Urban Institute*, www.urban.org/sites/default/files/2023-02/The%20State%20of%20Baby%20Bonds.pdf.

Browne, R. S. (1970). Barriers to black participation in the American economy. *The Review of Black Political Economy, 1*(2), 57–67.

Browne, R. S. (1972). The economic case for reparations to Black America. *The American Economic Review, 62*(1/2), 39–46.

Browne, R. S. (1974). Wealth distribution and its impact on minorities. *The Review of Black Political Economy, 4*(4), 27–38.

Brownlee, W. (1985). Wilson and financing the modern state: The revenue act of 1916. *Proceedings of the American Philosophical Society*, 129(2), 173–210. Retrieved May 11, 2021, from www.jstor.org/stable/986988.

Brumley, J. (2022). "Most Americans Hang out with others who are a lot like them." Baptist News Global. Retrieved at Most Americans hang out with people who are a lot like them – Baptist News Global. Retrieved August 23, 2022.

Bryce, H. J. (1974). Are most blacks in the middle class? *The Black Scholar, 5*(5), 32–36. www.jstor.org/stable/41066302.

Burd, S. (2017). Moving on up? What a groundbreaking study tells us about access, success, and mobility in higher ed. *New America Foundation Policy Paper, October, 26*.

Burd, S. (2020). Crisis point: How enrollment management and the merit-aid arms race are derailing public higher education. New America.

Bureau of Internal Revenue. (1935). *Statistics of income for 1933*. US Treasury Department. www.irs.gov/statistics/soi-tax-stats-archive-1916-to-1933-statistics-of-income-reports.

Bureau of Labor Statistics. (n.d.) *Historical CPI-U*. Retrieved June 20, 2024, from www.bls.gov/cpi/tables/historical-cpi-u-201710.pdf.

Burke, M. (2019). Great Time for a GRAT. *Journal of Accountancy*. Retrieved June 25, 2021, from www.journalofaccountancy.com/issues/2019/oct/wealth-transfer-grantor-retained-annuity-trusts.html

Burlew, A. K. H., Banks, W. C., McAdoo, H. P., & Azibo, D. A. Y. (Eds.). (1992). *African American psychology: Theory, research, and practice*. SAGE Publications.

Carey, H. C. (1853). *The slave trade, domestic and foreign: Why it exists, and how it may be extinguished*. A. Hart. Reissued 1872.

Carlton, G. (2022). "A Brief History of the SAT: America's Most Popular College Entrance Exam." Retrieved June 30, 2023, from bestcolleges.com.

Carnegie, A. (1889). The gospel of wealth. North American Review.

Castoro, A. A. (2015). Wealth transition and entitlement: Shedding light on the dark side of a charmed life. *The Journal of Wealth Management, 18*(2), 9–12. https://doi.org/10.3905/jwm.2015.18.2.00.

Cavalluzzo, K., & Wolken, J. (2005). Small business loan turndowns, personal wealth, and discrimination. *The Journal of Business, 78*(6), 2153–2178.

Chachere, B., & Udinsky, G. (1990) R. F. America (Ed.). (1990). *The wealth of races: The present value of benefits from past injustices* (No. 132). Greenwood Publishing Group.

Charles, K. K., & Hurst, E. (2002). The transition to home ownership and the black-white wealth gap. *Review of Economics and Statistics, 84*(2), 281–297.

Charron-Chénier, R., Fink, J. J., & Keister, L. A. (2017). Race and consumption: Black and White disparities in household spending. *Sociology of Race and Ethnicity, 3*(1), 50–67.

Chen, R., & DesJardins, S. L. (2010). Investigating the impact of financial aid on student dropout risks: Racial and ethnic differences. *The Journal of Higher Education, 81*(2), 179–208.

Chiteji, N. S. (2010). The racial wealth gap and the Borrower's Dilemma. *Journal of Black Studies, 41*(2), 351–366.

Christensen, R. (2010). *The paradox of Tar Heel politics: The personalities, elections, and events that shaped modern North Carolina*. University of North Carolina Press.

Clemans-Cope, L., Garrett, B., & Hoffman, C. (2006). *Changes in employees' health insurance coverage, 2001–2005*. Henry J. Kaiser Family Foundation.

Clinton, W. J. (1995). Remarks at the Franklin D. Roosevelt 50th Anniversary Commemoration in Warm Springs, Georgia Online by Gerhard Peters and John T. Woolley, The American Presidency Project www.presidency.ucsb.edu/node/220738.

Clinton, W. J. (1996, June 4). *Princeton University Commencement Speech*. [Speech audio recording]. Retrieved July 11, 2023, from www.c-span.org/video/?72708-1/princeton-university-commencement-speech.

Cohen, L. (2003). *A consumers' republic: The politics of mass consumption in postwar America*. Vintage Books.

Collins, C., Fitzgerald, J., Flannery, H., Ocampo, O., Paslaski, S., & Thomhave, K. (2021). *Silver spoon oligarchs: How America's 50 largest inherited-wealth dynasties accelerate inequality*. Institute of Policy Studies.

Collins, W. J., & Margo, R. A. (1999). *Race and home ownership, 1900 to 1990* (No. w7277). National Bureau of Economic Research.

Collins, W. J., & Margo, R. A. (2003). Historical Perspectives on Racial Differences in Schooling in the United States. Working Paper 9770 www.nber.org/papers/w9770 *National Bureau of Economic Research.*

Collins, W. J., & Margo, R. A. (2011). Race and home ownership from the end of the civil war to the present. *American Economic Review, 101*(3), 355–359.

50 Congressional Record. (1913).

53 Congressional Record. (1916).

55 Congressional Record. (1917).

64 Congressional Record (1924).

75 Congressional Record (1932).

97 Congressional Record (1951).

Cooper, J. (2010). Ghosts of 1932: The lost history of estate and gift taxation (July 23, 2009). *Florida Tax Review, 9*(10). Available at SSRN: https://ssrn.com/abstract=1438181.

Cooper, D., & Dynan, K. (2016). Wealth effects and macroeconomic dynamics. *Journal of Economic Surveys, 30*(1), 34–55.

Copeland, C. (2014). Employment-based retirement plan participation: Geographic differences and trends, 2013. *EBRI Issue Brief, 405.*

Craemer, T., Smith, T., Harrison, B., Logan, T., Bellamy, W., & Darity Jr, W. (2020). Wealth implications of slavery and racial discrimination for African American descendants of the enslaved. *The Review of Black Political Economy, 47*(3), 218–254.

Crooks v. Harrelson, 282 U.S. 55 (1930).

Cumming v. Richmond County Board of Education. 175 US 528 (1899). https://tile.loc.gov/storage-services/service/ll/usrep/usrep175/usrep175528/usrep175528.pdf.

Curs, B. R., Singell, L. D., & Waddell, G. R. (2007). The Pell program at thirty years. In J. C. Smart (Ed.), *Higher education: Handbook of theory and research* (Vol XXII, pp. 281–334). Springer.

Danhof, C. H. (1941). Farm-making costs and the "safety valve": 1850–60. *Journal of Political Economy, 49*(3), 317–359. www.jstor.org/stable/1824734.

Darity Jr., W. A. (1975). Economic theory and racial economic inequality. *The Review of Black Political Economy, 5*(3), 225–248.

Darity Jr., W. A. (2008). Forty acres and a mule in the 21st century. *Social Science Quarterly, 89*(3), 656–664.

Darity Jr., W. A. (2022). Position and possessions: Stratification economics and intergroup inequality. *Journal of Economic Literature, 60*(2), 400–426.

Darity Jr., W. A., & Frank, D. (2003). The economics of reparations. *American Economic Review, 93*(2): 326–329.

Darity Jr., W. A., & Mason, P. L. (1998). Evidence on discrimination in employment: Codes of color, codes of gender. *Journal of Economic Perspectives, 12*(2): 63–90.

Darity Jr., W. A., & Mullen, A. K. (2020). *From here to equality: Reparations for Black Americans in the twenty-first century*. UNC Press Books.

Darity Jr., W. A., & Myers Jr., S. L. (1998). Persistent disparity. *Books.*

Darity Jr., W. A., Guilkey, D. K., & Winfrey, W. (1996). Explaining differences in economic performance among racial and ethnic groups in the USA. *American Journal of Economics and Sociology, 55*(4): 411–426.

Darity Jr., W. A., Hamilton, D., Paul, M., Aja, A., Price, A., Moore, A., & Chiopris, C. (2018). What we get wrong about closing the racial wealth gap. *Samuel DuBois Cook Center on Social Equity and Insight Center for Community Economic Development, 1*(1), 1–67.

Delisle, J. (2017). The disinvestment hypothesis: Don't blame state budget cuts for rising tuition at public universities, *AEI: American Enterprise Institute for Public Policy Research*. Retrieved September 9, 2021, from https://policycommons.net/artifacts/1296939/the-disinvestment-hypothesis/1900195/. CID: 20.500.12592/4v2ctq.

Demakakos, P., Biddulph, J. P., Bobak, M., & Marmot, M. G. (2016). Wealth and mortality at older ages: A prospective cohort study. *Journal of Epidemiology and Community Health*, *70*(4), 346–353.

Deming, D., & Dynarski, S. (2009). Into college, out of poverty? Policies to increase the postsecondary attainment of the poor (Working Paper No. 15387).

Derenoncourt, E., Kim, C. H., Kuhn, M., & Schularick, M. (2022). Wealth of two nations: The US racial wealth gap, 1860–2020. NBER Working Paper 30101.

Desmond, M. (2016). *Evicted: Poverty and profit in the American city*. Crown.

Deverell, W. F. (1988). To loosen the safety valve: Eastern workers and western lands. *The Western Historical Quarterly*, *19*(3), 269–285.

Dewey, D. (1958). Review 5: No title. *Southern Economic Journal (pre-1986)*, *24*(4), 494–496.

Dilliard, I. (1941). *Mr. Justice Brandeis, great American: Press opinion and public appraisal*. The Modern View Press.

DiRusso, A. A. (2009). Testacy and intestacy: The dynamics of wills and demographic status. *Quinnipiac Probate Law Journal*, *23*, 36.

Dobbs, G. R., & Gaither, C. J. (2023). How much heirs' property is there? Using lightbox data to estimate heirs' property extent in the US. *Journal of Rural Social Sciences*, 38, 10–28.

Dortch, C. (2023). Federal Pell Grant Program of the Higher Education Act: Primer. CRS Report R45418, Version 2. Updated. *Congressional Research Service*.

Douglass, F. (1876). Speech of Frederick Douglass at the 1876 Republican Convention. https://thelionofanacostia.wordpress.com/2016/05/16/speech-of-frederick-douglass-at-the-1876-republican-national-convention/ Accessed on August 8, 2021.

Dukeminier, J., & Krier, J. E. (2002). The rise of the perpetual trust. *UCLA Law Review*, *50*, 1303.

Duquette, N. J. (2019). Founders' fortunes and philanthropy: A history of the US charitable-contribution deduction. *Business History Review*, *93*(3), 553–584.

Dynarski, S. M. (2003). Does aid matter? Measuring the effect of student aid on college attendance and completion. *American Economic Review*, *93*(1), 279–288.

Dynarski, S. M., & Scott-Clayton, J. E. (2006). The cost of complexity in federal student aid: Lessons from optimal tax theory and behavioral economics. *National Tax Journal*, *59*(2), 319–356.

E. H. S. (1921). Constitutionality of taxation of realized capital increase under federal income tax acts. *University of Pennsylvania Law Review and American Law Register*, *69*(3), 253–259. https://doi.org/10.2307/3314252.

Easterlin, R. A. (1976). Population change and farm settlement in the northern United States. *Journal of Economic History*, *36*(1), 45–75.

Economic Policy Institute. (n.d.) *State of America Working Data Library*. Wages by Education. 2022. Retrieved July 27, 2023, from www.epi.org/data/#?subject=wage-education.

Edlin, A. S. (1993). Is college financial aid equitable and efficient? *Journal of Economic Perspectives*, *7*(2), 143–158.

Edwards, R. (2009). Changing perceptions of homesteading as a policy of public domain Disposal. *Great Plains Quarterly, 29*(3), 179–202. https://digitalcommons.unl.edu/greatplainsquarterly/1229.

Employer Health or Accident Plans: Taxfree Protection and Proceeds. (1954). *The University of Chicago Law Review, 21*(2), 277–286. https://doi.org/10.2307/1597927.

Fairlie, R. W., & Robb, A. M. (2010). *Race and entrepreneurial success: Black-, Asian-, and White-owned businesses in the United States.* MIT Press.

Farrand, M. (Ed.). (1911). *The records of the Federal Convention of 1787* (Vol. 3). Yale University Press.

Federal Estate and Gift Taxes: Public Hearings Before the Committee on Ways and Means. 94th Congress. (1976). Testimony by S. S. Surrey. www.google.com/books/edition/Federal_Estate_and_Gift_Taxes/E7A6lcwdH8gC?hl=en.

Federal Housing Administration. (1936). *Underwriting Manual: Underwriting and Valuation Procedure under Title II of the National Housing Act with Revisions to April 1, 1936* (Washington, DC), pt. 2, sec. 2, Rating of Location.

Federal Reserve Board of Governors. (2022). *Financial Accounts of the United States-Z.1.* Retrieved August 21, 2022, from www.federalreserve.gov/releases/z1/20230309/html/default.htm.

Feiveson, L., & Sabelhaus, J. (2018). How does intergenerational wealth transmission affect wealth concentration? FEDS Notes.

Finkelman, P. (2009). The American suppression of the African slave trade: Lessons on legal change, social policy, and legislation, *Akron Law Review, 42*(2), Article 4. Available at: http://ideaexchange.uakron.edu/akronlawreview/vol42/iss2/4.

Finkelman, P. (2012). Slavery in the United States: Persons or Property? Retrieved June 23, 2023, from https://scholarship.law.duke.edu/cgi/viewcontent.cgi?referer=&httpsredir=1&article=5386&context=faculty_scholarship.

Fishback, P. V., LaVoice, J., Shertzer, A., & Walsh, R. (2020). *Race, risk, and the emergence of federal redlining* (No. w28146). National Bureau of Economic Research.

Fleury, J. B. (2012). Wandering through the borderlands of the social sciences: Gary Becker's economics of discrimination. *History of Political Economy, 44*(1), 1–40.

Flippen, C. (2004). Unequal returns to housing investments? A study of real housing appreciation among black, white, and Hispanic households. *Social Forces, 82*(4), 1523–1551.

Flowers, L. A. (2011). Attaining the American dream: Racial differences in the effects of Pell grants on students' persistence and educational outcomes. Kirwin Institute for the Study of Race and Ethnicity.

Fogel, R. W., & Engerman, S. L. (1974). *Time on the cross: The economics of American Negro slavery.* W. W. Norton & Company.

Forbes Magazine. (2023, November). America's Largest Privately Held Companies, 2023. Retrieved June 20, 2024, from www.forbes.com/largest-private-companies/list/#tab:rank.

Franklin, R. S. (1991). *Shadows of race and class.* University of Minnesota Press.

Friedberger, M. (1983). The farm family and the inheritance process: Evidence from the Corn Belt, 1870–1950. *Agricultural History, 57*(1), 1–13.

Friedman, M. (1957). *Theory of the consumption function.* Princeton University Press.

Galenson, M. (1972). Do blacks save more? *The American Economic Review, 62*(1/2), 211–216.

Ghilarducci, T., & James, H. (2016). A Comprehensive Plan to Confront the Retirement Savings Crisis. The New School Retirement Equity Lab, Schwartz Center for Economic Research, The New School. Retrieved May 7, 2019, from tinyurl.com/y2v42df6.

Gittleman, M., & Wolff, E. N. (2004). Racial differences in patterns of wealth accumulation. *The Journal of Human Resources, 39*(1), 193–227. https://doi.org/10.2307/3559010.

Gladieux, L. E. (1995). Federal student aid policy: A history and an assessment. *Financing Postsecondary Education: The Federal Role, October*, 43–60.

Goldfarb, S. J. (1994). An inquiry into the politics of the prohibition of the international slave trade. *Agricultural History, 68*(2), 20–34. www.jstor.org/stable/3744400.

Goldin, C. (1998). America's graduation from high school: The evolution and spread of secondary schooling in the twentieth century. *The Journal of Economic History, 58*(2), 345–374.

Goode, R. (1960). Imputed rent of owner-occupied dwellings under the income tax. *The Journal of Finance, 15*(4), 504–530.

Goodwin, I. J. (2010). How the rich stay rich: Using a family trust company to secure a family fortune. *Seton Hall Law Review, 40*(2), 2.

Gordon, A. (2005). The creation of homeownership: How new deal changes in banking regulation simultaneously made homeownership accessible to whites and out of reach for blacks. *The Yale Law Journal, 115*, 186–226.

Gravelle, J., & Jackson, P. J. (2005). *The exclusion of capital gains for owner-occupied housing*. Congressional Information Service, Library of Congress.

Grebler, L., Blank, D. M., & Winnick, L. (1956). Long-term changes in cost and terms of mortgage financing. In *Capital formation in residential real estate: Trends and prospects* (pp. 220–237). Princeton University Press.

Gregory, K. D. (1973). Brief report of the State of the Black Economy, 1973. *The Review of Black Political Economy, 3*(3), 3–16.

Grubb, F. (2010). US land policy: Founding choices and outcomes, 1781–1802. In D. Irwin and R. Sylla (Eds.), *Founding choices: American economic policy in the 1790s* (pp. 259–290). University of Chicago Press.

Gutter, M. S., & Fontes, A. (2006). Racial differences in risky asset ownership: A two-stage model of the investment decision-making process. *Journal of Financial Counseling and Planning, 17*(2). Available at SSRN: https://ssrn.com/abstract=2232188.

Hadden Loh, T., Coes, C., & Buthe, B. (2020). Separate and unequal: Persistent residential segregation is sustaining racial and economic injustice in the US. Brookings.

Hall, B. (2024, May 19). Show me the money: How billionaires influence public education in North Carolina'. Greensboro News and Record. https://greensboro.com/opinion/column/bob-hall-show-me-the-money-how-billionaires-influence-public-education-in-north-carolina/article_dbc8ac54-113a-11ef-a8cd-3f68fecaa4f5.html.

Hamilton, D., & Chiteji, N. (2013). Wealth. In P. L. Mason (Ed.), *International Encyclopedia of race and racism* (2nd ed.). Macmillan Reference.

Hamilton, D., & Darity Jr., W. A. (2010). Can 'baby bonds' eliminate the racial wealth gap in putative post-racial America? *Review of Black Political Economy, 37*(3–4): 207–216. https://doi.org/10.1007/s12114-0109063-1.

Hamilton, D., & Darity Jr., W. A. (2017). The political economy of education, financial literacy, and the racial wealth gap. *Review*, *99*(1), 59–76.

Hamilton, D., Austin, A., & Darity Jr, W. A. (2011). Whiter jobs, higher wages: Occupational segregation and the lower wages of black men.

Hartford Courant. (1997, February 8). President Clinton strikes out with tax credit. Retrieved August 4, 2023, from www.courant.com/1997/02/08/president-clinton-strikes-out-with-tax-credit-for-college/.

Hauptman, A., & Rice, L. (1997). Coordinating financial aid with tax credits. *Brookings Institution*. Retrieved July 21, 2023, from www.brookings.edu/articles/coordinating-financial-aid-with-tuition-tax-benefits/.

Hays, C. L. (1999, July 3). Forrest Mars, Sr., 95, creator the M&M and a candy empire. *New York Times*.

Heiner v. Donnan, 285 U.S. 312 (1932).

Heller, D. (2013). The role of Pell grants in an era of rising tuition prices. Reflections on Pell: Championing Social Justice Through 40 Years of Educational Opportunity. The Pell Institute for the Study of Opportunity in Higher Education.

Henderson, C. (2020). Heirs property in Georgia: Common issues, current state of the law, and further solutions. *Georgia Law Review*, *55*, 875.

Henderson, L., Herring, C., Horton, H. D., & Thomas, M. (2015). Credit where credit is due?: Race, gender, and discrimination in the credit scores of business startups. *The Review of Black Political Economy*, *42*(4), 459–479.

Herbold, H. (1994). Never a level playing field: Blacks and the GI Bill. *The Journal of Blacks in Higher Education*, *6*, 104–108.

H. R. Rep. No. 82-586, at 27 (1951). SERIALSET-11497_00_00-001-0000-0000.pdf (govinfo.gov).

Hull, C. (1948). *The memoirs of Cordell Hull* (Vol. 1). Macmillan Company.

Hungerford, T. L. (2006, September). Tax expenditures: Trends and critiques. Congressional Research Service, the Library of Congress.

Hylton v. United States, 3 U.S. (3 Dall.) 171 (1796).

Internal Revenue Service. (n.d.). *Estate Tax Filing Year Tables*. Retrieved May 29, 2023, from www.irs.gov/stan.d.)tistics/soi-tax-stats-estate-tax-filing-year-tables.

Internal Revenue Service. (n.d.). *Taxable Estate Tax Returns as a Percentage of Adult Deaths, Selected Years of Death, 1934–2019*. Retrieved May 20, 2023, from www.irs.gov/statistics/soi-tax-stats-historical-table-17.

Jackson, K. T. (1987). *Crabgrass frontier: The suburbanization of the United States*. Oxford University Press.

Jacobsen, E. (n.d.). A (Mostly) Brief history of the SAT and ACT tests. Retrieved July 4, 2023, from www.erikthered.com/tutor/sat-act-history-printable.html.

Jacobson, D., Raub, B., & Johnson, B. (2007). The estate tax: Ninety years and counting. *SOI Bulletin*, *27*(1), 118–128.

Jeszeck, C. A. (2019). Retirement security: Most households approaching retirement have low savings, an update. Retrieved June 20, 2024, from www.gao.gov/products/gao-19-442r.

Johnsen, D., & Dellinger, W. (2018). The constitutionality of a national wealth tax. *Indiana Law Journal*, *93*, 111.

Joint Committee on Taxation (JCT). (2015). History, Present Law, and Analysis of the Federal Wealth Transfer Tax System. JCX-52-15.

Joint Committee on Taxation (JCT). (2019). Estimates of Federal Tax Expenditures for Fiscal Years 2016–2020. JCX-55-19. Government Printing Office.
Joint Committee on Taxation (JCT). (2022). Estimates of Federal Tax Expenditures for Fiscal Years 2022–2026. JCX-22-22. Government Printing Office.
Jones, A. H. (1980). *Wealth of a nation to be: The American Colonies on the eve of the revolution.* Columbia University Press.
Jones, J., & Schmitt, J. (2014). *A college degree is no guarantee* (Vol. 8). Center for Economic and Policy Research.
Jones-Correa, M. (2000). The origins and diffusion of racial restrictive covenants. *Political Science Quarterly, 115*(4), 541–568.
Joulfaian, D. (1998). *The federal estate and gift tax: Description, profile of taxpayers, and Economic consequences.* Office of Tax Analysis, US Department of the Treasury.
Joulfaian, D. (2007). The Federal Gift Tax: History, Law, and Economics. OTA Papers, *100.*
Journal of Political Economy. Washington notes. Vol. 23, no. 10. (1915).
Kahn, C. H. (1960). Personal deductions in the federal income tax. NBER Books.
Kahng, L. (2013). Path dependence in tax subsidies for home sales. *Alabama Law Review, 65,* 187.
Kamin, D. (2024, June 1). She made an offer on a condo. Then the seller learned she was black. *New York Times.* A 14.
Katznelson, I. (2005). *When affirmative action was white: An untold history of racial inequality in twentieth-century America.* W. W. Norton & Company.
Keisler-Starkey, K., & Bunch, L. N. (2020). *Health insurance coverage in the United States: 2019.* US Census Bureau.
Kihss, P. (1970). 'Benign Neglect' on Race is Proposed by Moyniham. *New York Times.* March 1, pp. 1, 69.
Klaman, S. B. (1961). *The postwar residential mortgage market* (Vol. 8). Princeton University Press.
Klarman, M. J. (1998). The Plessy era. *The Supreme Court Review, 1998,* 303–414.
Klebs, S. (2020). Why should we double the Pell grant. *Third Way.* Retrieved August 2, 2023, from www.thirdway.org/memo/why-we-should-double-the-pell-grant.
Klein, C. A. (1998). A requiem for the rollover rule: Capital gains, farmland loss, and the law of unintended consequences. *Washington and Lee Law Review, 55,* 403.
Klein, W. A. (1963). An enigma in the federal income tax: The meaning of the word gift. *Minnesota Law Review, 48,* 215.
Knowlton v. Moore, 178 U.S. 41, 78–83. (1900).
Kopkin, N. (2017). Does racial prejudice affect black entrepreneurship?: Evidence exploiting spatial differences in prejudicial attitudes. *Applied Economics, 49*(31), 3045–3066. https://doi.org/10.1080/00036846.2016.1254336.
Kornhauser, M. E. (1985). The origins of capital gains taxation: What's law got to do with it. *Southwestern Law Journal, 39,* 869.
Kousser, J. M. (1980). Separate but not equal: The Supreme Court's first decision on racial discrimination in schools. *The Journal of Southern History, 46*(1), 17–44.
Kraus, M. W., & Tan, J. J. (2015). Americans overestimate social class mobility. *Journal of Experimental Social Psychology, 58,* 101–111.
Kraus, M. W., Rucker, J. M., & Richeson, J. A. (2017). Americans misperceive racial economic equality. *Proceedings of the National Academy of Sciences, 114*(39), 10324–10331.

Kraus, M. W., Onyeador, I. N., Daumeyer, N. M., Rucker, J. M., & Richeson, J. A. (2019). The misperception of racial economic inequality. *Perspectives on Psychological Science, 14*(6), 899–921.

Kurtz, J., & Surrey, S. S. (1970). Reform of death and gift taxes: The 1969 treasury proposals, the criticisms, and a rebuttal. *Columbia Law Review, 70*(8), 1365–1401.

Laband, D. N., & Lentz, B. F. (1983). Occupational inheritance in agriculture. *American Journal of Agricultural Economics, 65*(2), 311–314. https://doi.org/10.2307/1240880.

Ladd, H. F. (1998). Evidence on discrimination in mortgage lending. *Journal of Economic Perspectives, 12*(2), 41–62.

Langbein, J. H. (1989). The twentieth-century revolution in family wealth transmission. *Occasional Papers from the Law School, the University of Chicago, 25*, 1.

Laurenti, L. (1960). *Property values and race*. University of California Press.

Lee, J. (2013). "The Early Years of the Pell Grant", Reflections on Pell: Championing Social Justice Through 40 Years of Educational Opportunity. The Pell Institute for the Study of Opportunity in Higher Education.

Levin, S. (2021, April 17). A beach town seized a black couple's land in the 1920s. Now their family could get it back. *The Guardian*. www.theguardian.com/us-news/2021/apr/17/bruces-beach-willa-charles-manhattan-beach-la-county.

Levine, P. B., & Ritter, D. (2022). *The racial wealth gap, financial aid, and college access* (No. w30490). National Bureau of Economic Research.

Light, J. (2011). Discriminating appraisals: Cartography, computation, and access to federal mortgage insurance in the 1930s. *Technology and Culture, 52*(3), 485–522.

Lindsey, V. W. (2002). The charitable contribution deduction: A historical review and a look to the future. *Nebraska Law Review, 81*, 1056.

Lomax, R. G., West, M. M., Harmon, M. C., Viator, K. A., & Madaus, G. F. (1995). The impact of mandated standardized testing on minority students. *Journal of Negro Education, 64*(2), 171–185.

Long, B. T., & McPherson, M. (2007). *The impact of federal tax credits for higher education expenses* (pp. 101–168). University of Chicago Press.

Lowenstein, H., & Kisska-Schulze, K. (2018). A historical examination of the constitutionality of the federal estate tax. *William & Mary Bill of Rights Journal, 27*, 123.

Lowndes, C. L. (1960). Federal taxation and the supreme court. *The Supreme Court Review, 1960*, 222–257.

Luckey, J. (2003). A history of the federal estate, gift and gst yaxes *CRS Report*.

Lui, M., Robles, B., Leondar-Wright, B., Brewer, R., & Adamson, R. (2006). *The color of wealth*. United for a Fair Economy.

Ma, J., Pender, M., & Libassi, C. J. (2020). Trends in college pricing and student aid 2020. College Board.

Malveaux, J. (1991). Missed opportunity: Sadie Tanner Mossell Alexander and the economics profession. *The American Economic Review, 81*(2), 307–310.

Maremont, M., & Scism, L. (2010, October 3). Shift to wealthier clientele puts life insurers in a bind. *Wall Street Journal*.

Marketti, J. (1990). Estimated present value of income diverted during slavery. In R. F. America (Ed.), *The wealth of races: The present value of benefits from past injustices* (No. 132, pp. 107–124). Greenwood Publishing Group.

Markoff, S., Ain J., Chelwa G., & Hamilton, D. (2022). *A brighter future with baby bonds: How states and cities should invest in our kids*. Prosperity Now.

Marshall, R. (1974). The economics of racial discrimination: A survey. *Journal of Economic Literature, 12*(3), 849–871.

Masnick, G. (2001). Homeownership trends and racial inequality in the United States in the twentieth century. Joint Center for Housing Studies, Harvard University. W01-4.

Mason, D. L. (2010). Homeownership is colorblind: The role of African American savings and loans in home finance, 1880–1980. In *Business History Conference. Business and Economic History On-line: Papers Presented at the BHC Annual Meeting* (Vol. 8, p. 1). Business History Conference.

Mason, P. L. (2023). *The economics of structural racism: Stratification economics and US labor markets.* Cambridge University Press.

Massey, D. S., & Denton, N. (1993). *American apartheid: Segregation and the making of the underclass.* Harvard University Press.

Mathews, J. (1970). Studies in race relations in Georgia, 1880–1930. Unpublished PhD dissertation. Duke University.

Mattheis, R., & Raz, I. T. (2019). There's no such thing as free land: The homestead act and economic development. Working paper. Available at: https://scholar.harvard.edu/iraz/publications/homestead-act-and-development-american-west.

May v. Heiner, 281 U.S. 238 (1930).

McMichael, S. L., & Bingham, R. F. (1923). *City growth and values.*

Mehlhorn, D. (1998). A requiem for blockbusting: Law, economics, and race-based real estate speculation, *Fordham Law Review, 67,* 1145. Available at: https://ir.lawnet.fordham.edu/flr/vol67/iss3/4.

Miller, M. C. (2011). Land and racial wealth inequality. *American Economic Review, 101*(3), 371–376.

Modigliani, F., & Brumberg, R. (1954). Utility analysis and the consumption function: An interpretation of cross-section data. In K. K. Kurihara (Ed.), *Post-Keynesian economics.*

Morsell, J. A. (1973). Black progress or illiberal rhetoric? The Crisis, 200–203.

Mortenson, T. G. (1988). Pell grant program changes and their effects on applicant eligibility 1973–74 to 1988–89. ACT Student Financial Aid Research Report Series, 88-1.

Moylan, M. (2019). A profitable yool: The act of 1807's failure at ending the slave trade in antebellum America.

Mullainathan, S., & Shafir, E. (2009). Savings policy and decision-making in low-income households. In R. M. Blank, & M. S. Barr (Eds.), *Insufficient funds: Savings, assets, credit, and banking among low-income households* (pp. 121–145). Russell Sage Foundation.

Munnell, A. H., Tootell, G. M., Browne, L. E., & McEneaney, J. (1996). Mortgage lending in Boston: Interpreting HMDA data. *The American Economic Review, 86*(1), 25–53.

Myers Jr., S. L., & Chan, T. (1996). Who benefits from minority business set-asides? The case of New Jersey. *Journal of Policy Analysis and Management, 15*(2), 202–226.

Myers Jr., S. L., & Chung, C. (1996). Racial differences in home ownership and home equity among preretirement-aged households. *The Gerontologist, 36*(3), 350–360.

Myers Jr., S. L., & Ha, I. (2018). *Race neutrality: Rationalizing remedies to racial inequality.* Lexington Books.

Myrdal, G. (1944). *An American dilemma; the Negro problem and modern democracy* (2 vols.). Harper & Row.

National Advisory Commission on Civil Disorders. (1968). Kerner Commission Report. Department of Justice. www.ojp.gov/ncjrs/virtual-library/abstracts/national-advisory-commission-civil-disorders-report.

National Archives. (2021). The Homestead Act of 1862. Retrieved July 22, 2021, from www.archives.gov/education/lessons/homestead-act.

National Center for Education Statistics (NCES). (2020). Table 331.95. Retrieved July 21, 2023, from https://nces.ed.gov/programs/coe/current_tables.

National Center for Education Statistics (NCES). (2023). Loans for Undergraduate Students and Debt for Bachelor's Degree Recipients. Condition of Education. U.S. Department of Education, Institute of Education Sciences. Retrieved July 20, 1923, from https://nces.ed.gov/programs/coe/indicator/cub.

National Center for Health Statistics. (2019). National Health Interview Survey, *Long-Term Trends in Health Insurance Coverage, 1968–2018.*

National Federation of Independent Business v. Sebelius, 567 U.S. 519 (2012).

Neal, L. (1990). A calculation and comparison of the current benefits of slavery and an analysis of who benefits. In R. F. America (Ed.), *The wealth of races: The present value of benefits from past injustices* (No. 132). Greenwood Publishing Group.

"Newspaper Account of a Meeting between Black Religious Leaders and Union Military Authorities" (1865). Freedmen and Southern Society Project. Retrieved December 5, 2024, from https://freedmen.umd.edu/sampdocs.htm.

New York Trust v. Eisner, (1921). 256 U.S. 348.

Nicholls, W. H. (1960). Southern tradition and regional economic progress. *Southern Economic Journal*, *26*(3), 187–198. https://doi.org/10.2307/1054951.

Nier III, C. L. (2011). *Race financial institutions, credit discrimination and African American home ownership in Philadelphia, 1880–1960.* Temple University.

Nixon, R. (1970). Special Message to the Congress on Higher Education. Retrieved June 19, 2023, from https://nces.ed.gov/programs/digest/d20/tables/dt20_331.95.asp on 8/30/2021 at www.presidency.ucsb.edu/documents/special-message-the-congress-higher-education-0.

Oliver, M. L., & Shapiro, T. M. (2006). *Black wealth, white wealth: A new perspective on racial inequality.* Taylor & Francis.

Olson, K. W. (1973). The G. I. bill and higher education: Success and surprise. *American Quarterly*, *25*(5), 596–610. Accessed August 18, 2021. https://doi.org/10.2307/2711698.

Onkst, D. H. (1998). 'First a negro… incidentally a veteran': Black World War Two veterans and the GI Bill of rights in the Deep South, 1944–1948. *Journal of Social History*, *31*(3) 517–543.

Onyeador, I. N., Daumeyer, N. M., Rucker, J. M., Duker, A., Kraus, M. W., & Richeson, J. A. (2021). Disrupting beliefs in racial progress: Reminders of persistent racism alter perceptions of past, but not current, racial economic equality. *Personality and Social Psychology Bulletin*, *47*(5), 753–765.

Ozanne, L. J. (1987). Tax policy for pensions and other retirement saving. *Congressional Budget Office*, the Congress of the US.

Painter, N. I. (1992). *Exodusters: Black migration to Kansas after reconstruction.* New York: W. W. Norton & Company.

Paul, M., Zaw, K., & Darity Jr., W. A. (2022). Returns in the labor market: A nuanced view of penalties at the intersection of race and gender in the US. *Feminist Economics, 28*(2), 1–31.

Pell Grant Preservation and Expansion Act of 2021, S.2081, 117th Congress. (2021). Available at: www.congress.gov/bill/117th-congress/senate-bill/2081.

Pew Research Center. (2021, August). Deep divisions in Americans' views of the nation's racial history – and how to address it. Retrieved August 22, 2022, from www.pewresearch.org/politics/2021/08/12/deep-divisions-in-americans-views-of-nations-racial-history-and-how-to-address-it/.

Plessy v. Ferguson, 163 U.S. 537 (1896).

Pollock v. Farmers' Loan and Trust, 157 U.S. 429 (1895).

Power, P. (1983). Apartheid Baltimore style: The residential segregation ordinances of 1910–1913. *Maryland Law Review, 42*(1983), 289. Available at: http://digitalcommons.law.umaryland.edu/mlr/vol42/iss2/4.

Projector, D. S. (1968). *Survey of changes in family finances*. Board of Governors of the Federal Reserve System.

Public Citizen. (2015). Billionaires' bluff: How America's richest families hide behind small businesses and family farms in effort to repeal estate tax.

Quadagno, J. S. (1994). *The color of welfare: How racism undermined the war on poverty*. Oxford University Press.

Radford, W. (1977). Comment, generation-skipping transfers and the tax reform act of 1976. *SMU Law Journal, 31*(2). https://scholar.smu.edu/smulr/vol31/iss2/5.

Ransom, R. L., & Sutch, R. (1986, May). The Decline in Fertility and the Life Cycle Transition in the Antebellum States1. In *paper for the All-UC Group in Economic History conference, Laguna Beach* (pp. 262–263).

Ransom, R. L., & Sutch, R. (1990). Who pays for slavery? In R. F. America (Ed.), *The wealth of races: The present value of benefits from past injustices* (No. 132, pp. 31–54). Greenwood Publishing Group.

Revenue Act of 1916, 39 Stat. 756, September 8, 1916. Retrieved July 27, 2021, from https://govtrackus.s3.amazonaws.com/legislink/pdf/stat/39/STATUTE-39-Pg756.pdf.

Rice, S. (2021). Ambassador Susan E. Rice Video Remarks at "It starts with us: Forging the future of federal leadership" Virtual Event. Retrieved July 4, 2023, from www.whitehouse.gov/dpc/briefing-room/2021/02/22/ambassador-susan-e-rice-video-remarks-at-it-starts-with-us-forging-the-future-of-federal-leadership-virtual-event/.

Rippy, J. F. (Ed.) (1936). *FM Simmons, statesman of the new South: Memoirs and addresses*. Duke University Press.

Rivlin, A. (1978). Veteran educational benefits: Issues facing the GI Bill. Congressional Budget Office.

Roberts, S. (2017). "Lois Dickson Rice, Trailblazing Executive Behind Pell Grants, Dies at 83." *New York Times*. January 18, 2017.

Roosevelt, T. R. "December 3, 1907: Seventh Annual Message" Miller Center, University of Virginia. December 3, 1907. https://millercenter.org/the-presidency/presidential-speeches/december-3-1907-seventh-annual-message.

Rosenbloom, J. L. (2018). The colonial American economy (2018). Economics Working Papers: Department of Economics, Iowa State University. 18002. https://lib.dr.iastate.edu/econ_workingpapers/40.

Rothstein, R. (2017). *The color of law: A forgotten history of how our government segregated America*. Liveright Publishing.

Ruggles, S., Flood, S., Sobek, M., Backman, D., Chen, Grace A. C., Richards, S., Rogers, R., & Schouweiler, M. (n.d.). IPUMS USA: Version 15.0 [dataset]. IPUMS, 2024. https://doi.org/10.18128/D010.V15.0.

Sanchez, R., & Chandler, C. (1997). Education aid at what cost? Clinton's $50 billion plan has skeptics even on campus. *Washington Post*. February 3. Retrieved August 4, 2023, from www.washingtonpost.com/wp-srv/politics/special/tax/stories/tax020397.htm.

Saunt, C. (2004). The paradox of freedom: Tribal sovereignty and emancipation during the reconstruction of Indian territory. *The Journal of Southern History*, *70*(1), 63–94.

Scholey v. Rew, 90 U.S. 331, 348. (1875).

Scholz, J. K., & Levine, K. (2004). US black-white wealth inequality. In K. Neckerman (Ed.), *Social inequality* (pp. 895–929). Russell Sage Foundation.

Scofea, L. (1994). The development and growth of employer-provided health insurance. *Monthly Labor Review, 117*(3), 3–10. Retrieved April 22, 2021, from www.jstor.org/stable/41844254.

S.441-American Opportunity Account Act. (118th Congress, 2023–2024). Retrieved August 2, 2023, from www.congress.gov/bill/118th-congress/senate-bill/441/text.

Senzaki, R. S. (1976). Exploring some of the conceptual changes behind the estate and gift tax provisions of the tax reform act of 1976. *Loyola of Los Angeles Law Review*, *10*, 785.

Shanks, T. R. (2005). The homestead act: A major asset-building policy in American history. In M. Sherraden (Ed.), *Inclusion in the American dream: Assets, poverty, and public policy* (pp. 20–41). Oxford University Press.

Shapiro, T. M. (2004). *The hidden cost of being African American: How wealth perpetuates inequality*. Oxford University Press.

Shapiro, T. M. (2017). *Toxic inequality: How America's wealth gap destroys mobility, deepens the racial divide, and threatens our future*. Basic Books.

Shelley v. Kraemer, 334 U.S. 1 (1948).

Shirtsleeves to Shirtsleeves. (2019). Boyd Wealth Management. Retrieved June 22, 2021, from https://boyd-wealth.com/blog/shirtsleeves-to-shirtsleeves.

Simmons, F. M. (1936). *FM Simmons, statesman of the new South: Memoirs and addresses*. Duke University Press.

Simon, J., & Neal, L. (1974). A calculation of the black reparations bill. *The Review of Black Political Economy*, *4*(2), 75–86.

Snowden, K. (2013). Mortgage banking in the United States, 1870–1940. Research Institute for Housing America Research Paper, (13-02).

Snyder, T. D. (1993). *120 years of American education: A statistical portrait.* US Department of Education, Office of Educational Research and Improvement, National Center for Education Statistics.

Solomon, D., Maxwell, C., & Castro, A. (2019). Systemic inequality: Displacement, exclusion, and segregation. *Center for American Progress*, 7.

Southern Illinoian. (1983, 28 September). "15 Billionaires Top New List of America's Rich."

Spratlen, T. H. (1974). The record and rhetoric of black economic progress. *The Review of Black Political Economy*, *4*(3), 1–30.

Steinbaum, M. (2020). The student debt crisis is a crisis of non-repayment. Jain Family Institute.

Stewart, D. M., & Johanek, M. (1996). Chapter XIII: The evolution of college entrance examinations. *Teachers College Record, 97*(5), 261–286.

Student Aid Programs: Subcommittee on Postsecondary Education, Committee on Education and Labor, U.S. House of Representatives, 98th Cong. (1984) (Testimony of Rudolf Penner). www.cbo.gov/publication/19892.

Students for Fair Admissions v. Harvard, 600 U.S. 181 (2023).

Surrey, S. S. (1958). The federal income tax base for individuals. *Columbia Law Review, 58*(6), 815–830.

Surrey, S. S. (1968). Speech to money marketeers, New York City, November 15, 1967; see for excerpts, Annual Report of the Secretary of the Treasury for the Fiscal Year 1968, p. 322.

Surrey, S. S. (1970a). Federal income tax reform: The varied approaches necessary to replace tax expenditures with direct governmental assistance. *Harvard Law Review, 84*(2), 352–408.

Surrey, S. S. (1970b). Tax incentives as a device for implementing government policy: A comparison with direct government expenditures. *Harvard Law Review, 83*(4), 705–738. https://doi.org/10.2307/1339837.

Surrey, S. S. (1976a). At home: Tax expenditures. *Challenge, 18*(6), 53–54. Retrieved June 10, 2021, from www.jstor.org/stable/40719371.

Surrey, S. S. (1976b). Reflections on the tax reform act of 1976. *Cleveland State Law Review, 25*, 303.

Surrey, S. S., & McDaniel, P. R. (1978). The tax expenditure concept: Current developments and emerging issues. *Boston College Law Review, 20*, 225.

Swinton, D. H. (1990). Racial inequality and reparations. In R. F. America (Ed.), *The wealth of races: The present value of benefits from past injustices* (No. 132, pp. 153–162). Greenwood Publishing Group.

Terrell, H. S. (1971). Wealth accumulation of black and white families: The empirical evidence. *The Journal of Finance, 26*(2), 363–377.

Testimony on Student Aid Programs: Subcommittee on Postsecondary Education, Committee on Education and Labor, U.S. House of Representatives, 98th Congress. (1984). (Testimony of Rudolf Penner). Retrieved January 9, 2025, from www.cbo.gov/publication/19892.

Thaler, R. H. (1999). Mental accounting matters. *Journal of Behavioral Decision Making, 12*(3), 183–206.

The Colored Nomination in the Second Judicial District. (1878, July 7). *Wilmington Post*, p. 2.

The Preemption Act of 1841. 5 Stat. 453 (Chapter 16).

The White House (.gov). (2023). Table 2.5 Composition of "Other Receipts": 1940–2028. Retrieved August 2, 2023, from www.whitehouse.gov/wp-content/uploads/2023/03/hist02z5_fy2024.xlsx.

Thomasson, M. A. (2003). The importance of group coverage: How tax policy shaped US health insurance. *American Economic Review, 93*(4), 1373–1384.

Toder, E., & Khitatrakun, S. (2017). Estimates of a proposal to establish guaranteed retirement accounts, financed by reduced limits on current law contributions to defined Contribution retirement saving plans. *Tax Policy Center.*

Turner, J. A. (1999). Pensions, tax treatment. *The Encyclopedia of Taxation and Tax Policy.*

Turner, M. A. (2002). Discrimination in metropolitan housing markets: National results from phase I of HDS2000.

Turner, S., & Bound, J. (2003). Closing the gap or widening the divide: The effects of the GI Bill and World War II on the educational outcomes of black Americans. *The Journal of Economic History, 63*(1), 145–177.

Tuskegee University Archives Repository. (n.d.). *Lynching Stats Year Dates Causes.* Retrieved July 16, 2021, from http://archive.tuskegee.edu/repository/digital-collection/lynching-information/lynchings-stats-year-dates-causes/.

Tyson, T. (2006). The ghosts of 1898. *The Raleigh News and Observer.*

Umbricht, M. (2016). Helping low-income and middle-income students: Pell grants and the higher education act. *Higher Education in Review.*

Underwood Simmons Tariff Act of 1913. 38 Stat. 114.

US Census Bureau. (1936). *Mortality Statistics 1933.* Department of Commerce. www.cdc.gov/nchs/products/vsus/vsus_1890_1938.htm.

US Census Bureau. (1952). *1950 Census of Housing Volume 4 Residential Financing: Mortgaged Nonfarm Properties.* Department of Commerce. Retrieved May 15, 2023, from www.census.gov/library/publications/1952/dec/housing-vol-04.html.

US Census Bureau. (1962). "School Enrollment of the Population of the United States: 1960." Retrieved July 2, 2023, from www2.census.gov/library/publications/decennial/1960/pc-s1-supplementary-reports/pc-s1-29.pdf.

US Census Bureau. (1963). 1960 Census of Housing Volume V Residential Finance. U.S. Department of Commerce. Retrieved May 17, 2023, from https://usa.ipums.org/usa/voliii/pubdocs/1960/pubvols1960.shtml.

US Census Bureau. (1975). *Historical Statistics of the United States: Colonial Times to 1970.* Retrieved August 21, 2022, from www.census.gov/library/publications/1975/compendia/hist_stats_colonial-1970.html.

US Department of Education. (n.d.) *Student Financial Assistance FY 2024 Budget Request.* Retrieved August 2, 2023, from www2.ed.gov/about/overview/budget/budget24/justifications/p-sfa.pdf.

US Department of Treasury. (2016, September 23). *Freedmen's Bank Forum.* Video. www.yorkcast.com/treasury/events/2016/09/23/freedmansbank.

US Department of Treasury. (2023). *Tax Expenditures, FY2024.* Office of Tax Analysis. https://home.treasury.gov/policy-issues/tax-policy/tax-expenditures.

US Department of Veterans Affairs. (1957). *Annual Report.* Retrieved August 19, 2023, from www.va.gov/vetdata/docs/fy1956.pdf.

US Department of Veterans Affairs. (1963). *Annual Report.* Retrieved August 19, 2023, from www.va.gov/vetdata/docs/fy1963.pdf.

US Internal Revenue, Statistics of Income. (1916). Retrieved from https://fraser.stlouisfed.org/title/statistics-income-61/1916-20384.

US Internal Revenue, Statistics of Income. (1918). Retrieved from Statistics of Income, 1918 | FRASER | St. Louis Fed (stlouisfed.org).

Ventry, D. J. (2010). The accidental deduction: A history and critique of the tax subsidy for mortgage interest. *Law and Contemporary Problems, 73*(1), 233–284.

Waggoner, L. W. (2014). From here to eternity: The folly of perpetual trusts. https://repository.law.umich.edu/law_econ_current/76/

Wall Street Journal. (1920). Answers to Inquirers: "Intelligent inquiry is the public's greatest safeguard", September 11, 1920, at 2.

Watson, R. L. (1960). A political leader bolts – FM Simmons in the presidential election of 1928. *The North Carolina Historical Review*, *37*(4), 516–543.
Watson, R. L. (1967). Furnifold M. Simmons: "Jehovah of the tar heels"? *The North Carolina Historical Review*, *44*(2), 166–187. www.jstor.org/stable/23518041.
Watson, R. L. (1978). A testing time for southern congressional leadership: The war crisis of 1917–1918. *The Journal of Southern History*, *44*(1), 3–40.
Watson, R. L. (1989). Furnifold Simmons and the politics of white supremacy. *Race, Class and Politics in Southern History: Essays in Honor of Robert F. Durden*.
Wattenberg, B. J., & Scammon, R. M. (1973, April). Black progress and liberal rhetoric. *Commentary*, *55*(4), 35–44.
Weller, C. (2019). African Americans face systemic obstacles to getting good jobs. Center for the American Progress. www.americanprogress.org/article/african-americans-face-systematic-obstacles-getting-good-jobs/
Welsh, N. H. (2018). Racially restrictive covenants in the United States: A call to action. *Agora Journal of Urban Planning and Design*, 130–142
Wheeler, J. B. (2013). *A campaign of quiet persuasion: How the college board desegregated SAT® test centers in the deep South, 1960–1965*. Louisiana State University Press.
Wiese, A. (1999). Black housing, white finance: African American housing and home ownership in Evanston, Illinois, before 1940. *Journal of Social History*, 33(2), 429–460. https://doi.org/10.1353/jsh.1999.0079.
Wilkerson, I. (2020). *Caste: The origins of our discontents*. Random House.
Williams, R. B. (2016). *The privileges of wealth: Rising inequality and the growing racial divide*. Routledge.
Williams, R. B. (2017). Wealth privilege and the racial wealth gap: A case study in economic stratification. *The Review of Black Political Economy*, *44*(3–4), 303–325.
Williams, R. B. (2018). Wealth privilege: Reprising the Jim Crow System. *Intergenerational Responsibility in the 21st Century*, 83.
Williams, R. B. (2022). Federal wealth policy and the perpetuation of white supremacy. *The Review of Black Political Economy*, *49*(2), 130–151.
Williams, J., & Wilson, V. (2019). *Black workers endure persistent racial disparities in employment outcomes*. Economic Policy Institute.
Williams, R., & Preisser, V. (2005). *Philanthropy, heirs, and values: How successful families are using philanthropy to prepare their heirs for post-transition responsibilities*. Robert D. Reed Publishers.
Williamson, S. H., & Cain, L. P. (2021). Measuring Slavery in 2020 dollars. www.measuringworth.com/slavery.php.
Wilson-Gorman Tariff of 1894. 28 Stat. 509 (Ch. 349).
Wolff, E. N. (1981). The accumulation of household wealth over the life-cycle: A microdata analysis. *Review of Income and Wealth*, *27*(1), 75–96.
Wolff, E. N. (2018). *A century of wealth in America*. Harvard University Press.
Wolfman, B. (1985). Tax expenditures: From idea to ideology. *Harvard Law Review*, *99*(2), 491–498. https://doi.org/10.2307/1341132.
Woo, J. H., & Choy, S. P. (2011). Merit aid for undergraduates: Trends from 1995–96 to 2007–08. Stats in Brief. NCES 2012-160. *National Center for Education Statistics*.
Xu, J., Murphy, S., Kochanek, K., & Arias, E. (2022). *Mortality in the United States, 2021*. CDC. www.cdc.gov/nchs/products/databriefs/db456.htm.

Yao, R., Gutter, M. S., & Hanna, S. D. (2005). The financial risk tolerance of blacks, Hispanics and whites. *Journal of Financial Counseling and Planning, 16*(1), 51–62.

Yellin, E. S. (2013). *Racism in the nation's service: Government workers and the color line in Woodrow Wilson's America.* UNC Press Books.

Zaritsky, H. (1977). The estate and gift tax revisions of the tax reform act of 1976. *Washington and Lee Law Review, 34*(2), 353–408.

Zelenak, L. A. (2018a). Leaving it up to treasury: Congressional abdication on major policy issues in the early years of the income tax. *Law and Contemporary Problems, 81*, 137.

Zelenak, L. A. (2018b). *Figuring out the tax: Congress, treasury, and the design of the early modern income tax.* Cambridge University Press.

Zhao, B. (2018). State disinvestment in higher education: The impact on public research universities' patent applications.

Zucchino, D. (2020). *Wilmington's Lie: The murderous coup of 1898 and the rise of white supremacy*. Atlantic Monthly Press.

Index

For EU product safety concerns, contact us at Calle de José Abascal, 56–1°, 28003 Madrid, Spain or eugpsr@cambridge.org.

www.ingramcontent.com/pod-product-compliance
Lightning Source LLC
Chambersburg PA
CBHW020243301225
37488CB00007B/97

* 9 7 8 1 0 0 9 3 6 7 8 6 8 *